FAIRWAY DREAMS

MAINSTREAM / SPORT

FAIRWAY DREAMS

A DECADE IN PROFESSIONAL GOLF

LAUREN St JOHN

MAINSTREAM
PUBLISHING

EDINBURGH AND LONDON

First published in Great Britain in 2001 by
MAINSTREAM PUBLISHING COMPANY
(EDINBURGH) LTD
7 Albany Street
Edinburgh EH1 3UG

ISBN 1 84018 368 3

A catalogue record for this book is available
from the British Library

Typeset in Caslon and Futurist
Printed and bound in Great Britain by
Cox and Wyman Ltd

CONTENTS

FOREWORD

I first met Lauren St John in 1988, in the clubhouse at Royal Lytham, during the Open Championship. She was waiting to interview a couple of players and I was drinking tea with a friend. We chatted for a while and I can recall thinking . . . 'Lovely girl . . . Cannon fodder.'

Not generally being thought of as arrogant or patronising, I have mused many times, as I have eaten these words, on just how I could have formed such a mistaken opinion. I should have known better. Coming as she does from Zimbabwe, where sport is a religion and unreconstructed laddishness is genetically programmed into the male psyche, she was only too well equipped to take anything that the European Tour might throw at her. Like the redoubtable Liz Kahn before her, she was no respecter of the status quo and, in bringing the fresh eye of the outsider to bear on our cosy world, she performed a service to golf writing, and rose in the process to become a respected journalist and author.

The PGA European Tour, like its American cousin, is in some ways the ultimate men's club. Unlike other Tours, however, ours retains a healthy atmosphere of genuine cameraderie. Players who fight each other tooth and nail on the course enjoy close friendships off it, and support from colleagues in times of stress is never far from hand. Add to this travelling circus a smattering of wives and loved ones, a hundred or so caddies, and a clutch of psychologists and coaches and you have all the ingredients for a strange brew of emotions.

A golf tournament is a slowly evolving drama where the player stands uniquely alone in the spotlight. There is no hiding place among team members. We all play on the same stage on the same day, and rarely are souls laid so bare as when coming down the stretch in a major golf tournament. What golfer at his or her own level has not shared this rollercoaster ride of despair and elation that is the lot of most professional golfers at some time? It's what makes the game so compelling and also what makes the relationship between reporter and player such an intimate one.

The golfing press are an integral part of our circuit. They are our natural confidants, feeling for us when our dreams are shattered, and rejoicing with us when they are fulfilled. They are given insights into our lives and thoughts that come from the deepest parts of us, and the best of them can enlighten us with their perceptions.

In her years on Tour, Lauren has interviewed many great players, but she has always had a soft spot for the journeyman. In this book, you can follow the exploits of both, and enjoy stories of some great characters who will be remembered, but possibly not for their play.

A good friend, now a correspondent on an Irish paper, once asked me: 'Do you think you need to be a good player to be a golf reporter?'

'No,' I said. 'You need to be a good writer.'

Good writing on any subject is a joy to read. Sports writing with a literary dimension is a rare bird indeed, and sadly our continued thrall with the sporting hero as celebrity does little to staunch the flow of ghost-written articles and books. Thankfully, there are still some who can inspire us with the precision of their observations and the quality of their prose.

DAVID JONES
JUNE 2000

SHOOTING AT CLOUDS

A KIND OF MADNESS WITH RULES

> golf n. outdoor game in which a small hard ball
> is struck with clubs into a succession of holes

I never set foot on a golf course until I was 18, and then for all the wrong reasons.

Before that day, I can only ever remember coming into contact with the game of golf on three occasions. I know I was transfixed by a tournament which Gary Player won and which I watched in black and white on our old farm television. Why it held my interest I have no idea, because I had never seen golf played before. I hadn't a clue what the object of the game was and the programme was punctuated, as were all television programmes in Zimbabwe at that time, by the rolling of the picture – whereupon my dad was prevailed upon to go out into the garden and adjust the aerial – and extended musical interludes, all preceded by the notice: 'We apologise for the break in transmission.'

The second occasion was at boarding school. My two best friends and I discovered that we could skip up to half a day's lessons three or four times a week (employing the time more usefully by sitting discussing life in the sunshine, with our feet dangling in the pond on the edge of the eleventh at Chapman Golf Club, Harare) as long was we produced the odd painting as evidence that these hours hadn't been wasted. Our art teacher, you see, was a great champion of our cause and a willing conspirator in these escapades.

Such was my lack of interest in the game that in all the years we did this it never occurred to me to be more than slightly curious about those little groups of men who strode so briskly past us up the pristine fairways; or glowered at us as they entered the leafy glade at our backs and commenced beating at bushes and crashing among the branches, or even gazed hopelessly into the black depths of the pond. It didn't occur to me to be curious for the simple reason that I thought golf was a game, like bowls, which was only enjoyed by old men. No one I had ever come across played golf, not within our family or outside of it. At home, we all did things that normal farming families in our area did. We rode horses, we fished, held braais (barbecues), swam, dipped cows, inspected tobacco barns and hunted with a spotlight in the dead of night. Golf was never included among our pastimes. I was midway through journalism school when I had my third encounter with the game. I had met a man whom I was most intrigued by and asked him not long afterwards: 'What do you do in your spare time?'

'Well, I play rugby and I play golf.'

Now rugby is a respected pursuit where I come from, but golf is a different matter altogether. 'Golf?' I scoffed. He went down several notches in my estimation. I can remember laughing rather derisively and then saying something inane like: 'What on earth do you see in a game which involves nothing except walking around for hours hitting balls with sticks?' It was the beginning of the end of that particular relationship.

Nevertheless, I was sufficiently interested to allow myself to be talked into going to Chapman Golf Club with a college friend of mine to watch her boyfriend play. We spent an exhausting afternoon in pursuit of his match, running unwittingly across greens and fairways incurring the wrath of dozens of golfers, before being drenched by a sudden thunderstorm. We gave up the search and stalked sodden and sullen-faced off the golf course. I suppose the fact that I went straight back for more just goes to show that the little streak of lunacy inherent in every golfer was lying dormant in me, just waiting for a chance to emerge.

It manifested itself at my very first golf lesson.

'This is a golf club,' said Andrew, a scratch golfer who had volunteered unwisely to teach me the game. 'This is how you grip it. Right you are, there is the fairway. No, no, not that way. This way. Good. Now hit the ball.'

I think he underestimated how little I knew about the game. The full extent of my golfing know-how at the time was that you should swing the club back as far as you possibly could and then smash the ball as hard as you possibly could. Then, of course, it would fly like an arrow several hundred yards along the fairway and you would go and hit it again. For 18 holes.

Ten air shots later, it was beginning to come home to me that there was more to the game than met the eye, and to Andrew that he had taken on a lost cause. This pattern continued for nine holes. I would flail at the ball with increasing desperation until I eventually made contact. Having watched it hurtle diagonally along the ground into the bushes, I would go and hunt for it, while Andrew played out the hole. I might have a putt or two and then we would repeat the whole scenario on the next tee.

And so began my love affair with golf. When I came off the course I felt three overriding emotions: humiliation, anger and astonishment. Golf was not like I expected it to be. Not at all.

Andrew shot away in a cloud of dust, anxious to escape before I requested another lesson. I wandered thoughtfully into the town centre where I found a second-hand bookshop. There, in amongst the Dick Francis, the Harold Robbins and the Mills and Boons, I found a battle-scarred copy of Brian Huggett's *How to Play Better Golf*. With the assistance of this, a box of golf books (containing everything from a complete collection of Jack Nicklaus to Ben Hogan and Tommy Armour) given to me by a friend whose father had been an addict, an antique five-iron and a box of air-flow balls, I taught myself to play in the garden. Thrilled at the prospect of my taking up a hobby less dangerous than show-jumping or snake collecting, my parents immediately rushed out and bought me a set of second-hand golf clubs – Slazenger Lady Panthers. Within two months I was a member of Chapman Golf Club. My first handicap was 18.

I graduated from college; I cursorily scanned the appointments pages; I came to the conclusion that work would interfere with golf. Help came in the shape of an entrepreneur who owned a business which masqueraded as a promotion company. I was recruited to run it. Our days went thus:

7 a.m.	To the office. Brief, frantic burst of activity. Flying visits to printers, originators, clients.
10 a.m.	Telephone tussles with clients, bailiffs and bank managers.
10.30 a.m.	Golf.

I was very fortunate to live in a country where it is possible to play golf 365 days of the year, where full membership of the best golf club in the capital city is less than £50, and where green fees for members are the approximate equivalent of ten pence. There was only one snake in this apparent Garden of Eden. My temper.

Nobody who takes up golf with serious intent does so without uncovering a side of their personality hitherto unknown to them. It may be that they are remarkably resilient in the face of adversity or have vast untapped reserves of patience and determination. Or they might, like me, discover that they are perfectionists with short fuses – two of the most completely unsuitable traits an amateur golfer could have the misfortune to possess.

I began playing with a group of low handicappers and scratch golfers who seemed to throw clubs as a matter of course. I watched and learned. Soon I could discipline a club with the best of them. Let me tell you, a recalcitrant three-wood sent soaring in a series of graceful somersaults over a fir tree is one of the most satisfying spectacles in the world. But the satisfaction gained from a horrifying display of temper on the golf course – one where you might have broken every club in your bag, sworn in five languages, and taken a foot-long divot out of the green – is short and bittersweet, and all you are left with is a sick and guilty feeling in the pit of your stomach because you know you've violated a kind of sacred code.

I never really grew out of it though until I'd spent a season on the European Tour. Once you've watched a man with his whole life riding on a round of golf suffer seven kinds of disaster and still observe the etiquette of the game and conduct himself like a gentleman, you tend to look at your own feeble efforts from a different perspective. You have to keep reminding yourself that you are only playing the hardest game in the world for pleasure, a professional golfer plays it for a living.

Henry Longhurst used to say that the way we are introduced to golf influences our attitude to the game for the rest of our lives. I agree. If I had grown up in a golfing family and had taken the playing of it for granted, I don't think I would have become as obsessed with it as I am, although I think I would always have enjoyed it because the whole idea of it appeals to me. I love it that you can play golf every day of your life and never master it. I love the complexity and mysteriousness of the golf swing, and I love it that you can play the same hole on the same golf course a thousand times and never play it the same way twice.

Sometimes, though, I think I'm attracted to the people in golf as much as I am to the game. Where else would you find top sportsmen with their livelihoods or dreams at stake, selflessly giving up their time to help their chief rivals only moments before they go out onto the golf course? In what other walk of life is a man called upon to be his own judge? Where else is he asked to be so scrupulously honest that even when he has infringed a rule which no one else could possibly know he has, he will still call a penalty on himself? What other successful professional sport has retained the clean, wholesome image than this game has, and hung on through thick and thin to such old-fashioned values as honour and loyalty?

Nowhere else but golf.

I became a golf writer for all of these reasons. And I became a golf writer on the European men's professional Tour because I wanted to work with the best players in the world.

In 2000, the Professional Golfers' Association European Tour boasted a prize fund of £52 million – an increase of more than £51 million since 1970. Some 25 per cent of tournaments are worth over £500,000, and ten to 12 are worth over £1.5 million. But the Tour has grown long as well as rich. In 2000 the season began in South Africa in the second week of January and ended in Argentina in December. Every week on the European Tour, nearly 150 players of more than 14 different nationalities compete: some to win the tournament, a handful with the eventual aim of winning the Order of Merit, some merely to earn enough money to retain their cards.

I wanted to write the story of their lives. I wanted to go beneath the superficial glamour of the PGA European Tour, to know what made the best players as good as they are, where their motivation and talent comes from, what fuels their desire? What separates major winners? Why does a man who has never won a tournament and who only scrapes the most meagre living from the game want to play tournament golf so much? I wanted to write about everyone: about the rookies, the journeymen, the stars, the characters and the legends. What do they think about? Care about? Dream about?

So here it is, the PGA European Tour and the extraordinary people who populate it.

1

PARADISE LOST

La Manga, Sunday, 3 December 1989. When the Tourists have gone and endless summer days have given way to the slow, wet Spanish winter, the 37 Bar at La Manga provides an unlikely refuge for a new, more solemn group of people: the players of the European Tour Qualifying School. The time they spend here is short – little more than a week in some cases – yet its importance cannot be overestimated. Many of their lives depend on its outcome.

The media have done well to furnish the gloss picture that is the European Tour. We see Ian Woosnam driving a Porsche; Nick Faldo, in a Savile Row suit standing in front of his Wentworth mansion smiling his perfect smile, or collecting his MBE, or kissing the Open Championship trophy; and more numbers after Seve Ballesteros's name on the career money list than there are in the London telephone directory. Seldom is it mentioned just how few succeed. Seldom do we read statistics of how many players never get as far as the Tour; of how short the period of grace is for most of those players who do, before they are forced back to the School by the strength of the competition coming behind them; of how many veterans find themselves washed up on the stony beach of life in middle age having devoted 30 or 40 years to the game – with nothing to show for it and a family to support. Reality, in professional golf, is harsh.

Still they come. And for every one that touches that big brass ring there are a hundred who don't. So, unlikely as the 37 Bar might be, refuge it certainly is: a sanctuary for souls bruised at La Manga, school of hard knocks.

Beneath fading portraits of Hogan, Snead and Palmer, players sprawl, killing time in between practising or playing.

They come from every walk of life and a dozen countries. The only common bond between any of them is golf and a simple desire to be the best in a sport which accepts nothing less. The talk here is incessant. The players compare swing theories, swap Tour stories and offer one another consolation or advice when their rounds are done. All day long and way into the night they drink tall glasses of hot chocolate and milky coffee, play interminable card games and listen to Anne Murray, John Denver and Don McLean's 'American Pie'.

Some initiates have the white, pinched look of people who have bitten off far more than they can reasonably expect to chew. Others exude confidence and the fresh-faced optimism of youth.

Graham Whale, a young Essex county player turned professional, brushes his straw-blond hair from his eyes and looks around him. 'This is a shit place,' he announces. 'I've decided that already. Don't wanna come here too often. Wanna get through and get going.'

Strange how one place can be so many things to so many different people. For some players, just reaching La Manga can seem an achievement in itself. Poised on the threshold of their dream, they imagine that the School is only a short bridge which has to be crossed before they are home and dry. For veteran Tour players it represents a low point in their career, a threat to their livelihood and a symbol of the demise of their game. To players who return year after year it can become a mentally insurmountable barrier.

Since Jeremy Bennett was made Rookie of the Year on the European Tour in 1981, he has been back to the School six times.

'Obviously it costs a lot of money,' says Bennett, who manages, nevertheless, to look like a walking advertisement for designer clothing, 'but, yes, I get more nervous and just feel so bad the first round or two than any other time of the year.

'I remember feeling exactly the same thing last year. I wasn't doing very well in the first round and I was thinking, "I can't do this. I don't know why I'm doing it. I can't enjoy this pressure at all, I can't play properly." And then I got going again. I had been four over at one time in my first round and I finished one under so that wasn't so bad. But I didn't really play my proper game until the third or fourth round when I started getting more relaxed. I suppose it's the same for most people.'

Never had the examination hall of the European Tour been more full of chancers and dreamers and every other player who ever aspired to take over from Ballesteros, Nicklaus or Palmer. Twelve million pounds is an irresistible lure.

The PGA European Tour tries to weed out those unlikely to make the grade early on by making the entry requirements for the School as stiff as possible. Unless a player has exempt entry by virtue of finishing at the top of the Satellite Tour Order of Merit or in the top 120 on the regular Tour it is necessary for him to pre-qualify at a selected course in Britain. If he fails there, he can have one more bite at the cherry – this year the odds are even shorter. In 2000, there were 800 pre-qualifying entrants with 168 making it through to the school and just securing their cards. In 1989, there were 588 pre-qualifying entries and 109 exempt entries to La Manga. Only 50 would win their cards.

The price of attempting to qualify is in itself a significant deterrent. La Manga costs in the region of £1,500: £400 for the entry fee, £500 for a professional caddie and the remainder for flights, accommodation and food. Pre-qualifying adds another £1,000 to the bill – a lot to lose if you don't make it through.

Ultimately, the Qualifying School is the fairest test of a player's heart, but not necessarily of his game. Most courses on the Tour force the golfer to manufacture shots with every club in his bag; hence, the best shot-makers are the best players. The courses at La Manga are long and wide open and have a tendency to reduce the tournament to a putting contest.

Getting through La Manga is not confirmation that a player will succeed, just as not getting through isn't proof that he won't. The School is just the first pinnacle in a game full of mountains. Each ensuing climb is higher and harder; majors are reached by way of cliff faces. Those who reach the top are those with one philosophy: winning isn't everything – it's the only thing.

At its best, La Manga is a depressing place. There is too

little for the players to do and nowhere for them to go to escape from the pressure, from each other, or even from themselves. At its worst, it becomes a kind of cemetery – a place where dreams go to die.

'Colditz,' was how a caddie at the Portuguese Open described it when I mentioned I was going.

'Colditz?' I said in surprise, imagining stone walls and shell-shocked faces.

'Colditz,' he insisted. 'It's a nightmare, that place. Nothing there except two golf courses and a lot of depressed people.'

In the cold light of day La Manga was dank and gloomy. Grey sheets of rain fell on the empty villas whose inhabitants had taken their leave like snow geese with the coming of winter. I decided that the caddie hadn't been joking. When it slowed to a drizzle, I walked down the hill to the 37 Bar.

It is possible to spend most of every day in its dim, smoky warmth, drinking endless mugs of coffee and listening to stories of past Schools. One such account recalls an occasion where several of the pros got together and paid another player to drive a car through the glass doors of his hotel, across the foyer and into the swimming-pool.

Another, more infamous, tells of a player – a member of a Ryder Cup team – who missed his card one year when the School was still held in Portugal. He rushed straight up to his apartment and proceeded to smash every movable object and hurl it out the window. Not content with that, he leapt into his car, raced down to the end of the pier and drove it off the ramp, smashing it down, turning it around and doing it all over again. The police, so that story goes, caught up with him in the end, and escorted him from the country.

Over the years pros have been known to break their golf clubs as well as their television sets, drive over their golf bags in cars, throw them off cliffs and even set fire to them. When veteran Danny Goodman failed to qualify, he and David Jones went to the top of the cliffs above La Manga and hit Goodman's entire bag of practice balls into the sea to the sound of the Allman Brothers' 'Hard Cross to Bear'.

Wayne Player, son of Gary, flew over from America in 1985

to pre-qualify at Foxhills Golf Club. He teed up in the most unsociable weather conditions Britain has to offer and hit a shaky drive down the first. Undaunted by a three-putt, he proceeded calmly to the second where he hit his tee shot into the rough. Having found the ball and played his approach shot, he discovered that it wasn't his at all. He was penalised two shots. His own ball came to light under a bush in an unplayable lie. He took a drop under penalty and carried on to the next hole, determined not to be beaten.

On the third hole, he hit a perfect tee shot. Sadly, the flight of his ball coincided with that of 40 ducks. There was a small explosion of feathers in mid-air, then ducks and ball succumbed to the forces of gravity. Under the rules of golf, such an occurrence is considered rub of the green. At the fourth, Player played the wrong ball again – and was penalised a further two strokes.

I could go on. Suffice to say that Player shot 84, 71 to miss the pre-qualifying mark by two shots.

Monday, 4 December

By mid-afternoon, the conversation in the 37 Bar has reached a pitch where it is no longer possible to hear the roar of the deluge outside. Condensation on the window panes obliterates the landscape outside.

Scotsman Gary Collinson, his black hat still wet from his round, looks as though he is on the verge of breaking down. His eyes are over-bright, his voice unsteady.

'I feel I've aged about 30 years out here,' he says. 'Since I've been here I've had nightmares every night. I'm scared of flying. I keep dreaming about planes crashing.'

Collinson considers what he will do when he misses the cut tomorrow. It seems a foregone conclusion. He is lying 13 over par after three rounds and the cut isn't expected to be much higher than plus five.

'Give up.' He's not joking.

His brother Bob, who is caddying for him this week, came to the School once, missed his card by a shot and decided that if that was all there was to tournament golf he wasn't interested.

'I've got a club job now,' explains Bob, 'and I can still play the Scottish Tour, and that does me. If I have a good year I can make some money at that, and I can still get home every night and see my kids.'

For some players, getting a club job is an option they are prepared to contemplate. Others consider themselves tournament pros and wouldn't do it if they were starving. 'I couldn't do that,' Gary says disparagingly, snapping out of the reverie into which he has fallen. 'Selling golf balls.'

'That's the life they choose,' says Bob dourly. He clearly has little regard for a Tour pro's life himself. 'It must be very soul-destroying, though. I mean, it's being able to cope with all the disappointments. There's certainly more downs than ups.'

Gary Collinson made what he feels was a tactical error by playing too many practice rounds. He played seven rounds of golf before the tournament started and wasn't over par once. When the gun went off, his game fell to pieces.

'What went wrong?'

'Just my head,' Collinson says, 'it's gone. I haven't had a good meal in ten days. I've been out to restaurants but the food over here's crap. It's terrible.'

Between nightmares and mosquitoes, Collinson hasn't been getting much sleep. 'I've been bitten all over. Killed about 20 every night. Terrible. They keep going up into your ears. And the beds are so uncomfortable. Too small.'

The only plus this week, as far as I can make out, is that Gary and Bob shared an apartment with caddies instead of players.

'Some guys,' says Bob, 'you know, they have a post-mortem of their round and that's the last thing you want to hear – how every shot went.'

Rooming with caddies, they found time to have a drink and go out, not closeting themselves in their apartments the way that some players do, letting imaginings grow larger than life.

Gary Collinson smiles wistfully. 'The way I played this week, if I hadn't laughed, I'd have shot myself. I still think you've got to get out and have a few beers and try to relax.'

'Why change the habits of a lifetime?' agrees Bob.

PARADISE LOST

The rain delays have caused a chain reaction. Every golfer here is playing two incomplete rounds a day, the tail end of yesterday's round and the beginning of tomorrow's. It plays havoc with your mind and your game. Richard Fish, who was supposed to tee off at 8.46 this morning, didn't get away until nearly eleven o'clock and then in driving rain.

'Awful conditions,' he says crossly. His short blond hair is standing up in wet spikes. Out on the course he and his partners were knocking the ball along, struggling to concentrate; just biding time, really, until an official came to stop play. Nobody came. Fortunately, Fish is more fatalistic than most people here. 'It's all part of this week,' he says, blaming himself for not playing well, rather than the Tour or the elements. 'You just have to accept it and play the best you can.'

For some people, the European Tour School eventually becomes a way of life, an event which rolls around every December – like Christmas. Richard Fish holds the record for the most number of visits to the School. Eleven. On the surface, you wouldn't think it's the end of the world when he doesn't get his card. He laughs about it, shrugs it off and somehow survives until the end of the next year when he can try again. But the school takes a lot out of you each time you go through it. Nobody ever emerges unscathed.

'I enjoy playing,' he says when I question his perseverance, the extent of his self-belief. 'I think I'm a very slow learner – that's what keeps me going.'

This is golf at its cruellest. Perhaps it is ultimately easier on your soul if you come to the School a couple of times and finish nowhere. Eventually you could come to terms with the fact that you were never going to make it. But in golf there is no clear division between those players who are almost good enough to be tournament professionals and those who are. There are people who hover for years on the periphery of the Tour; some years they make it, some years they don't.

It can make you crazy. One pro I spoke to said that he resorted to a new scheme each year in an attempt to improve his golf. Out of season he had taken up weight-training and marathon running, experimented with anabolic steroids and changed coaches about as often as he changed shirts. He had made progress, but it was the slow progress of a man walking through a mire.

Talking to him I was reminded of something an American player said: 'You get to the point in your life where you keep trying to chase after this dream of getting on the Tour and making all this money everybody's making, and playing in front of all these people . . . and you've got to make a decision. Maybe it's time to give it all up and do something else.'

Tuesday, 5 December

Tuesday is D-day. It is a day for shattered dreams, the abrupt dissolution of illusion, the end of a lifetime of hope. Today is the four-round cut. The players who miss it get nothing: no tournaments whatsoever. The more fortunate are PGA-qualified and have a club job or a sponsor to fall back on, but others have to make money any way they can.

'I've done some incredible jobs,' remarks Nick Mitchell, a Satellite Tour player. 'I've sold roof-sheeting, cleaned toilets, done night jobs . . . anything just to keep playing.'

The rain does nothing for those players who still have a chance to make it. They mill around uneasily, watching for a break in the clouds. Players without a prayer look pale and exhausted. Their eyes are full of the fear of failing their friends and families back home.

Everyone has a different approach to the School. Some players like to arrive just the day before, believing that familiarity breeds contempt and creates swing problems at La Manga. Others are only happy if they can play both courses in their sleep. Tour player David Ray prepared for La Manga just as he would for any European tournament.

'Some people,' says Ray, who is dressed rather strangely in a golf shirt and a blue-striped tie, 'come out here and they hit thousands and thousands of shots, and they're just not used to doing that. I know two guys who arrived eight days before the first round and they played every day. By the time you tee it up on Saturday you're cuckoo, really.'

Disadvantaged by the 'psychological blow' of returning to

the School for the third time – after having won it in 1983 – Ray has resorted to eating two raw carrots a day, one on the practice ground and one on the tenth tee. Carrots contain a substance called beta-carotene – also found in beta-blockers – which is supposed to calm the nerves. Sam Torrance started the trend after finding carrots immensely beneficial to his nervous system during the 1989 Ryder Cup, and Ray claims they have cured his yips. He brought 60 of them with him to La Manga.

Later I walked down to the practice ground.

Richard Fish tips another ball miserably from the bucket as I go by. 'Know anything about the golf swing?' he says to me, then answers his own question. 'No.' He calls over Stuart Smith.

'Am I too inside?' he asks.

'A little bit,' says Smith, examining his backswing critically.

'Fucking game,' says Fish.

On the wall behind the scorer's table back at the clubhouse, someone has taped a message. It is crudely printed in red ink and says: 'THE CUT +4'.

Wednesday, 6 December

Graham Whale is the picture of dejection, balanced on a bar stool and hunched over the grand piano. His face, propped on his elbows and reflected in the shiny black surface, is wan, his manner devoid of its usual arrogance. Whale missed the cut by two shots, which is one situation he has no intention of getting used to. He feels that there has to be a cut-off point, that you can't keep coming back to the School every year chasing a hopeless ideal.

'You can't keep going and you've got to be realistic,' says Whale, with players like Richard Fish, who has missed his card again, in mind. 'That's what separates me from a lot of people, hopefully – I'm realistic. I've got my feet stuck firmly on the ground.'

Golf has long hours of enforced boredom in which to dwell on lost opportunities. At the School, a momentary loss of concentration, a single bad lie, a putt that skips out the back door, these are the things that could cost you your dream. Graham Whale has no such excuses. When it really counted he lost his nerve.

'I lost the control I had. I was cruising, no sweat. Hit it nicely, good rhythm. Three-putted one hole – I missed a putt of about 18 inches – and it threw me, completely threw me. All of a sudden it became emotional. Everything became an effort, rather than being simple.'

Perhaps there is no other week in golf where players are forced to be so selfish, so abstemious, so tunnel-visioned as the week of the School. It can have an adverse effect. The result of each shot can begin to prey on your mind until it eats away your concentration altogether.

'If you hit a bad shot here you feel it more,' says Whale, 'because it's that much more important. It's harder to chip it close and the hole gets a little bit smaller. I just get too anxious over it. I had plenty of chances on the way in to get out of it, I just never really got it going for me.'

For most of his life things have come easily to Whale. Having prepared for the School by playing on the South African circuit, he was confident it would fit smoothly into the same pattern.

'I never thought I was going to miss the cut until the last ten holes. Always thought I was in. If you're worried about making the cut, you're not worried about playing the tournament. I came here to win it. Didn't come here to make the top one hundred.'

Whale smiles self-consciously.

'You see, I've got this thing. I'm not in golf for the money. I'm a glory seeker. I love the attention, love it. I can't help it. Out there in Africa for the first time, signing autographs for little kids, talking to spectators; I've got no hassle with that. And I come down here and for four days I was in there and fighting, when I could have shot 80 in the first round and been out of it.'

He laughs ironically. Whatever else he might be, Whale is a survivor. 'You live to fight another day,' he says philosophically. 'I mean, I shed a few tears about it, sat in a corner and cried. But you come back and you fight – you've got to. The only hard thing about it all is you've let people down. I've let my father down. I've got nothing to feel ashamed of because I put everything on the line and it didn't come off . . . That hurts, knowing that you weren't good enough. I wasn't good enough because I wasn't experienced enough.'

Not every story at La Manga is a sad one. After two years in the wilderness, recovering from short game yips and the doubtful policies of too many teachers, Michael McLean finally reached the other side. He won back his playing card.

McLean, who is nicknamed Nobbie on the Tour, is one of the most likeable people in pro golf. He's so small and appears to be so shy that you wonder where he finds the courage needed to make it in this sport (the reality is a little different). But his motivation is his hatred of losing, his inability to accept mediocrity. 'Something in me always makes me fight back.'

The School was his last resort. If he hadn't won back his Tour card this year, he would have had to give up the game. What he would have done then, McLean has no idea.

'You cross that bridge when you come to it,' he says quietly. Golf is the only thing he knows.

'The hard thing about this week is concentration and doing it under pressure. Because under this pressure you could play around the easiest golf course there is and it would be difficult. It's a test. I mean, I was really wound up about the whole thing. I was really unsure of myself. I didn't know whether I'd be able to get it back. Whatever happens now I feel I've achieved my goal.'

Thursday, 7 December

There is an ancient truck with no sides at La Manga which is known as the Gua-Gua (Wa-Wa) bus. It keeps a schedule familiar only to itself and makes a tortoise-slow journey from the hotel and golf club to the apartments at Bellaluz and back. Bad weather of any description renders it more or less useless, so you spend a lot of time walking. That was how I met Mickey Yokoi.

Yokoi, a Californian of Japanese origin with a keen line in card tricks, had decided that it might be fun to try and qualify for the School this year. He was confident that he'd breeze through, and that he and his wife could spend the following year getting to know Europe in between tournaments. He didn't anticipate missing the cut, or the heartache that comes with it.

'If I'd known it was going to be [as lonely as] this,' he says, 'I wouldn't have roomed by myself. To try to qualify, usually, you've got to be away from people, because if you've got a room-mate that's not doing too well, then he kind of drags you down with him. They talk about how bad they're playing – everything's negative – and I hate to be around people who are negative. But I'm all by myself and there's no television in the room.' He holds up his Walkman. 'If I didn't have this music to listen to [Kenny G], I'd just drive myself crazy in this room. I never read, but I've read over a thousand pages this week.'

Yokoi missed a lot of putts in the third and fourth rounds and they cost him dearly. Five holes into the last round he began to think he was out of the tournament but managed to claw his way back. 'I got myself so I was five over with four holes to play. I figured if I just parred in I'd make it . . . I had no idea the cut was going to go down that low. The first person I talked to was a friend of mine and he said four over made it and my heart just went down. I thought, "Oh, no!"'

If they miss the cut, some players sit around with their head in their hands. Yokoi is a 30-year-old bundle of frenetic energy and has to work it out of his system. On different days he has pumped iron down at the gym, driven around some of the poorer surrounding areas and gone go-karting.

'There are worse things going on in the world than me not qualifying,' he points out, and cites the fate of an American player as an example. In the fourth round, the player was even par with three holes to play. He three-putted the sixteenth, three-putted the seventeenth, and hit his drive out of bounds on the eighteenth to miss the cut by a shot.

'You're always thinking about qualifying,' comments Yokoi, 'and that's not what you wanna think about. You wanna think about playing really well. In a tournament, you're always looking to win, but in the qualifying you're always looking to be ahead of the last spot. So your whole idea's different.'

THURSDAY P.M.

As soon as the four-round cut is made at La Manga there is a perceptible change in atmosphere. The players who miss it often break down and cry publicly. They either feel suicidal or they feel enraged. Anybody who can escape flies away from La Manga on the first available plane. Those that can't are trapped here – reluctant witnesses to the triumphs and failures of the remaining players.

On Wednesday, you can feel rebellion brewing in the air. But it is still a day of mourning, of coming to terms with grief. On Thursday there is a revolution. All the pent-up emotions and frustrations of every player who ever fantasised about winning the Open Championship explode like a cork from a champagne bottle. From that moment on they party.

West German Heinz-Peter Thuel won the School with a record 15 under par, so the Germans and the Swedes took over the steakhouse and celebrated raucously in one corner of the room. After spending much of the evening running in and out of the restaurant consulting sheets of paper, spraying each other with champagne and almost setting the place alight with flaming kebabs, they burst into song. It is traditional, Mikael Krantz informed us later, for the Swede who finishes highest at the School to be made to sing solo at the dinner given by the Swedish Federation.

Back at the 37 Bar, a party was in full swing. The pianist who had been hired for the week struggled to keep pace with her requests. She was completely surrounded by players in varying states of inebriation, and the banging on the piano drowned out all but the occasional note of music. By the time she had sung 20 renditions of 'American Pie', her voice was showing a distinct lack of emotion. David Ray's caddie annoyed her by seizing the microphone and treating us to his own version of 'Candle in the Wind', then David Ray sang a French song, which wasn't really in keeping with the occasion.

Mikael Krantz wove an erratic path over to the table where I sat talking to Paul Carman and a couple of other players. He and two fellow Swedes had been given a fortnight's release from the army to attend the School and he had managed to win back his card.

'I'm so happy,' he says to Paul Carman. 'I'm just so happy.' He looks around the bar at the players trying to exorcise the demons of this week, and shakes his head. 'This place is a fucking nightmare,' he observes.

It is after midnight and the bar is full of people sharing that exact sentiment.

FRIDAY, 8 DECEMBER

From first light on the final day a nervous crowd gathers around the scoreboard. Forty-eight cards are awarded automatically but the last two have to be fought for in a play-off. Nobody wants to be on the borderline. It is a situation comparable to that of a runner reaching the finishing line of a marathon, only to be told he has to run another mile before the outcome can be decided.

Of the 50 players who win Tour cards, only a handful will retain them. At the end of every season the top 120 money winners are exempt for the following season. The rest have to return to the School. To find the players with a fighting chance of success you don't need to look much further than the top ten finishers at La Manga because the lower down the ladder you go the less the number of tournaments allocated to each player.

When Jeremy Bennett won the 43rd card a few years ago, it entitled him to seven tournaments, only three of which he had practice rounds for. Bennett calculated that he would have had to finish 30th or better in every tournament he played to make the top 120 in the Order of Merit. The mental and financial strain of playing the Tour under those circumstances can be crippling. As Bennett says, 'You must be hungry, but you mustn't be desperate.'

Sudden death is the most appropriate term in golf. At La Manga, it gives the play-off the sinister significance of a Russian roulette game. The nine players tied on two under par competed for the final two places. José Rozadilla and Scotsman Russell Weir walked back after the first extra hole – victor and victim respectively. Rozadilla birdied and earned his card. Weir bogeyed to miss it.

On the second hole, Carl Stronberg leaves a five-foot birdie putt for his card short. Having traversed their way safely through the traps laid by the Qualifying School, some players lose their nerve. One by one, like the storyline of an Agatha Christie novel, they are eliminated. After the last green only Spaniard Santiago Luna and Keith Jones, a supremely confident young Englishman, are left standing.

Luna makes his putt. He stands under a palm tree on the fringe of the green and closes his eyes. Jones ignores the fine mist rain which has begun to fall and walks over to his putt with a catlike grace. The ball rushes towards the hole, teasing him, and then slides on by. For a split second his composure slips and agony crosses his face. Then he picks himself up, congratulates the speechless Luna and walks away without a backward glance.

Perhaps the only way for a player to survive the blows that professional golf inflicts is to use them to strengthen himself, to make him more determined. 'You almost have to go through this pain before you can get to the ecstasy at the other end,' said the Irishman Des Smyth once.

The Qualifying School might be the hardest lesson in professional golf, but it's only the first.

In the grey light of evening I stood on the balcony of the 37 Bar and looked out over the rain-scarred courses and the silver strip of sea on the horizon. Of the events of the past week no visible trace remained. The souls of those players who died on the killing fields of La Manga had been blown to the four winds.

2

CONQUISTADOR

'The longer you play the more certain you are that a man's performance is the outward manifestation of who, in his heart, he really thinks he is.'

HALE IRWIN IN *STROKES OF GENIUS*
BY THOMAS BOSWELL

Majorca, Spain, March 1990. Today is one of those cobalt-blue spring days where the sunshine has the hard brightness of a mint coin and the air is so bitingly cold that it hurts you to draw breath.

On such days even my boundless enthusiasm for the practice ground tends to wane and this morning, a practice day, so has that of a large group of players. Instead, we sit huddled before a video in the rustic warmth of the Son Vida clubhouse, watching highlights from past US Masters Championships. Between them the players can anticipate every shot so they provide a running commentary.

'Nicklaus takes an eight-iron here,' Roger Davis says. 'Hits it back left of the green.'

'He holes a ridiculously difficult putt here,' supplies a caddie. 'Watch this . . . There! . . . Did you see the borrow on that?'

Out of the corner of my eye, I see Severiano Ballesteros enter through the distant clubhouse door. His handsome countenance is customarily dark and brooding, and he wears the absorbed expression of a man intent on his own affairs. His is a strong face, one that would not look out of place on a statesman, a lawyer or a successful businessman. It has an actor's capacity for dramatic expressions, looking by turns stricken, enraged or joyful, and it reflects the climate of his mood with the accuracy of a weather barometer.

Right now, as I watch, it softens. Ballesteros drops to his knees beside an old armchair in the lounge outside. A fat tabby cat, warm from the fire, rolls on her back so he can rub her furry belly. After a time, he stands up and comes quietly into the room where we are gathered. He watches the clips from the 1987 Masters.

'That was a very conservative shot for Greg,' he comments, watching the Shark's approach to eleven, the play-off hole where he lost to Larry Mize's 40-yard chip-in. 'That really cost him the tournament.'

'He should have gone for the pin,' agrees Davis.

'That's what I mean,' says Ballesteros. 'It was too conservative. It was the same when he played Bob Tway.'

His own image flashes on to the screen. Ballesteros watches himself hit a fatal four-iron into the lake on fifteen in 1986. Covertly, everyone watches him for reaction.

'That shot saved Jack,' observes Ballesteros casually and without embarrassment.

Strange how the effects of a single shot can last a lifetime. They say that Tony Jacklin was never the same after Trevino holed his chip shot at the penultimate hole of the Open in 1972 to snatch certain victory from his grasp. They say that when Tom Watson chipped in at the seventeenth to defeat Jack Nicklaus in the 1982 US Open at Pebble Beach, the Golden Bear took the best part of four years to recover. There are those who will tell you that Hubert Green still loses sleep over the three-foot putt he missed for victory at Augusta in 1978. Green went back to that green after it was all over, leaving Gary Player – the winner on the second play-off hole – to his celebrations, and played that putt again. When it didn't count, he made it easily.

Green, and the rest of that sad band of players more famous for the way they lost a major than some people are for the way they won, knows how one stroke can sear the mind. Sometimes the scars inflicted take years to heal. Sometimes they don't heal at all.

On that fateful day in April 1986, Ballesteros waited on the fifteenth fairway at Augusta National with a four-iron in his hand. Ahead of him, Bernhard Langer took an age to putt out on the green where Jack Nicklaus had just carded an eagle to move within a shot of him. How long he waited for the green to clear, Ballesteros has no idea, but it was a long time. Long enough to break his rhythm and interfere with his concentration.

When he finally played his shot, Ballesteros did something which had cost him dearly in previous majors and would again. He pull-hooked – into the creek. An audible gasp accompanied the curved flight of his ball into its watery grave. A deathly hush followed. As the ripples spread across the glassy surface in ever-decreasing circles, Ballesteros made bogey. Then he bogeyed the next. The fire which had burned bright in him at the start of the day had been doused. When Nicklaus came after him with an inward half of 30, one of the greatest back nines in the history of golf, Ballesteros had no reply. He finished fourth.

And so began a long dry season. The next year, Ballesteros three-putted the first extra hole of a play-off for the Masters against Norman and the ultimate winner, Mize. In the Open Championship he fared no better. He finished sixth in 1986 and 50th in 1987.

It was a time when majors seemed beyond the reach of Ballesteros, when it began to look as though the greatest player in Europe had gone into an early decline. Newspapers and golf journals began to print articles under headings such as: 'Is there a way back for Ballesteros?'

Those were years when the Spaniard became increasingly moody, prone to frequent outbursts on and off the course. The greybeards shook their heads and pondered the problem. It was true that Ballesteros had been devastated by the death of his father, Baldomero, and it had taken its toll on his game. But was it also the fault of his brothers who caddied for him and with whom he had constant heated rows? Was his tempestuous relationship with Carmen interfering with his golf? Had he lost his putting stroke? Or had he tempered his game so much that he was in imminent danger of playing too cautiously?

All these things might, in part, have been true, although

none of them prevented him from winning titles throughout the world all the while. But golf is a game where a player is measured by major victories alone. And because Ballesteros measures himself in much the same way, doubts began to gnaw at his mind.

'Really, I lost a lot of confidence,' he says in retrospect, 'because once the time goes by, you know, it makes you think a little bit. And you say, "well, it's been four years without winning a major championship, maybe I'm not going to win any more".'

His laughter now holds a note of incredulity as though he can scarcely believe he ever thought such a thing. He shrugs. 'It happens. It's like when you're playing badly for long periods of time, you start to think, "Have I lost my form?"'

Shoulders hunched, dark forearms placed together on the wooden table-top, Ballesteros's stare is hawk-like in its intensity and makes one experience feelings similar to that of a rabbit hypnotised by headlights. Under this penetrating gaze, questions threaten to vanish from my mind without trace and I have to make a conscious effort to grab them by the tails, like eels, and hang on to them.

Ballesteros has not the slightest intention of being intimidating. On the contrary, he is relaxed and amiable as he discusses the arduousness of winning majors in the modern era.

'There are four majors a year and there's a lot of good players today. You watch Norman. Norman has been playing great for the last six or seven years and he has won only one major. Norman has been the favourite in every [major] tournament for the last three years and he hasn't won one yet. That tells you how difficult it is.'

In professional golf there are two kinds of pressure. There is the kind a young player feels when he's starting out on Tour, when he's struggling to survive financially and competitively. Then there's the kind of pressure that follows a major championship victory: pressure to maintain that level of play, to be a contender in every major championship thereafter, to win another major, to prove yourself time and time again.

Before he won the Open Championship for the third time at Royal Lytham in 1988, Ballesteros was bowed under the weight of this last. 'The first one was difficult, but I think the second one is much tougher. Much tougher. There's no question.'

For that reason, his victory at Lytham, his fifth major, was as much over himself as it was over the Zimbabwean Nick Price. 'It was very important for me to win,' said Ballesteros, who rated his last-round 65 as one of the best of his career, 'because I can now remember how I played today and forget about that shot at Augusta.'

Immediately afterwards, having cast off the shroud of public opinion which had threatened to smother him, Ballesteros became a changed man. He no longer looked sullen and bad-tempered, glowered at spectators or snapped the heads off reporters and caddies. He was no longer at odds with the universe. He began to rejoice once more in his own ability and it showed in his game. The old Ballesteros magic came back: the swashbuckling play, the daredevilry, the arrogant assumption that anything in golf was possible, however improbable.

In 1988, in only 24 outings, he won an incredible seven titles on three continents and finished in the top ten in eight other tournaments, topped the Order of Merit, and knocked Greg Norman right off his perch as number one in the Sony world rankings. A further three European victories in 1989 took his total number of titles to 62.

Now, confidence restored, Ballesteros says: 'I think if I can get ten majors, that would be good. I'd be happy.'

Contemplating the probability of any contemporary player winning as many majors as Nicklaus has (20) seems to afford him some amusement. 'Well, it's possible but it's not likely,' Ballesteros says, black eyes crinkling at the notion. 'I think there's more pressure in the majors today than there was maybe 15 or 20 years ago, and also the competition is more close. That's why it's become more difficult. If you look at the record, in the last ten years there have been only two or three players that have peaked and that proves how tough the competition is now.'

Severiano Ballesteros was born on 9 April 1957, in the tiny

Spanish town of Pedrena. The youngest son of a peasant farmer, he grew up running barefoot and free in the wild and rugged beautiful country of northern Spain. Times were hard, but they instilled in him the strength of character and resilience in the face of adversity that such beginnings often do. His education was rudimentary.

At the age of seven he was given his first golf club. Made by Manuel, one of his three golf professional brothers, it was fashioned from the head of an old three-iron and a stick which served as a shaft.

Ballesteros's love affair with golf was instantaneous. Forbidden to play at the exclusive Real Club de Golfe de Pedrena, which adjoined his father's land, he taught himself the game on the beach along the Bay of Santander. As soon as he was able, he began caddying. In his free time he and the other caddies held fierce competitions along the seafront, using pebbles for golf balls. Playing and practising off impossible lies over near insurmountable obstacles, Ballesteros learnt to imagine shots and then manufacture them. Armed with only his makeshift three-iron, he learnt to see and play more shots than most professionals could manage with a full set.

His most precious childhood memory remains, to this day, that of stealing away, aged 12, from the tiny, windowless room where he slept and playing the empty golf course at dawn.

His aspirations were simple. 'When I was small I never thought about winning. I was never even thinking about the majors. I was thinking I'd like to be the best.'

Such attitudes are as often inherited as they are inherent. Ballesteros's father was a champion rower, renowned for his strength and courage. His uncle, Ramon Sota, was Spain's best golfer. Sadly, Ballesteros rarely had a chance to play with him because their careers were on diverging paths. While Sota was playing tournaments his nephew was still caddying, and when he retired Ballesteros's own career was just beginning.

It wasn't so much a beginning as an explosion.

At 19, in his third year as a tournament player, Ballesteros entered the final round of the 1976 Open Championship at Royal Birkdale two strokes ahead of Johnny Miller, whom he had led for three days. At that age his game was less tempered, almost uncontrolled. He worked on extremes: wild drives, Houdini-like escapes, bold, attacking iron play and superlative chipping and putting. He fought like a tiger for four days, only faltering at the last through misadventure. He finished runner-up to Miller and tied with Nicklaus.

Those were the days when tournament golf was as slow and primly conservative as a Renoir painting. Golf clubs were the domain of the rich, major championships were the preserve of a handful of great players and tournament fields were made up of nameless, faceless golfers with indifferent golf games and few distinguishing features.

Ballesteros was an entirely new entity. Fiery and brilliant and as darkly good-looking as a movie star, he refused to conform to the existing mould of a tournament professional. He couldn't and wouldn't play the odds on the golf course. He played to limits far beyond the comprehension of most other golfers. He had imagination, vibrancy and irresistible charm, and he arrested the attention of a complacent public.

But he carried the legacy of his poor background with him like a burden. He had a roughness about him; he was gauche. He had a social chip on his shoulder, accentuated by his struggles with the English language, which gave rise to many misunderstandings. At that time there were a lot of other Spanish players on the Tour with only a very basic grasp of English, all of whom had the same problem. They developed an intriguing system of coping with situations such as interviews, ordering in restaurants and asking chambermaids about the laundry service. Whichever Spaniard was highest on the Order of Merit in a particular group would speak, and the rest would act dumb. Which was all very well until they changed positions on the money list.

Willie Aitchison, Lee Trevino's caddie, remembers going out for a practice round with Severiano and his elder brother, Manuel, around that time. 'My first impression of Seve was this scruffy kid. He hit the ball all over the golf course. But whenever he got to the middle part of his game and his short game, it was magic. You could see there was something different about the way he stroked the ball on the green and the way he played chips.'

Just how different, Ballesteros was to prove. For three successive years, 1976 to 1978, he was leading money-winner in Europe. Then in 1979 at Royal Lytham, aged 22 years and three months, he won the Open Championship.

Cruel winds sucked and swirled and tore at the links of Royal Lytham that week, lending her the means to flaunt all her wiles. Ballesteros went out in the worst of the conditions on the first day and shot 73. On the second day, he recovered with a 65 to move to within two shots of Hale Irwin, the tournament leader. 'He did what?' was Irwin's disbelieving response on hearing this news. But the third round brought rain and it was all the pair of them could do to shoot 75.

Ballesteros hit the ground running on the final day. He birdied the first hole and watched Irwin three-putt the second to take the lead. He played with reckless abandon, gambling with certain disaster and staking his life on an almost occult ability to escape from the inescapable. He went to the turn in 34. Irwin trailed in his wake with an outward half of 37 and an eventual tally of 78.

All week at the 339-yard thirteenth, Ballesteros had been trying different clubs. To reach the green with a driver it was necessary to fly the bunker, a carry of 300 yards. This time he just turned to his caddie, Dave Musgrove, and said: 'We'll go for it today.' By now Ballesteros was flying. Veins coursing with adrenalin, he hit a drive which was unlucky to catch the top of the bunker and go in. His recovery spun off to the right of the green. From there he holed out for a birdie three. Irwin watched open-mouthed.

Then came the sixteenth. At this stage in a major championship, most players would have thought it prudent to observe caution and taken an iron off the tee at this treacherous hole. Not Ballesteros. He took a driver and smashed his tee shot 40 yards off line and into a car-park. But according to Musgrove, Ballesteros had planned his round much more carefully than it would appear. He had studied the rough on every hole. Playing from the car-park meant he was coming back into the wind. From the fairway it was nearly impossible to stop the ball on the green where the pin had been positioned. Given a free drop from an Austin-Healey,

Ballesteros landed the ball 20 feet from the flag and holed the putt for birdie. He finished with a score of 70 for an aggregate 283, winner by three shots, and in so doing became the youngest Open champion this century and the first Continental to win the championship since Arnaud Massy of France in 1907.

'Why do I want to win?' says the mature Ballesteros in the manner of someone who has never known what it is not to want that. 'Well, it's difficult to describe how much satisfaction you have inside when you beat everybody. It's the goal. It's just what you try to achieve.'

In the spring of 1980, Ballesteros became the youngest winner of the Masters and the first European champion. Three years later he claimed the green jacket once more, overcoming the formidable trio of Watson, Stadler and Floyd in the process.

'When Seve gets going,' Ben Crenshaw said famously, 'it's like matching a model T Ford against a Ferrari. He plays shots that the rest of us can't even imagine.'

It was at this point, speaking from his position at the pinnacle of world golf, that Ballesteros approached the US Tour Commissioner, Deane Beman. He wanted the requisite number of tournaments foreign players had to compete in to be lowered to 15. Beman complied. Then came St Andrews and the Open Championship. Ballesteros won there in 1984, dashing Watson's hopes of a Scottish hat-trick and of matching Harry Vardon's record of six Opens. Subsequent demands on his time were such that Ballesteros decided to ignore his 15 tournaments commitment and to play in just eight US events. Enraged at having his authority flouted, Beman banned him from the 1986 PGA Tour season.

That was the year fate struck its cruel blow at the US Masters; the year that Ballesteros's reputation in the majors went into sharp decline; when he became sulky and irritable, convinced that everyone and everything was conspiring against him.

Ballesteros dismisses the memories of that low period in his life with a lift of his shoulders.

'I think you have to make many mistakes and you have to struggle. This will make you a little bit more hungry to win –

no question. In anything in life, I think. If things come very easily you don't appreciate them. I know some players that have the potential and the ability, but because they're making the [good] life so easily and they're making so much money, they just . . .' he purses his lips in a characteristic expression of contempt. 'You know.'

'There are many good players but they are not champions in their hearts. To be a champion it has to be inside. Some people they have that naturally and other people they don't. That's why they don't become champions.'

Events, seasons and years rush by at such speed in golf that they are almost self-effacing. Only the majors stand out as yardsticks, recognised measures of greatness. In such a protean environment, the players who leave an indelible mark on the game are people with a single work ethic: 'To be a champion you have to live for what you do. For golf or football or any sport, you have to think and you have to live all the time for that, otherwise it's impossible to be a champion. And you must like it.'

Ballesteros's words hang in the air, heavy with the weight of conviction.

'Some people,' he continues, 'want to become champions, and when they become a champion – once they have that and all the tension and the pressure that comes with it – they cannot take it any more. So they escape from it. That's why they come down.'

But there is a price to be paid for becoming a world champion. No one reaches the pinnacle of any sport without paying for it. Not ever. To Ballesteros, an intensely private man, giving up his personal freedom and any semblance of a normal life was the ultimate sacrifice.

'I went through a very tough time. I think when I became famous I feel like I lost a big part of myself. This is the most difficult thing that could happen to anybody . . .' He pauses, searching for words to express the hurt that it has caused him.

In that respect, marriage to Carmen Botin, the daughter of one of Spain's wealthiest bankers, has helped him enormously. Ballesteros, you see, is a man to whom family means everything. Throughout his brilliant career, his brothers have been there for him, watching from the wings. Manuel was the guiding influence in the early stages of his playing life. Vicente has coached him and caddied for him, and all four of them are heavily involved in the family firm. After all these years, Ballesteros will still go to his brothers for advice on his game before he goes to anyone else.

'My brothers help a lot. They are the only ones that know my swing because they saw me grow up. Everybody else, they don't know my swing. To teach someone that plays good golf is very difficult unless you know their swing.'

Like his brothers, Carmen is always there behind the scenes, calmly supporting him, as far removed from the stereotype of a golfer's wife as is imaginable. Her hair is dark and straight and her face, like Ballesteros's, is more striking than conventionally good-looking. When she smiles it lights up her whole face, just like it does his. Ballesteros was denied her hand for 12 years because her parents didn't think a man with his peasant background was good enough for her. Only when he had amassed a fortune and earned a reputation consistent with their own high standards did they relent. Seve and Carmen were married in November 1989.

'Marriage helps in many ways, no question,' observes Ballesteros, whose leisure time is spent cycling, fishing, playing cards with his friends and watching television and videos. 'I think,' he says, 'it settles you down a little bit. It's much better.'

Of all our modern players, Ballesteros most exactly embodies the spirit of the game.

'As a golfer, as a striker of the ball, Seve's supreme,' said Tony Jacklin. 'You can see that without knowing anything about golf. It's his balance, his poise. He's exciting . . . The game lives in him. He can create atmosphere wherever he is. That's what charisma is about.'

'Seve's a great inspiration,' enthuses Rodger Davis. 'I think his attitude and charisma are fantastic. Myself, I think he's the best player in the world at the moment. He's the complete golfer . . . I think you just get a guy that comes along once every ten years that has that indefinable "it". You can't teach it – someone just has it. Now that's not saying that guys like Faldo or Greg Norman aren't great players, but there are certain people – Nicklaus had it, Hogan, Palmer – they just have something. It's hard to put your finger on what it is.'

'Let me tell you something about Seve,' said ex-journalism graduate Chip Beck at the 1989 World Match Play. He was collapsed against a radiator in the press tent, recovering from a severe Ballesteros mauling (Ballesteros won nine and eight). 'He's a tough competitor; he's a great competitor. He could probably play hurt and beat most people in the world.'

It is as much the myth as the man which intimidates his foes. 'Everybody gets nervous,' says Ballesteros of his apparent invincibility on the golf course. 'I think that anytime you don't have any nerves out on the course it's because you aren't interested in the game. Sometimes it helps. Not every shot, every hole, but sometimes. I think especially when you play the last few holes and you're close to winning. I think a little pressure helps. But it's the kind of pressure everybody is looking for. It's sweet pressure, you know. I like that. I don't know about the others, but I like it.'

In years to come, in the annals of golf, Ballesteros is one of the criteria against which all others will be judged. Who else in today's uniform ranks of up-and-coming players is likely to take every facet of the game to its nth degree the way he has?

In the players' lounge at Son Vida, I put the question to Ballesteros. 'I know one,' he replies with a twinkle in his eye, 'but I think I'm not going to tell you.'

'In that case,' I say, 'how much longer do you intend to keep playing before you start thinking about retiring?'

'Retiring?' Ballesteros says, horrified. 'What else can I do? I don't know. I don't have any . . .' He laughs and shakes his head vigorously to dispel the image. 'No, no, no, I don't want to think about that. I'd like to play forever.'

'Like Gary Player?'

'Not like Gary Player. No, no, no, that's not my way. Because I think one day I will like to stay home and not travel so much. Travelling is very tough. But definitely, I will like to play for as long as I can.'

At length, Ballesteros strides from the clubhouse on his way to practice, frowning at some private thought.

'Seve,' shouts Harry Pichannick, a tiny white-haired Irish caddie. The Spaniard stops in his tracks, his face relaxing into a grin. 'I'm going to put money on you to win the Open this year,' HP tells Ballesteros, 'but not the Masters.'

He speaks to Seve as though he doesn't think the man can understand English. 'Your putting – no good.'

Ballesteros assumes a menacing scowl. 'Why not the Masters?' he demands in mock annoyance. Ian Wright, his caddie, stands behind him like a bodyguard, legs astride, hands on hips. He listens to the exchange with amusement.

'Oh, no,' says HP. 'Those greens – too slick for you.'

Ballesteros turns on his heels and starts to walk down the steps. 'HP,' he says sternly, 'in a few months, I quote you back.'

World Match Play, Wentworth, September 1990. But Ballesteros didn't win the US Masters. He wound up a forgotten sixth. And at the US Open, after shooting 73, 69, 71 in the first three days to enter the final round only four strokes behind the leaders, Ballesteros sank his tee shot in the lake at the second and blew out with a 76. At the Open and US PGA Championships, he never even made the weekend. His European Tour appearances have been erratic, to say the least. Out of 12 starts he has had just one victory (in the Majorcan Open), two missed cuts and seven top-ten finishes.

It has not been a year upon which Ballesteros will look back with fond memories. From the start it was dominated by a multitude of distracting dilemmas. The first thing that happened was the announcement that Carmen was expecting a baby, after which Ballesteros became increasingly preoccupied and progressively less attentive on the golf course.

Then there was the business of the venue for the 1993 Ryder Cup. Ballesteros led the bid for the event to be held at Club de Campo in Madrid, using tactics which those familiar with his arguments with Beman would recognise ('If the Ryder Cup doesn't go to Spain, I might lose interest in the game' and 'if Samuel Ryder was alive today he would be for Spain'). But in the end, although everybody agreed with Ballesteros that he had done more than any other player to promote golf in Europe, it was decided that the Ryder Cup should return to the

Belfry in 1993, with Club de Campo pencilled in as a possible venue for 1997.

After that there was an announcement of a swing change which would be implemented under the guidance of Vicente in the months following the Madrid Open in April. This statement was as good as retracted at the Open Championship. And then, finally, he and Ian Wright, his caddie, parted company at the English Open.

Ballesteros came into the press tent to be interviewed at the start of that week looking like a man with the weight of the world on his shoulders. He sat down behind the microphones and stared fixedly at the tablecloth, dejection in every line of his body.

'My concentration is not good,' he said in reply to a question about his game.

'Why is that, Seve?'

Ballesteros cleared his throat. He shifted in his chair. His expression was hunted. 'Well, I don't really want to go any farther than that,' he said at last. 'That's all I want to say. I don't really like to think about why this and why that. It's not necessary. Let's concentrate on the English Open. It's the only important thing right now.'

'Apart from the concentration problem, are you happy with the way you're playing?'

Ballesteros eyes his persecutor miserably. 'I say-a that I just don't want to go over that.'

He refused to talk about the US PGA, or to discuss past events in any shape or form. We proceeded along the narrow route of the English Open. We exhausted topics such as the weather and the golf course. When a reporter tried to get him back on to the subject of his poor form, Ballesteros snapped: 'Listen, I come here to play and to enjoy this golf tournament . . . I always play the best I can. It's important to win, but it's not the aim of my life and it will not be the aim of my career.'

'You seem unhappy,' someone else tried, after further attempts to get a dialogue going had been foiled.

'Unhappy? I'm not unhappy. I'm just not happy with the way things are going for me in golfing matters.'

Unable to advance or retreat, we eventually reached stalemate.

CONQUISTADOR

As the year has gone on, people have begun to talk about Ballesteros in the past tense, in the way that they have about Sandy Lyle through his slump, Bernhard Langer in the throes of the yips, and the Spaniard himself before he won at Royal Lytham. Even the players are beginning to talk in the same way, which is a bad sign. At the Belfry, Sandy Lyle said, 'Seve is a very proud man and he wants to dominate golf like he did through the '80s. He's struggling to come to terms with the fact that Faldo is the man of the moment.'

'He's lost his aggression on the golf course,' observed Wright, 'that natural sparkle. That will to play golf wasn't there this year.'

By far the most interesting theory I've heard on the subject is that of Ted Pollard, martial arts expert and fitness adviser to the Tour. Pollard believes the deterioration of a major golfer starts with his eyes. He says that once you reach a certain age your eyesight becomes impaired, and unless you correct it immediately by getting glasses or contact lenses your brain gradually adjusts itself to cope with this new visual information. And if all of a sudden the visual information that a golfer gets, with regard to club selection, lines of putts, etc., begins to alter, then he cannot continue to play in the same way.

At Wentworth, however, regarding us genially from his roost on the press conference platform, Ballesteros (blissfully unaware that his eyesight may be worsening by the minute) appears to be in quite the best mood I've ever seen him in. It may well be the product of his new-found status as father, bottle-washer and nappy-changer – his son was born on 20 August – but whatever the cause, this new sunny disposition is infinitely better than the state of depression he has been in for much of this year.

Two things have come out of the arrival on earth of the Ballesteros baby. One is the rather odd rumour that Seve calls him Baldomero (the boy's official name and that of Seve's father) while Carmen calls him Xavier, which I haven't placed too much store by. The other is the joke:

'Why did Carmen take so long in labour?'
'Because the baby was demanding appearance money.'

Oblivious to such idle chatter, Ballesteros watches Tony

Greer, the World Match Play press officer, shuffle his papers and pens.

'Your thoughts?' asks Greer, peering at Ballesteros through the milk-bottle thickness of his glasses.

'You want my thoughts?' Ballesteros asks the attendant press corps. 'I don't really have anything to say.' He pauses to let the comment sink in and then relents. He smiles widely. 'Well, it's always nice to play match-play, and of course I like Wentworth.'

'Could we have the Ryder Cup here?' a reporter asks, goading him.

Ballesteros refuses to rise to the bait. 'We can have the 1997 Ryder Cup at Wentworth.'

'Is it important to you to win the World Match Play this year?' Ballesteros has won this event four times, one short of Gary Player's record of five. 'I would like to win it anytime . . . To win the World Match Play is difficult, but to win the World Match Play five times like Gary did is something more difficult.'

'Are you playing well enough to win?'

'I played good enough last week [the Lancôme Trophy] to win, and I played good enough at the Belfry [the English Open] to win.' In fact he won neither.

'The odds are 11/1 against you,' a scribe tells him. 'Is that good?'

Ballesteros shrugs, half-amused. 'Maybe.'

He is in playful mood. We throw conversational tennis balls at him and he bats them merrily back.

At intervals our eyes drop below the level of the table, where he performs an intricate juggling act with a small brown ball, mauling it, stretching it, tossing it. Eventually he throws it at Tim Glover (the *Independent* correspondent), who gives it to me as a souvenir. I examine it closely. It turns out to be a piece of bread kneaded, the way a child does, into a dough-ball.

Ronan Rafferty, whom Ballesteros meets in the first round tomorrow, is playing very well and the Spaniard knows it will be a tough match. We remind him of his opening draw in the 1983 World Match Play when his opponent was Arnold Palmer. The match went to sudden-death after 18 holes and Ballesteros won at the 21st.

'Of course,' said the journalist who raised the subject, 'he was young then.'

'Who?' Ballesteros asks with a grin. 'Arnold Palmer or me?'

Ballesteros has an outstanding record in the World Match Play, having won all four finals he has played in. 'Better than Sandy Lyle,' he says wickedly when it is mentioned. Prior to his victory in this tournament in 1988, Lyle had the unfortunate record of having played in four finals and lost every one.

'Do you think that you should have been seeded?' asks a reporter, raising a controversial issue. Ballesteros is unseeded for only the third time in 15 consecutive starts in this event.

'Well,' says Ballesteros, 'if you go by the record, I've won this tournament four times. Some people should think about that. But I'm not upset about that. I'm just hurt.'

A tabloid reporter captures his attention. 'Do you get upset when you read in the papers that people think that you are finished, that you might never win again?'

There is a moment's horrified silence, the kind that always follows the voicing of the unthinkable.

'What?' says Ballesteros, doubting his own hearing. Unbelievably, he takes it with perfect equanimity. He even smiles at the man who asked the question. 'I don't get upset, no. I say that they don't have any idea what they are writing about. That is what I say.'

Emboldened by his calm response to this polemic the reporters become more and more daring. What is the matter with him in that case, they ask. Why hasn't he won a tournament since the Majorcan Open in March?

'I'm quite confident that I'm going to win before the year is finished,' replies Ballesteros. 'I have that feeling.'

But they persist. What has been the problem? Why hasn't he performed well in the majors?

'I don't have to prove anything to anybody,' says Ballesteros, letting their taunts slide off him like water off a duck's back. 'I have to prove it to myself. My record speaks for itself . . . I think over the years I have proved to everyone what I can do when I play well. I have nothing to prove anymore.'

'What do you have to prove to yourself?'

'Well, my career's been very steady and quite good over the last 14 years, and I feel that I have to win over the next few weeks to continue that, that's all.'

'What happens if you don't win?'

'NO!' shouts Ballesteros (but not angrily), cutting the question short. 'I will. I will win. You want to have a bet with me. I'll give you four to one.'

'Go on, Brian,' chorus the press in unison. 'No,' cries the Reuters reporter indignantly. 'I want him to win.'

Ballesteros's face is alive with merriment. He looks down upon the man as indulgently as a headmaster who has had to reprimand a favourite pupil.

'I know you do,' he assures Brian.

3

NOMADS

D.A. Russell plays the Blues. The soulful sound of his harmonica filters into the antiseptic atmosphere of the airport lounge. On this grey, still day, the gods have conspired to delay us. Other people throw up their hands in despair or erupt into towering rages when the television monitors confirm this. The pros, all veteran travellers, ignore the coughs and squeaks emitted by the loudspeaker – alluding vaguely to air traffic controllers and high winds in distant places – and head upstairs to the smoky innards of the bar.

Russell occupies centre-stage. He holds a captive audience. The faces of John McHenry, Stephen Hamill, Wayne Riley and Steven Bottomley are enraptured. A ragged line has formed around them as people press forward to pay for drinks and the air is heavy with the mixed aromas of strong coffee, cheap liquor and Continental cigars. Riley whoops and dances a jig, stamping his feet on the floor. Here, freed from the pressures of the tournament environment and out of their work clothes (lambswool sweaters off the golf course are taboo), the pros seem much younger; in their jeans and sweatshirts they look like students.

Fellow travellers give them a wide berth. 'Hooligans,' I suppose they must be thinking. They can't know that some of these players have known more heartache and hardship than many people twice their age; that sometimes the only way to stop yourself crying in professional golf is to laugh. Moments like this are their release.

Riley, for instance, has good cause to celebrate. He came within one shot of losing his Tour card this week (Portuguese Open 1989). After the first round he was four over par and it was unlikely the cut was going to be more than one over. I found him down on the range one night, alone except for the mosquitoes. Illuminated by the floodlights, he stood hitting balls like shooting stars into the darkness. 'Can I tell you something?' said Riley stopping suddenly, his face rigid with determination. 'If I miss the cut tomorrow and lose my card it doesn't matter, because I know that every week I've gone out there and I've done my best.'

He shot 66 the next day to make the cut and keep his card.

Other members of this happy group were not so fortunate. Russell, McHenry and Bottomley might be enjoying themselves now, caught up in the general end-of-term spirit (this is the last tournament of the year for most players), but all three have lost their playing cards and will have to return to the School. At the back of everyone's mind lurks the fear, however subconscious, that this time might be the last time.

FRANCE, APRIL 1990

If it's Wednesday, it must be Cannes.

After a while on Tour, you begin to think like that. Each week partially erases the last so that all you are left with is fragments; colours, faces and places blur in your mind like a kaleidoscope. You reach the stage where you have to go through a kind of ritual every morning to establish where you are and what day it is. Weeks are no longer divided into weekdays and weekends, but travel days, practice days, pro-am days and tournament days.

But when I look from my window this morning, there's no mistaking the blue of the Côte d'Azur, the rows of designer shops and, in the distance, the theatre where the film festival is to be held in a fortnight's time. Location: Carlton Hotel, Cannes. Pro-am Day.

Tour travel is not real travel. It's an endless succession of views from windows: from the plane, the bus, the hotel room. Paris, London, Rome – we could be in any one of them for all the impression we get of each place. The way in which we travel screens us from the real world; the problems that the ordinary Tourist encounters pass us by. For the most part, we go on packages organised for the Tour by three companies. We are met at the airport, whisked by coach or courtesy car to our hotel, and fetched and carried daily to and from the golf club. The hotels we stay in are mostly large and splendid.

The price of Tour travel is not low. A player's expenses per week, including accommodation, food and caddie, average out at around £1,000. Australian, African and American players have to bear the extra cost of long-haul airfares and maintaining second homes. Australian Peter McWhinney says that it costs him approximately Aus$100,000 (around £40,000) a year to play the Tour. Most Tour pros play between 18 and 30 tournaments a season, over 150 players following the circuit to some 14 countries. Package prices vary from week to week. The Desert Classic trip to Dubai costs around £600 for flight and accommodation, which wasn't particularly expensive given the distance to the United Arab Emirates and the quality of the hotel we stayed in. Traveleads' quote for two weeks in Madrid for the Madrid and Spanish Opens was £1,600 for a single room, which was unusually high. Randy Fox's charge of £250 for the Dutch Open, based on shared accommodation, transfers and flight, was exceptionally low.

Ten years ago, half the Tour travelled by car or caravan. Ian Woosnam did, so did D.J. Russell, D.A. Russell and Denis Durnian; David Jones slept in the back of his van. Tony and Lucienne Charnley are about the only people who still prefer to take a caravan to British and Continental events. 'The only good thing about being in a hotel,' claims Tony Charnley, 'is that they make the beds.'

The Charnleys' caravan has all the basic amenities of a small home, including a television, radio cassette player, books and Lucienne's knitting. 'I had a discussion with Ronan Rafferty who said he'd never go in a caravan,' says Charnley. 'And basically, I proved to him that what he has in his hotel room is less than what I have in my caravan. But it's just a case of people like that, unless they're spending £1,000 a week, they don't feel they're doing their job properly.'

Continuous travel requires a certain hardiness and great adaptability to changes in climate, language and food. Even after taking adequate precautions you are always vulnerable to colds, viruses and stomach bugs. In Majorca in 1990, about 20 players ended up with severe food poisoning after eating chicken sandwiches on the practice ground. Peter Smith had to be rushed to hospital, haemorrhaging from the stomach, and Jamie Spence collapsed on the golf course.

Partly for this reason, we tend to stick to familiar restaurants. Half a dozen favourites in every town tend to be common knowledge – McDonald's in the centre of Madrid is one such place – and most of the players will eat there. Personally, that's one of the things I like best about Tour life, but there are people who make a point of eating or staying in places where they know they won't find anyone connected with the Tour.

The good side of life on the European Tour far outweighs the bad. There is the golf, the humour and the companionship and, although we seldom see the cities we go to, the opportunity is still there. In Monte Carlo, for example, we are annually invited to the palace to meet Prince Rainier, Princesses Stephanie and Caroline and Prince Albert. This year (as usual) only a handful of players went, most people passing up the opportunity in favour of watching the World Cup on television.

Each place has its own accompanying rituals. In Dubai, we went to the market and bought fake designer T-shirts, watches and cassettes, and walked through the Gold Souk alongside black-veiled women, Arab sheikhs, expatriates and poverty-stricken migrant workers. In Düsseldorf, we ate chicken with our hands at a street café. In Valencia, we drank bitter coffee in neon-lit dive bars, sampled every ice-cream on their grubby menus and shopped for porcelain figurines.

It is a strange, nomadic existence, enjoyable in its way, but also very artificial and very insular. The Tour is an environment which encourages reclusivity and selfishness, because if you choose you need never have any other life. If you are not the type of person who keeps abreast of current affairs, world wars could literally pass you by.

'Things happen in Britain,' says Yorkshireman Gordon J. Brand, 'and we miss them completely. Six months later, someone will mention something and I'll say, "I don't remember hearing about that. Is radiation fatal, then?" I don't particularly go and find newspapers when I'm away. Some players do but they keep them to themselves because they're so expensive.'

At any one time on Tour there doesn't seem anything more important in life than who is leading the tournament. It is a life that doesn't require a lot of thought. Get on the plane, go to the tournament, go home, pack, catch another plane. Your years are mapped out for you, so are your weeks and your days.

David Llewellyn, conditioned by years of travelling to do things automatically, once even managed to get on the wrong plane. It was only because one of the other players spotted him disappearing through the wrong exit gate that he was rescued at all. Otherwise he would have found himself in Cyprus on arrival, an altogether different destination from the one where he was headed.

GERMAN OPEN, DUSSELDORF, AUGUST 1990

Randy Fox describes himself as 'a baby-sitter, cook and bottle-washer, priest, rabbi, psychologist and pimp'. Others might add to the list. In truth, he is a Jewish-American, one-man travel operator, with a round, pale face with spots of high colour on the cheekbones, an excitable nature and scarcely any hair.

Fox has, he says, always been a golfer by profession, but never a player. In the hippie days, he used to tuck his hair away and teach golf at night to get himself through graduate school in Buffalo, New York. What was he doing there? Many, many things. Avoiding the Vietnamese war, but mainly studying what we call English. A Masters degree led to an associate professorship at the university, until things got 'very hot and frustrating in the ivory tower' at which point Fox went back to being a golf pro. When he tired of the sterile atmosphere of American clubs, he became a travel guide for a Californian who was bringing American players over to Europe. Eleven years ago he started his own company, Pro Travel, on the European circuit.

Of course, Tour travel was different in those days. The players used to stay on the Continent for five weeks at a stretch; they didn't come home every Sunday like they do now. The old system of pre-qualifying for every tournament was still in existence then, so that players failing to qualify on the Monday of each week would be forced to spend the days in between incarcerated in the hotel.

'They went crazy,' recalls Fox, with a slight shudder. 'I remember my very first trip – they ran out of natural gas and there was Tony Jacklin needing a shave and looking like he hadn't had one in weeks. The airlines were on strike, so we chartered a plane to Malaga and the great three – Simon Hobday, Bobby Lincoln and [the late] Vinnie Baker – had a little bit too much to drink and the pilot threatened to put the plane down if they didn't behave themselves. When we landed, we lost Baker and I found him two or three days later sobering up somewhere.' Baker had got himself into trouble in a bar and had to be bailed out of jail.

'We got to Spain and the hotels were on strike . . . There was no food. We ate shredded lettuce for three days . . . From there we flew to Italy, and from Italy to Leon. We had a young German player with us, who was a pre-qualifier and who had no money in those days. His name was Langer. I remember checking in at Leon and they wanted to overweight us. Instead, I talked them into averaging the players' weight with that of a group of 40 nuns. But it was Langer's ticket that they had held back. He was the one that would have had to pay all the money.'

If stories like that don't convince prospective clients of Fox's attributes as guardian angel abroad, he pulls out his old Tour favourite – Brian Sharrock's incredible journey, which has, he says, done more than any marketing campaign to demonstrate to young professionals the pitfalls of travelling alone.

Brian (Save a Shilling) Sharrock was a Tour player in the mid-'70s. He was scrupulously careful with money; so much so that, given the choice of flying or driving from Madrid to the south of Sardinia for the Italian Open one season, Sharrock decided to drive. He set off for Marseille one Friday afternoon, only to discover on arrival that there was no ferry to Sardinia for three days and he had to fly after all. The only flight available by that time was one to the northern tip of Corsica, which he had no alternative but to take.

In Corsica he hired a car and drove like Ayrton Senna the

length of the country. He spent Saturday night in a hotel and went down to the harbour at the crack of dawn the following morning to try to get a boat to Sardinia. A surly French-speaking sea captain seemed to be the only living soul in existence. The language barrier was prohibitive and at one point threatened to put paid to the whole expedition. But eventually Sharrock's rantings and gesticulations won through and the man agreed to take Sharrock across the water – for a price.

When they reached the other side, the captain flagged down a passing Mini, engaged in an animated discussion with the driver and proceeded to load Sharrock's luggage into the car. Sharrock followed it gratefully. The driver then got behind the wheel, drove 600 yards down the road to a bus stop, dumped a surprised Sharrock, his suitcase and his golf bag on the roadside and hurtled away. When the bus finally came, some three hours later, it only took Sharrock as far as the town centre. He then caught a train to Is Molas, the tournament venue, where he arrived at 11 p.m. having spent a small fortune. The luckless Sharrock took a wrong drop at a water hazard in the first round of the tournament and was disqualified.

Fox talks rapidly in an American twang, reeling off ten stories in the time it takes most people to think of one. A party was thrown in Barcelona to celebrate a Scottish player's second-place finish, which resulted in a room being trashed at the Ritz and a Jaguar being damaged by a milk bottle flung from a window. Mark James and Ken Brown, who were sitting innocently in their room while all this was going on, lit a fire in the artificial fireplace because they were cold, and ruined the wallpaper. Buses have also broken down and drivers have fallen asleep, and Fox has arrived in countries at midnight on Easter Monday with his group, to find no coach waiting there to collect them.

'We found Mac O'Grady and Danny Goodman [who broke 28 putters and his caddie's ankle one year] riding in the undercarriages of buses several times. I don't know what they were doing . . . Mac once raced us from the airport in Madrid back to the hotel (12 kilometres) and beat us. He was a jogger in excellent shape . . . Another time in Madrid, we were going round a roundabout near the Palace Hotel and the undercarriage of the bus opens up and a golf bag falls out. Sure enough, it's Tony Johnstone's. There's clubs all over the street. So Tony jumps out and starts yelling and screaming as Tony was prone to do in those days.'

Fox goes on and on without pausing for breath.

'The Tour has,' he says, 'evolved into a high-pressure [big] money business with a lot of very serious young players who are born into playing pro golf . . . who are very alike and get more clonish every year. When we started, a lot of them were club pros and there were a couple of hell-raisers who got fined thousands. There was Ken Brown and Mark James, who got fined for every conceivable thing, from refusing to salute the flag to wearing jeans at the official Ryder Cup dinner, to refusing to sign autographs. There were others and there was action on the Tour. I'm not saying it was better. It wasn't. But there was a lot of hell-raising, a lot of girl-chasing, a lot of groupies, a lot of drinking.'

There are few groupies now – unless you count the adolescent autograph hunters who sometimes hang around the practice ground – and not much revelry.

Only one recent incident stands out as being particularly unsavoury. Mikael Krantz, a young Swede, went out one night at the 1990 Irish Open and had quite a bit to drink. No one, including Krantz, is entirely sure what happened next, but he allegedly left a bar at midnight and then was seen leaving it again at about 3 a.m., which would seem to indicate that he went back again. In any case, when he turned up the next morning to play with John Morgan and Keith Waters, he was clearly still inebriated. But he did, according to Waters, manage to play eighteen holes without inconveniencing his partners in any way.

But Morgan felt that his own round had been disrupted and duly reported Krantz, thus breaking a time-honoured code of loyalty between players. The story was blown out of proportion in the papers, particularly by the Swedish press, and Krantz lost his sponsor. Morgan was strongly criticised by the rest of the Tour for being, among other things, a hypocrite, although he continued to insist, without a shred of evidence, that he had believed Krantz to be high rather than drunk.

The fact that the episode aroused such a furore just goes to show how quiet it is on Tour these days.

'There's nothing at all,' agrees Fox. 'They're very homogeneous; to an outsider, very boring unless you know them. Players nowadays are really concerned with making money . . . and with planning and preparation. The top priority today for staying in a hotel is satellite television in English. McDonald's is a high priority: if Mickey D's is close by, they'll stay at the hotel. Things have changed. Most guys don't go any further than the bar, whereas in the old days – the pre-AIDS days – they used to chase around the red-light districts looking and messing around.'

It's been suggested that Fox has on occasion put players in hotels in close proximity to the less salubrious areas of certain towns in order to keep them entertained.

'Categorically untrue,' denies Fox emphatically. 'Whatever hotel we chose, people would find the red-light district . . .'

'There used to be a lot of hell-raising and parties. Now, the only place where the players go out at night is Sweden. We had kids from the hotel there jockeying us back from the Café Opera [nightclub] at two or three in the morning. Yes, the guys get involved in Sweden, but it's a dating-type thing, not a heavy thing. In Switzerland, there's a traditional insane party on Tuesday night at the members' bar. It just started spontaneously two years ago. But generally it doesn't happen anymore. To be honest, the hotels are dead at 10.30. Everybody's watching TV.'

A camaraderie not found in any other sport exists on the European Tour, born of the unique, nomadic lifestyle of the players. It stems from the constant insecurity of playing a game as unpredictable as golf and from spending a lifetime in the company of others in search of the same dream, and it has the same strength and moral support system as a large family.

'One thing I do like about Europe is that there's no caste system on this Tour,' says Fox. 'You can find Sandy Lyle talking to Wraith Grant about cars, you can find Seve having dinner with rookies. Nick [Faldo] too, hard as that is for people to believe; Nick's best friend on Tour was Peter Thomas many years ago and two more unlikely friends you'd never see. But there's no caste system, which I've heard there is in America. If you win a tournament, you eat in one place; if you win a major, you don't talk to this one.

'However, the caste system among nationalities here is destructive. The Swedes will not go out to dinner – with a few exceptions – with anyone else. They refuse to stay in a room unless it's with another Swede. The Spaniards have never ever made any attempt to communicate with anyone else. The Italians are the same way. [Alberto] Binaghi and his friends eat Italian food at the same restaurant at a tournament every night. There's no attempt at variance whatsoever. The Americans are just so tight. And even among the British players, the Welsh don't want to room with the Scottish and the Scottish don't want to room with the English. The Aussies and the South Africans will sometimes get together. You know, it's more than which football team you like. They thrive on it.'

But you have to balance that against the complete lack of snobbery or bias among the players. Everybody, no matter who they are, looks out for everyone else. 'If you're stuck you can always turn to someone,' grins Gordon J. Brand, 'which I often tend to do because I'm not an organiser. I'm a follower. I hate it when I catch a plane that no one else is on. I don't know what to do. Where do you get the baggage? How do I get from the airport to the hotel when there's no buses there with Traveleads on the front?'

In general, everyone gets along. Real arguments or fights are rare. As Mark Roe says, if you took a survey among the players, you would find that only about 2 per cent of the players aren't popular and that everybody dislikes the same few people. But for the most part, professional golfers have an acceptance of each other, regardless of their colour, nationality or beliefs, that we could all learn from. On the US Tour, I've heard it said, you could go into a restaurant with 52 tables and there would be a player at each one. On the European Tour you don't ever have to be alone unless you want to be. 'You can be a loner or an extrovert,' says Brand, 'and it doesn't really matter, because there's always someone to suit your needs.'

Chris Moody can be slotted firmly under the category of extrovert. Donald Stirling, a Satellite Tour player, has a story which he tells about the time he bumped into Moody in a wine bar in Barcelona. After exchanging a few platitudes they sat down for a drink. The focal point of the bar was a huge magnum of champagne.

'Christ,' said Moody suddenly, 'I could nick that.'

'You're joking,' said Stirling, startled.

'If I get across this bar and take the champagne,' said Moody, 'you have to buy dinner.'

'Fair enough,' said Stirling, feeling that his money couldn't be safer in the Bank of England. In due course, first one barman then the other disappeared. In a flash Moody was round the bar and had the champagne tucked under his leather jacket. Stirling, who is a very serious pro with a habit of talking in a sort of half-whisper, couldn't believe his eyes.

Now over in the opposite corner of the room, oblivious to all of this, were three Irish professionals. 'Watch this,' said Moody gleefully. He strolled over to their table.

'Well, Eamonn,' Moody said to Darcy, 'we've had our differences in the past but I'd like to show you that there's no hard feelings.' And with that he produced the champagne and handed it over.

'Now the fun begins,' Moody said to Stirling when he returned to his chair.

The Irishmen were stunned. They stared at the bottle for several moments and then began to pass it around the table, trying to decide who should open it. Some time elapsed before the barmen caught sight of their prized possession, which was by then in the process of being opened. As one, they dropped what they were doing and raced around the bar, shrieking profanities in Spanish. An almighty row broke out. 'It's mine,' cried Darcy, clutching the bottle to his chest. 'It's ours,' screamed the barmen trying to wrench it from his grasp.

'Chris,' said Stirling, 'you'd better say something . . .'

But Moody was nowhere to be seen. As he well knows, when the going gets tough, the tough get going.

A lifetime spent on the road makes most players philosophical, resigned to a multitude of fates. As a group, they are quite extraordinarily patient (David Grice, the long-suffering Traveleads rep, would disagree), the result, I suppose, of years spent playing a game which requires so much of that virtue.

'There are people who aren't patient,' comments Brand, the winner of the 1989 Belgian Open and six Safari circuit titles, 'and they tend to stand out like a sore thumb. I always just sit and wait. Occasionally I'll have a ding-dong with someone, but it's a waste of time because you know it's nothing they can do anything about. It's always someone else's fault whom you can't get hold of. So you're better off just sitting there and saying, "I'm ready to go when you are." If you got upset every time something went wrong on Tour, you'd be a nervous wreck.'

Golf is full of wasted time. You can't actually do anything with it because you're always waiting for something to happen: waiting to tee-off, waiting to catch a plane, sitting out delays. Christy O'Connor, Eamonn Darcy, Gordon Brand Jnr, and Roger Chapman carry telescopic rods everywhere they go, and spend their spare hours fishing. Chris Platts, David R. (Doctor) Jones and Jamie Spence, occasionally joined by Sam Torrance, have a poker school; Keith Waters plays the stock market; Phillip Parkin and David Whelan play chess. Gordon J. Brand sketches.

'I used to draw the view from the hotel room, but then we started staying in cheaper hotels and we'd back on to the bins. So now I pick up magazines which sometimes have decent pictures in, or I take pictures of people's houses and draw them. I've not sold a picture yet but I might have to if I keep shooting 74s.'

Brand is completely deadpan. He speaks in a slow, broad Yorkshire accent and his humour is so dry that you have to listen carefully to pick it up. But he is quite effortlessly and unintentionally the funniest player on the European Tour. His jokes are so involved and take such an age to tell that by the time you reach the punchline you've forgotten the beginning. And yet they are ridiculously hilarious.

'I suppose,' intones Brand when we discuss the problem of too much time and not enough to do with it, 'you're not too conscious of trying to kill time because it's the same every week. You're only on the course for just over four hours. It used to be five, but now they've started fining players for slow play so we've had to get a move on, which means we've got more time to kill. I liked it when it was slow.'

At the American Express Open in Los Brisas earlier this year, we were trapped in a cyclone for three days. We literally couldn't leave the hotel. The tournament was temporarily abandoned and eventually cut to 54 holes. Our only source of in-hotel entertainment – an indoor swimming-pool – was destroyed when a palm tree, bent double by the wind, snapped off at the roots and came crashing through the roof. If Denis Durnian hadn't saved the hour by producing a portable video and 30 video tapes, we might have all been taken away in straitjackets.

It's at times like these when you need people like Wayne (Radar) Riley – who can lay claim to the feat of having been jailed three times by mistake – to entertain you with stories of past misdemeanours. Riley loves to shock. This he does rather brilliantly by doing such things as emptying his briefcase – which has 'National Sex Week' on the side and is filled with assorted trifles from sex shops and other dubious establishments round the globe – onto the table at inopportune moments.

In Montpelier, he woke up one morning at 8.27. Normally that wouldn't be a crime but his tee-off time happened to be 8.35 a.m. In any other profession he could have rolled over and gone back to sleep, then called in sick later. In golf, it meant leaping from the bed that instant, grabbing a handful of clothes and racing out of the hotel half naked. To the amazement of the courtesy car driver, Riley dressed on the way to the golf course and was just doing up his fly as he reached the first tee. He went out in three under par that day and holed in one to win a Volvo the next. By unfortunate coincidence, however, his licence had been endorsed when he was caught drunk driving a fortnight previously.

'What are you going to do with your car?' I asked when I saw him in Cannes the following week.

'I've given it away to charity,' said Radar brightly.

'What charity?' I said disbelievingly.

'Alcoholics Anonymous!'

Fairway Dreams

Riley might be a prankster, and a very good one at that, but he is only a beginner when compared to the double act of Mark Roe and Robert Lee. Roe, the 1989 Catalan Open champion, is hyperactive with a lean, athletic build and overlong blond hair. Lee, by contrast, is tall and broad shouldered with a close-crop of jet-black hair. He appears (misleadingly) to be the steadier of the two. They are best friends and the best practical jokers on Tour. Their humour, however, is not to everyone's taste. It involves a certain amount of food throwing and a lot of antics with potentially disastrous consequences.

One of their best-known adventures began with a typical argument between the two of them. It was around midnight and Lee had just finished a lengthy phone call to his girlfriend. Roe was starting to drift off to sleep so he turned the television off. Lee, who was wide awake, mischievously turned it back on. Roe turned it off and Lee turned it on. When Roe took the batteries out of the remote control and threw them away, Lee got up and switched the television on at the set.

Tired and more than a little bit annoyed, Roe decided to put an end to the quarrel once and for all. He got out of bed stark naked, fetched a pair of scissors out of his hold-all and cut the live wire. 'Robert said I was just shrouded in a cloud of sparks,' grins Roe now. 'The room was illuminated.' The scissors melted in his hand. Half asleep at the time, Roe only realised afterwards what he had done. Lee lay on the bed laughing hysterically, the way people do when they have had a narrow brush with injury or death. Roe was completely unharmed, but he had fused the entire floor of the hotel.

'You know what life's like out there,' says Roe, trying to explain the motive behind some of their madness. 'It can be very tedious. People don't really know what it's like. It's a hard way of life. You only have to look at the highs and lows. Robert, two or three years ago, was one of the best young players on the Tour and he was making plenty of money. And within a few years . . . well, he's made three cuts this year. There's a very fine line between success and failure. So if you have a little bit of fun – as long as it's not harmful – I think it's okay.'

The trouble is that many of their pranks come perilously close to ending in tears. A few years ago, during the course of a daily ferry trip back and forth from an event held in Santander, Roe and a few other players began hitting balls off the tow rope on the deck and scattering fishing boats. They did it all week and never hit a boat. But on the last day there were a lot of spectators on board and it developed into a show.

'I teed it up,' says Roe, 'and I saw this boat; it must have been 200 yards away. I hit a huge slice. It was never anywhere near the boat. But the wind was bringing it in, bringing it in. The people in the ferry, they were off their seats watching this ball. It pitched straight in this fishing boat and hopped over the side. And this guy has gone, "What's happening?" And he's pulled his rod over the other side and started fishing there.'

Now that story might have ended a little differently if the ball had actually hit the fisherman, and Roe was berated by the other players for that reason. But no harm was ever intended. What started out as fun just got out of hand. A lot of players get very annoyed by some of Roe's and Lee's stunts, but really it is just their way of letting off steam.

'We don't drink and we don't smoke either,' says Roe in their defence, 'and one thing we do is we work very hard at our golf, because at the end of the day it's a job. If we want to have some fun afterwards, that's fine. You know Robert used to love discos? Well, I got associated with him for that although I never went to a club with him. I used to go to bed at ten and Robert would come in at one or two in the morning. But then his life changed because he met Liz [Lee's fiancée]. He never goes out anymore. He's in bed by ten.'

Roe is a mass of contradictions. On the one hand, you have this serious young man who married his childhood sweetheart and lives in a listed house, who loves books like *Watership Down*, and whose main hobby is collecting golf memorabilia. And on the other, you have this 'hell-raiser', to borrow Fox's phrase. I mean, this is someone who has owned and damaged nine cars 'very badly', starting with a blue Austin 1800, which he drove straight through a golf club wall while practising handbrake turns in an icy car-park. He has emerged unscathed from every accident he has ever been in.

'That's the way we are,' explains Roe, who was a successful diver and gymnast in his teens, 'the way we seem to live life. All golf pros, when we get in a car we seem to think we're Emmerson Fitipaldi. We all love fast cars.'

A while ago there was a tournament held at Albarella in Italy, where there were no cars at all, only bicycles and tricycles. The golfers cycled everywhere. Of course, the temptation to tamper with the bikes was irresistible to Roe and Lee, who were unscrewing saddles and hiding bike parts and bicycles in trees.

South African John Bland, meanwhile, had soon tired of signing his tricycle in and out of the compound where they were kept and had taken to smuggling it into his apartment every night. After several days of watching Bland turn right out of the golf club and go racing down the street between two bollards and into his villa. Roe decided that he shouldn't be allowed to get away with it. So he moved the posts six inches closer together. Bland, of course, came down the hill at full pelt that evening, never expecting to find anything to have changed. His back wheels caught and buckled and he flew over the handlebars and landed in a heap in front of the bike. Bland sat up, dusted himself off and, according to Fox, said, 'I'll get that Mark Roe; I know it was him.'

'These things happen,' says Roe, laughing at the memory. 'You need all these stories to keep you sane out here. You've got to remember it's not a normal lifestyle on Tour. It's unnatural. You're living out of a suitcase . . . you don't see your family. It's hard, it's very hard. You're lucky to be able to work six months of the year and make enough money not to work the rest, but then again you have to be very good. Nobody gives you anything, do they? You get what you deserve out here, you know. You're in control of your own destiny. If you make mistakes, there's only you to blame.

'You are not going to be able to do it forever,' says Roe. He knows that Lee, winner of the 1985 Cannes Open, the 1987 Portuguese Open and the 1984 and '85 Brazilian Opens, will have to go back to the School this year. 'You're going to be doing it four, five, ten years at most. If you're fortunate enough to do really well when you play, and you make enough money to live on, then that's great. Otherwise, you've got to look for different avenues when you're finished.

'One thing's for sure, it's great experience in life. It's a great learning process.'

4

JOURNEYMEN

Dubai, February 1990. The face of Ian Mosey is world weary, weathered and unshaven. Unruly strands of hair escape from under his white cap, which he lifts by the brim when he pauses in practice to wipe away the sweat below. He has been on this practice ground since sunrise, only stopping for a coffee, and though his swing bears the raggedness of exhaustion he won't leave before dark. That is his commitment. He realises that only by reverting, at 39, to his boyhood regimen of endless practice, is he going to survive on the Tour.

'It's like starting again,' says Mosey ruefully. 'I'm like a rookie who wasn't good enough to play in the early '70s, and now my game isn't good enough to play in the '90s. If I want to continue playing, I have to work very hard at it.'

No other sport demands as much or gives as little in return. Golf makes room for so few élite that a player only has to be lacking in one single ingredient required in a champion – whether it be confidence, talent or determination – to be lost in the anonymity of the pack.

Players like Mosey, self-confessed journeymen, are golf's survivors. They have to be. Between them they bear the brunt of the blows the game deals, with less of the rewards that compensate the best players for the mental and physical hardships golf forces them to endure.

'I wouldn't think there's anyone who doesn't start out imagining that they're going to be a big star,' says David Jones, Mosey's friend and fellow-journeyman. 'But as you grow into it, you realise that it's not everybody who does and you can't set yourself deadlines and say, "If I don't win a tournament by such and such a time I'm going to stop." Because basically it's the love of the game that gets you into it in the first place. I mean, once you've been on the Tour a certain length of time the last thing you want is an ordinary job, even within golf. So you sort of amend your goals as you go along.'

Ultimate satisfaction in golf depends on a player's goals at the outset, whether he plays for money, glory or for the love of the game. Ian Mosey has always played for playing's sake. As he observes, the way to become a champion is to set your sights as high as you dare. To this day, Mosey has never raised his above the level of tournament player. His only claim to fame in a career spanning 18 years is victory in the Monte Carlo Open – the time it was rained out and cut to 36 holes. That might bother someone to whom winning tournaments is the ultimate goal, but not Mosey.

'I never had a problem with that,' he says, 'because although I used to tell people what I thought they wanted to hear, which was very positive, very ambitious, I really wanted to be a tour player . . . I was never a talented ball player. I never had the talent to be great.'

Not everybody's dream is as small.

'Last year a journalist asked me whether I'd feel I'd failed if I never won a tournament,' says Tony Charnley, a slender, unassuming man of Mosey's era. 'I said no at the time, but really I would.'

Charnley, whose career best since turning professional in 1974 was a share of second place in the German Open ten years ago, had ambitions of being a top player when he started out on tour. 'I wanted to win tournaments,' says Charnley, whose Dutch wife, Lucienne, has caddied for him since they were married. 'But when I started I thought I was a good player. Then I saw everybody else and I realised I wasn't very good at all.'

It took him a long time to learn to accept that, to adjust his expectations. Even now, he can't understand why he hasn't done better; he feels he is as good a player as anyone else on tour.

'I have thought about giving up,' Charnley confesses quietly, 'but then it's hard to know what to do. I don't really want to be a club pro. Four years ago I had a terrible year and my game was so awful I just got to the point where I didn't look forward to going away to play. I went to see Eddie Birchenough and I asked him – it's a difficult question to ask somebody – to tell me whether I should give up playing.'

Birchenough, who is pro at Royal Lytham, took Charnley for a coffee and asked him exactly what he wanted out of the game. Then he went out on the range and worked on Charnley's swing. Charnley has been going to Lytham for lessons ever since. In that time he has moved from 89th on the money list in 1985 (£11,857) to 47th place in 1989 (£62,953).

'I can remember Gary Player saying that you get out of the game what you put into it,' says Charnley, who has always worked hard in the belief that the more he practised, the better he would get. 'People say to me, "You've done well", but I don't feel I've done as well as I should have done. I'm my own worst enemy. Because if I felt I'd done well, perhaps I'd be more satisfied with what I've got to show for it.'

The 36-year-old from Derbyshire, who bought his first home last year, sighs. 'Deep down I really like golf and I want to do well. But then there's times when I think this is such hard work, there must be easier things I could do. But I know if I didn't play, I'd be unhappy.'

'Because you wouldn't have achieved your goal,' his wife puts in gently.

It's easy to look at players like Mosey and criticise. There is a consensus among people ignorant in the ways of the game that those players who appear to be playing the game merely to make a living are just taking up space. It is not their lack of ability that is objected to: it is their attitude. They are the players who often appear to be more concerned with enjoying life than striving for perfection, who are least often on the practice ground and most often out on the town, conspicuous by their lack of dedication and drive.

'They all say that they would like to win,' says American Ron Stelton, a journeyman by most people's standards, 'but their actions don't prove to me that they do. They don't work as hard as winners do, they don't take it as seriously . . . Some guys find it very important to also have a good time, and if their definition of a good time means going out to the pub or a disco, then they're going to pay a price for that.'

A similar attitude prevails among journalists and observers of the game. David Jones, quite rightly, is angered by it. 'The press tend to see it as a young pro would see it. What is the point of being out there if you don't think you can win at the very least? What is the point of being out there simply trying to make a living? If you don't feel you can win a tournament there's something wrong with you if you actually continue to do it. It doesn't basically seem to occur to most of the press and the spectator public that a professional sportsman may regard "success" as leading a life that he gets a great deal of pleasure and enjoyment out of, and making a pretty good living at it. Success is seen purely in terms of money amassed and titles amassed.'

In a way, journeymen are victims of the structure of the pro game. Because tournament golf is one of the few professions where monthly earnings are publicised, it is easy to point a finger at people who seem to be taking things easy. But to my way of thinking, if a golfer has been on the European Tour for any length of time, he must, by definition, be a good player and he must be working hard. He is, after all, one of the top 120 players in Europe. Nobody is capable of staying competitive on tour today unless they are putting in the hours on the practice ground, because they risk losing their playing card and having to return to the School. Professional golfers still make money the old-fashioned way – they earn it. No one in golf escapes without paying their dues. It's the nature of the game.

As Jones points out, 'There are people who have amassed vast fortunes and a great number of titles, and yet are very discontented human beings. In fact, there are people who have been a huge success at the game who appear to have abdicated their responsibility as normal human beings to be courteous and friendly towards people and lead a sociable life.'

'Now I could look at that and say they're very successful golfers but they're not successful people. You have to recognise if you're involved in the sport as a journalist or spectator that you don't want to be a big winner . . . to be out competing and playing on the Tour. All you need is the desire to be out there getting whatever you want to get out of it . . .'

Within the narrow confines of how followers of the game

perceive that a pro golfer should conduct himself, Jones, 43, born in Newcastle, County Down, has frequently been judged and found wanting. It has been said that if he practised harder, if he played more tournaments, if he was more dedicated, he would have done much better in his career.

'I've heard it said about many, many people. I've heard it said about Peter Alliss because he made a decision at one stage in his life that he could no longer handle the torture of being out there trying to compete when he hadn't got a putting stroke anymore. He diversified and went into broadcasting. I've heard it said that that's a cop-out. Well, I think that is absolute bullshit. Why does he have a responsibility to the people who write about golf and observe golf, to continue to torture himself because they think he should?'

Jones took up golf in his late teens and turned professional in 1967. He is the calmest and wisest person I know. On Tour he is regarded as a kind of mystic. He plays with great feeling for the game and for the love of it.

Yet even Jones, who has a balanced approach to most things and rarely allows himself to be influenced by the opinions of others, found himself believing at the age of 40 that he had reached a turning point in his career. A watershed. Without thinking why this should necessarily be, he started to look for options. He agreed to take on the position of national coach and began to do more company days and clinics. Now, three years on, having lost and regained his playing card, he does neither.

'I did realise then that this notion that the press and some of my friends were looking at me and saying, "Jesus, what is he still doing out there?" was making me start thinking that way. I suddenly thought, "Why the hell shouldn't I be out here?"'

'So once I'd started getting over the idea that because I no longer thought of myself as a potential winner every week, I had no right to be out here, I decided I was out here to enjoy myself. And the more I enjoy myself, the better I play and the more money I make. So that's obviously the way to look at it, not the other way round.'

'It's a question of how long you can remain competitive,' observed Mark James once. 'I think a lot of players lose the desire. Players like Brian Barnes, for example; he wasn't old when he left the Tour. Because you have to work hard, you have to keep fit and you have to practise. You have to keep moving, you have to retain an innate keenness for the game, otherwise it becomes too much hard work to actually play.'

No one understands that better than Mosey. Over the years, the endless grind and repetition of tournament golf has worn him down. Each season he has slid a little further down the rankings, a little nearer to losing his card. In 1989 he found himself clinging to the brink of the abyss. His marriage broke up after 13 years and he came within a whisker of going to the Qualifying School for the first time in his life, missing 19 cuts in 26 tournaments.

'It's sad that I did get down last year because I played so badly,' Mosey says in retrospect, 'because of all the players out here, I love the life most. I wanted to be a Tour player. I've been playing 11 months of the year for 15 years and I've been thinking about nothing else for 23 years. From the age of 15, this is all I've ever done. To the exclusion of everything. I've got no business interests. I've got no contracts. I just play. That's all I ever do. Unfortunately, that got the best of men. I got tired and just lost a bit of enthusiasm. I lost my game as well – I don't know which went first.'

Mosey is not uncompromising. It is an integral part of his character. After talking to friends at the end of last year he resolved to change his attitude, his swing and the practice routine. He started by kicking the habit many players have of flying home on Friday when he missed the cut, staying on at the tournament instead to hit balls. It was counter-productive. The intractability of his nature meant that, having thrown himself wholeheartedly into this new discipline, he found it desperately difficult to accept that it was going to fail.

'Mose is probably going through the phase that I went through a couple of years ago,' says Jones understandingly, 'where maybe it's hard to accept that you're not going to play as well as you've done in the past, and you find it hard, as I certainly do, to keep the work-rate up.'

'Once you've been on Tour a certain number of years you need to get away from it, and you can't. It's a treadmill. The very thing you need, which is a good sabbatical spell away, is the very thing you can't have. Because with the rankings we have now, if you take six months off, you come back and you're nowhere. You can't get into playing anything. So you're on this constant seesaw where, if you don't play, you're going to lose your ranking, and if you do play, you don't play well.'

So Mosey modified his routine. A coach once told him that he would gain more from playing than from hitting hundreds of practice balls. This spate of manic practising has borne out the theory. Mosey intends to go back to his old ways – at least as far as practice goes. But it isn't this which is worrying Mosey. It is the realisation that he has lost the main source of his motivation for golf: his love of the game.

Years ago a player accused Mosey of loving the competition more than he loved the game itself. At the time Mosey flatly denied it. Now he realises that the man was probably right. 'I think I played so much, I got it out of my system.'

'Mose says that because he played for such a long stint, he just put too much into it; he can't love it anymore,' says Jones, who recognises his friend's dilemma. 'I don't know. Maybe that's the way it is for him. There are other people who love the game enough to play every single week of their life ... But you know, after 20 years you don't feel like beating balls for eight hours anymore. Well, if you're not going to do that it's harder to be competitive, and if it's harder to be competitive then you fall into this negative way of thinking. It happens to everybody.'

'It's like me going out today and doing 81,' says Jones dryly. 'I mean, after four or five holes I'm thinking, "Jesus, what a shit-hole this place is." Basically, I'm saying it just as an excuse for not trying. But the bottom line is I know this is what I want to do.'

Most journeymen live on hope. As cruel as golf might be, it is also a game of miracles and anyone can win at anytime. Andrew Murray, a talented player stricken by spondylitis (a crippling disease), inspired a generation of players when he won the European Open at Walton Heath in 1989 having led the tournament from start to finish. So did Chris Moody, unlikely winner of the European Masters at Crans Montana in 1988.

Fairway Dreams

Moody is something of a legend as journeymen go. He has a unique ability to antagonise the most placid people on Tour ('You mean I've got a perverse sense of humour'), a talent for practical jokes and a weakness for beautiful women which will probably be his downfall. A student of the Henry Cotton approach to golf (have the best to play your best), Moody lives like a millionaire on a relatively meagre income. 'I play like a millionaire as well,' says Moody with a disarming grin, 'like I don't need the money.'

In mid-Tour he is taking a four-week break to go skiing in Crans Montana, to visit his coach David Leadbetter in Florida, and to get in a few extra flying hours before he takes his licence. When he returns, his new Mercedes 300CE will be ready for collection.

Suave and smoothly attired, blond hair closely cropped, gold chain winking at his throat, Moody looks as at home in the luxuriant space-age splendour of the Emirates Golf Club as Mosey looks out of place. He reclines in his chair, delighted, as always, to be the centre of attention.

'In a way I was just afraid of working,' says Moody, sipping a fruit cocktail through a twirled straw and trying to recall his aspirations on leaving school. 'Golf, as you know, is a lot of work, but it's different. I was never career-minded. I used to go for job interviews and it used to feel like I was volunteering to be admitted to prison. I used to feel claustrophobic.'

So Moody tried his luck on the Tour for 15 years with limited success. David Leadbetter, Faldo's coach, was the catalyst in Moody's uneventful career.

'Ambition made me go to him,' admits Moody sheepishly, having just spent ten minutes drawing an analogy between Sheikh Mohammed's money and playing golf to prove that he wasn't envious of better players. 'I looked at my game at the end of '87 and I thought, "With the game I've got I'm actually going nowhere." The previous three years I'd gone 50th, 60th, 70th in the Order of Merit and all I could see was carrying on in the same vein.'

'I just felt that I had struggled along enough, seeing people fiddling with this and working on that, and never really known what I was doing, and I thought if I'm going to get a solid game, someone else is going to have to show me how to do it. It might be the end of my career because, at 34 years old, how can you teach an old dog new tricks? But it doesn't matter because I'm not getting rich anyway.'

Eight months and as many missed cuts later, he became European Masters champion. 'I like the Nike slogan,' says the irrepressible Moody: "Just do it".'

CANNES, APRIL 1990

Nowhere in professional sport is the disparity between best and least greater than in golf. Each day, on the same golf course, millionaires and paupers play side by side. Mosey (whose career earnings at the end of 1990 were £291,344) and Ian Woosnam (whose earnings after 1990 were £2,061,738), practising next to one another in Cannes was a graphic illustration of the contradictions of the game.

Mosey's white shirt was crumpled and sweaty, his trousers baggy, his face unshaven. His mouth, shaded by the peak of his baseball cap, was set in grim determination. On the ground lay his slim green carry bag, clubs awry and still grimy from practice. He had no caddie that week.

Beside him, Woosnam looked sleek and well fed, immaculately turned out in a cream cashmere pullover and tailored trousers, every spare inch of clothing and equipment endorsed. His swing was smooth and effortless. He stared critically after each towering one-iron shot. Even Philip "Wobbly" Morbey, his caddie, polishing the club Woosnam had just used, appeared more prosperous than Mosey.

Mosey hit a shot fat. He bent down and gathered his clubs; the smile he gave me was weak. 'Well, if that's how it's going to be,' he said, 'I'm going to try putting.'

A hundred identical situations can be sketched. In any other walk of life such contrasts would create a breeding ground for resentment. On the Tour, nothing could be further from the truth. There is little jealousy or off-course rivalry between players. As desperately as each golfer wants to win for himself, he feels glad for anyone else who does.

But the endless toil and grind of golf without reward can

have the effect of a water torture on the soul. Bitterness can creep up on a player before he realises it's there.

'What you've got to remember,' says David Jones, 'is that as journeymen pro golfers we've had 10 or 15 years of being treated well, treated in many places that we go to like celebrities, following the sun, being able to do within reason exactly what we please, where and when we please, work hard when we want to, be lazy when we want to . . . Now there's not many people in that position and making money at it. So you've got to offset the dark sides that make you embittered against the positive sides.'

Mosey, born in Keighley, Yorkshire, hedges any questions on whether he harbours any resentment towards the top players by pointing out that the school he attended was concerned less with education than producing 'factory fodder'; that of all the children he grew up with, he made the most of the limited opportunities available to him. 'They knew they were going to do menial jobs and have dead-end lives. They knew that when they were 15. That was what the system did to them.'

In the manner of a boy who runs away to join the circus, Mosey escaped to follow his dream of playing the Tour.

More than most people, Mosey misses the good old days. It delights him to recollect how, for years, fish and chips were his stable diet, how everyone travelled by caravan or car, how little it was possible to spend at each tournament. 'My values are rooted in the wrong place for this lifestyle. I still think a pound is a lot of money.'

For him it was a great adventure.

'The job was to be out on Tour, to find a way of getting to the tournament. It wasn't getting on a plane and checking into a five-star hotel, then going out and winning £10,000.'

Even the bad old days seem pretty good to Mosey. He can recall playing the Madrid Open one year when the hotel was just an hour's drive from the course and there was only one bus a day: at six a.m. The players used to arrive at the course in darkness, and there they would have to sit on their golf bags until the caretaker arrived to open the clubhouse. First tee-off times were ten minutes after sunrise. Dew-sweepers went off without breakfast or hitting a single warm-up shot.

One of the tournaments Mosey dreaded most was the Spanish Open, played at La Manga, which at that time was nothing more than a wind-tunnel of empty concrete blocks built on a strip by the sea. In early April it was still bitterly cold and there was nothing for the players to do. Most days Mosey got by on a couple of oranges and a piece of cheese because he couldn't afford the restaurant at the golf club.

He was quietly eating his snack in the locker-room one morning when the attendant, an aggressive Spaniard who spoke no English, began to abuse him. 'I actually lost my mind,' recalls Mosey. 'I said, "Look, what do you want me to do? I can't afford the restaurant and you've shut the snack bar; I just want to have my orange." And in the end he fetched the manager who pacified him. But basically, it was like, "This club is not for people like you." I remember feeling really unhappy about that, because there was just no accommodation for the journeymen pros.'

Mosey's frank, unpretentious manner is his most endearing quality. He makes no excuses for being the way he is, offers no apologies for being careful or for dwelling on the past.

'What I'd like to know,' remarks one player, 'is how Mosey can still be wearing Musingwear shirts when they haven't been dished out for eight years? And why they still look so good?'

The answer is in Mosey's garage.

Phil Harrison brought up the subject one evening in Montpelier. Mosey, it seems, cherishes possessions in the same way he cherishes memories. His garage at his home in Sunningdale is a miniature pro shop, an Aladdin's cave of golf equipment. The walls are lined with boxes of unused shoes, sweaters, shirts, balls and golf clubs. Even the Footjoys that he saved up to buy when he first came out on Tour are there. They cost £27 at a time when you could buy a pair of shoes for a fiver and he just couldn't bring himself to wear them. The shirts are still wrapped in their polythene covers. 'Well,' says Mosey, fielding our gentle ribbing shyly, 'as soon as you take a shirt out of the plastic is just becomes another rag that you put in the washing machine.'

For most of us the Tour has an addictive quality as strong as that of any drug. David Jones admits he hadn't realised how hard it would be to relinquish it until he came face to face with the spectre of losing his card.

Mosey knows it already, but realises that he may have no choice in the matter unless his game improves. And because he has always relished the insularity of life on Tour and by choice has become reclusive, he now finds himself without contacts or contracts. These are things he could have taken advantage of when he played very well from 1980 to 1986, but he was so wrapped up in the game at the time he chose not to. As such, he has made no provision for the second half of his life.

He doesn't know the names of anyone on the periphery of golf: the reporters, the reps, the officials. When I approached him about an interview, he eyed me with deep suspicion and questioned me for a long time about what I was looking for. After ten minutes of assurances, he suddenly snapped: 'But who are you?'

'I don't think I'm that strange,' he says frankly, as though it's something he's given a great deal of thought to. 'It's just a life where people aren't necessary and I've got used to doing without people.'

On halcyon blue days like this, it is very easy to understand how a player can make a life out of pursuing an indeterminate goal.

Mosey's mood is buoyant, at once reflective and cautiously optimistic. In thinking of the past he is reminded of the reasons he chose to travel this long and winding road all those years ago. He tips himself back in the chair he dragged into the shade, so that the sunshine falls on his face, on the dark shadow around his jaw and the wry smile in his grey-green eyes.

'I think only time will tell whether I regret it. I do know for sure I only had one little self-doubt which must have been in about 1978. I had already been at it a long time and I was still pre-qualifying. I was on a long drive down from Newcastle, with no prospect of making any money and getting used to not making any money, and I thought: "Am I doing the right thing with my life?"'

'I took about a day to think it through and in the end what

I thought was, if I got to 40 and I was still a pro, if I knew that I'd tried very hard to get what I wanted, had a dream and followed a dream, well, I could live with that. Even if I'd made no money, I'd at least grow old knowing that I'd had a go at my one big ambition. A full-blooded go. I mean, everything brushed aside to be a Tour player. I had two bad years after that and then I started playing well, but I never thought about it again. I knew all along I could live with it either way.'

5

TRIUMPH AND ADVERSITY

Open Championship, St Andrews, Monday, 16 July 1990. There is a buzz in the air, a curious hum, an electricity which sends a shiver down my spine and makes me laugh out loud. The sky is blue, the wind is fresh and there is a pervading smell of sea salt, suntan lotion and history.

Nothing prepares you for your first visit to St Andrews. No photograph or oil painting, no television picture or film could make your body tingle the way the atmosphere does here. Standing on the Swilcan Bridge with the clubhouse before me and the most infamous hole in golf – the Road Hole, seventeenth – behind me, emotion rises up and threatens to overwhelm me. The greatest golfers who ever lived have crossed this burn; their shoes have rung on these stones. Before this week is out one of the men here now will become one of them, if he isn't already. I watch players putt out on the eighteenth green beneath the empty leaderboard and I wonder what they are thinking. What are their expectations? Their aspirations?

In 1978 Tommy Nakajima came to the penultimate hole of the Open Championship in contention for the tournament. On the green for two, Nakajima's first putt was a fraction too strong and his ball caught the slope and slid over the brim of the Road Bunker. Fearing the terrors of the Road more than that of the trap, Nakajima swung too cautiously and left his ball in the bunker – twice. Nakajima, who had taken 13 on the par-five thirteenth hole at Augusta only three months previously, grew desperate. He put everything he had into his third attempt and blasted free. One chip and two putts later Nakajima walked off the green with a nine.

The mysteries and ambiguities of the Old Course have not

abated with the passage of time. Technical advancements have not tamed her. In a world where golf-course architects are striving to create by artifice what St Andrews is by nature, the Old Course remains the blueprint: a hand-made analogy for the capriciousness of the game of golf itself.

Tony Jacklin went out in 29 in the first round of the 1970 championship, before a thunderstorm flooded the course and stopped play until the following day. When morning came, the spell had been broken. Instead, destiny decreed that it should be Doug Sanders who arrived at the eighteenth green needing a three-foot putt to win the Open, Sanders who should miss it, and he who should lose the ensuing play-off to Jack Nicklaus.

'I get asked if I ever think about that putt,' says Sanders, who has made a kind of emotional pilgrimage with his wife to St Andrews this year. 'I say I don't think about it too much. Sometimes I go five minutes without it crossing my mind.'

Six years after winning the last Open Championship held at St Andrews, Seve Ballesteros sits behind several microphones and a miniature flag of Spain and watches the world's press file into the interview room. He is a happy man. His black eyes crinkle at familiar faces; his mouth stretches into a helpless grin. These last two weeks spent fishing, practising, cycling and watching the Tour de France on television have relaxed him. He looks more contented than he has at any other time during this troubled year.

'It's always nice to be back to the place where I have such good memories,' smiles Ballesteros. 'I must say, to win the Open is something special, but to win at St Andrews, that's something very few people have the chance to do and I'm fortunate to be one of them.'

Can he recall every shot he played when he won here in 1984?

'Of course,' replies Ballesteros. Playing a practice round yesterday with his brother Vicente, he remembered every one of them.

'How did you play the thirteenth?' asks an American reporter, testing him.

'Why?' asks Seve, knowing it but rising to the challenge

anyway. His teeth flash in his brown face. 'The thirteenth? Four-iron to the right, nine-iron to 15 feet, two putts.'

The seventeenth hole was more significant, being the hole where the Championship was won. 'Vicente,' Ballesteros tells us, 'says it's the toughest par four he ever saw.' He himself agrees. 'I think the seventeenth; if there's a little bit of wind against, you must play it as a par five. But on a day like today, definitely you must make par.'

In 1984 Ballesteros came to the Road Hole tied with Tom Watson on 11 under par. Watson made bogey from the fairway. The Spaniard hit a driver up the left-hand side of the fairway and then, with an area no bigger than a postage stamp to work with, he hit a six-iron to 25 feet and two-putted. That approach shot, combined with the fact that he was only in one bunker the entire week – an achievement of some note at St Andrews – won him the tournament. 'The more I look at that shot,' says Ballesteros laughing, 'the more impressed I get myself. Because if you look where I was, to put the ball where I did on the green, I guess, was very lucky.'

'You are a lucky player,' a journalist points out.

'Yes,' says Ballesteros, acknowledging it matter of factly. 'Always have been.'

Some good fortune would not go amiss now. For most of the season Ballesteros has not played well, particularly in the majors. At the US Masters he was unhappy with his game. He found a lot of trouble and, unusually, had trouble extricating himself from it. He fell away without ever really presenting a threat.

At the US Open, the only news he made was when he sacked his caddie, Ian Wright. Wright was distraught. He is a very proud person and it wounded him deeply. Nevertheless, it had been building up for some time. Wright had angered Ballesteros earlier in the year by getting a contract with a vehicle manufacturer to drive a car which had something to the effect of, 'Ian Wright', who caddies for Seve Ballesteros, 'drives . . .' written on one side. Ballesteros was enraged and demanded that Wright give back the car immediately. No sooner had that row died down when Wright went out and got himself a lucrative contract with Boss clothing, which

Ballesteros is paid to wear, and which Wright was in immediate danger of losing if he no longer worked for the Spaniard.

To this day Wright denies being fired, but according to caddie-talk (which is almost certainly true in this instance), he turned to Vicente "Chino" Fernandez – the Argentinian who got him the job with Ballesteros in the first place – for help. Fernandez persuaded Ballesteros to take him back until the end of the year but couldn't convince him to let Wright caddie at the Open. So, despite the fact that Ballesteros's record in the majors whenever his brothers have worked for him is distinctly uninspiring, Vicente will caddie for him here.

Questioned on his poor form in the run-up to the Open, Ballesteros says he is playing much the same as he was going into the Championship in 1984 and not a lot worse than he was prior to winning at Royal Lytham two years ago. 'There's nothing wrong with my game,' he insists. 'There's nothing wrong with my swing. It's just a matter of confidence.'

The subject of his so-called swing change, aided and abetted by Vicente, is broached. For months the reporters have written of little else. Nobody can believe that a player of Ballesteros's calibre should want to remodel a swing which has won him nearly 70 tournaments world-wide. Ballesteros's good humour begins to evaporate. Apparently, the reports have been exaggerated. 'People keep saying I am changing my swing,' he says brusquely. 'Why should I change my swing when I've been the best player in the world for ten years? It's just small details. I think my swing has been good to me so far. It's just a matter of confidence.'

As Ballesteros says, his self-assurance will return with one great round. Out on the range this morning, he looked as though he was feeling shots again, not just hitting the ball. He should do well this week. He loves St Andrews with a passion, and a golfer always plays well on a course that he has a good feel for.

Colourful streams of people flow through the streets of St Andrews on to the sea of green. From my vantage point at the top of the stand beside the first tee, I can see for miles in any direction. To my left is the silver curve of the bay; in front of me is the grey outline of St Andrews, perched on its rocky promontory – an entire town given over to the golfing obsession; the course with all its famous landmarks – the Valley of Sin, Hell Bunker, Walkingshaw's Grave and The Elysian Fields – stretches away to the right. Below me, miniaturised in real life, is the Royal and Ancient clubhouse.

To this day women are not allowed through its portals. However, enough progress has been made in the outside world to force the octogenarian members of the R&A – who run the home of golf like a Masonic sect – to allow women journalists into the clubhouse during the week of the Open Championship. We are now allowed into the hallway, but no further. Once, when I summoned the nerve to ask if there was a ladies' toilet in existence, I was grudgingly escorted to the Royal and Ancient Powder Room: a standing-room-only facility located in the kitchens.

I can be very reticent when it comes to matters of sexual discrimination. I like to go where I please and be accepted and judged on my merits as a writer and a human being, and the fact that I can be barred from a clubhouse, of all places, on the grounds that I am a woman, infuriates me so much that I deem it safer to stay away. Sexual discrimination, in my opinion, has about as much place in today's world as apartheid does. Liz Kahn (another woman golf writer), on the other hand, believes in fighting for equal rights. She asked the R&A whether they made a policy in the past of not allowing women reporters into the men's locker-room and, having been informed that they hadn't, was in the process of asking the attendant at St Andrews whether he had seen Gary Player, when she was bodily evicted from the clubhouse. Michael Bonallack, secretary of the R&A, told her that she had made a mistake. She wasn't, he assured her, then or ever, likely to be allowed in the men's locker-room.

'When I die,' wrote Kahn, in her article on the incident (*Mail on Sunday*, 22 July), 'I have asked Mickey Walker, woman golf professional, to take my ashes to St Andrews and scatter them in the North room of the Royal and Ancient golf club. It may not be the Kingdom of Heaven, but it is probably the only way I will ever enter that hallowed ground. How Mickey will get in, I do not know.'

Down on the putting green, an Aussie three-ball posed obligingly for a photograph. 'You want to take a picture of me eating my rabbit food?' asks Ian "Hollywood" Baker-Finch, with a grin. He is eating prawn and salad sandwiches for brunch. His form is good and he is feeling optimistic about the week ahead, determined to make amends for 1984, when, having entered the last round joint leader with Tom Watson, he shot 79 and finished ninth. He has rented a house alone this week, giving himself space to breathe, to concentrate. 'That's the way I like it. That's perfect.'

The starter is working himself into a frenzy. He can't understand that the pros are pretty relaxed about practice rounds. He's having a fit because they're turning up late, swapping partners, or not turning up at all. Red-faced, he rushes up to Greg Norman, who is idly practising his putting while he waits to tee off. 'Mr Jones is not ready,' he worries.

'Right,' shouts Norman to his playing partners. 'We're out of here.'

He putts out his remaining balls. 'Hey, pooftah,' shouts a voice from the first tee. The Shark draws himself up to his full height. 'Barnsey,' he booms. He strides over to embrace Brian Barnes. They make an incongruous couple: Barnes, with what in all probability is a vodka and orange in his hand, his golf shirt fighting a losing battle with the waistband of his shorts, and Norman, every inch an athlete, the ultimate sporting success story.

In his press conference, Norman brimmed with confidence. Yes, he was playing wonderfully well. He had played consistently good golf all season. He had had only two bad rounds – the first at the US Masters, where he shot 78, and the third round at the Anheuser-Busch Classic, two weeks previously, where he shot 75. What department of his game was particularly good? Well, all of them. He only had to string four good rounds together and he'd be in with a chance on Sunday afternoon.

'I have good memories of last year, though I was disappointed,' says the Shark. 'I watched it last night on TV and I really felt that I did not play badly at all.'

Norman arrived at the eighteenth hole in the sudden-death play-off for the 1989 Open at Troon needing a birdie to win the Championship and a par to stay alive. Incredibly, his drive found a fairway bunker, his second shot found another, and his third was out of bounds. 'Unfortunately, my drive landed on a hard patch,' says Norman in retrospect. 'I had 318 yards to the bunker. To this day, I would not have hit any other shot.'

But that was just one shot and one major. If you had said at the start of Norman's illustrious career that by the age of 35 he would have won only one major championship, you would have been laughed out of town. If you had said he would have snatched defeat from the jaws of victory in at least four others, you would have been taken away in a straitjacket. Yet he has.

In the 1984 US Open, he shot a final round 69 to draw level with Fuzzy Zoeller and force a play-off, causing the amiable Zoeller to wave a white towel in surrender. The following day, after shooting a 75 to the American's 67, it was Norman's turn to wave the white towel. Two years later, shortly after bogeying the 72nd hole of the Masters to lose to Jack Nicklaus, he was beaten by Bob Tway in the US PGA Championship when Tway holed his bunker shot at the last. In 1987 Larry Mize holed his fluke wedge shot in the play-off to steal the Masters green jacket right from under the Shark's nose. And then Mark Calcavecchia got the better of him at Troon.

There have been others. It's got to the stage now where you don't wonder how Norman is going to win the tournament, you wonder how he's going to lose it.

Norman, to his credit, seems to have turned it around and made it into something positive rather than negative. 'If other guys hole their shots and pip me, I can't help that. I have no control over what they do. If they do it to me, it is a sign I am in contention more than anyone else. Maybe it makes me a better person, a better player, more resilient. I've had a lot of good out of it.'

The Great White Shark bares a row of white teeth. 'I'm holding fairly high hopes for myself this week.'

WEDNESDAY, 18 JULY

Nick Faldo went to his first Open Championship in 1973. Then aged 16, he drove up with his dad and stayed in a tent. 'I remember it was so cold, I walked around with my pyjamas on under my clothes. I watched Weiskopf practise in his street shoes. There was just something about the way he was swinging. I said to my dad: "He'll win."'

Strange that Tom Weiskopf might be looking at Faldo now and thinking the same thing.

Faldo looks like a champion – strong, fit and dominant. He removes his dark glasses and regards the press through deep-set blue eyes. He listens to the first question put to him, flicks irritably at an imaginary speck on the table in front of him and he fixes the reporter with a concentrated frown.

'What score's going to win it? What did Seve win it with? Twelve under? Who knows? If I knew that I'd be a stockbroker.'

'What lessons have I learnt from other majors? I take them all one at a time. After winning the Masters and missing by a stroke in the US Open, I just go at the majors as hard as I can. I think they're the most important thing in my career at the moment. That's what I channel all my thoughts into.'

Faldo's Open record is astounding. Besides his win at Muirfield in 1987, he has at various times finished third, fourth, fifth, sixth, seventh and eighth.

'I thrive on majors,' he says. 'When you get into a position to win it's nerve-racking, but that's what it's all about. Nicklaus used to look into the crowd on Sunday afternoon and say, "Isn't this great? This is what I've been working for." You've got to take a step back and look at yourself. You want to get into that position, so there's no point in being scared of it.'

Under cloudless skies, with only the mildest of sea breezes, the Old Course is as benign as a pussycat. If the weather doesn't change, somebody is likely to match Curtis Strange's course record 62, shot here in the Dunhill Cup a couple of years ago. 'There's not too many records you think too much about,' says the US Open champion, 'but having a course record at St Andrews, that's something special.'

When he first came to St Andrews as a Walker Cup player in 1975, Strange's immediate reaction was one of bewilderment – that of most uninitiated. 'I guess the first time you play here you come away feeling like everyone does, "What the hell was that?" But the more you play St Andrews, the more you appreciate it.'

'You have to defend yourself against the course off the tee,' said Ballesteros on strategy. 'Avoid the bunkers, then attack the course from there . . . You've got to put the ball in the right place, which is left, I think. This is the problem. It's the only golf course in the world where you have to play left.'

'Yes, you can bale out left all day long,' replies Strange, 'but the further left you go, the tougher your second shot is going to be . . . I think strength is very advantageous on this golf course. Strength being that you have to hit the ball a long way.'

'I found the Old Course disappointing in my early years,' recalled Tom Watson, 'because I thought the luck of the bounce was too prominent in scoring. Now I realise that this is the essence of the game and it's how it should be played. You have to take the bounces as they come and get to know them the best you can. I think it is the most difficult to know and understand of all Open courses because of the blindness and misdirection inherent in the course. At first I didn't understand it; I didn't like it. Now I love it.'

THURSDAY, 19 JULY

The worst of the Open Championship is that it is full of reporters from all around the globe – many of whom don't usually cover golf and don't know the first thing about it – in search of a bit of sensation. Scott Hoch and Nick Faldo, paired together in the opening rounds, were their first victims. The tabloids reported that Hoch, who missed a two-foot putt to lose the 1989 Masters to Faldo, as having said that he hated Faldo, that Faldo was universally disliked by other professionals and that the people in Faldo's home town would rather see Hoch win than Faldo.

'What was all that in the papers?' Trevino, who was talking to Canadian Danny Mejovik in the locker-room, asked Hoch.

'I said some things,' said Hoch miserably, 'but I never said all the bad stuff.'

He said as much to Faldo on the first tee. 'Don't worry about that,' said the Englishman. 'I don't read it, but I know exactly what's going on this week.' Years ago, an incident like that would have really got to Faldo. Today he just accepted it, reassured Hoch, and went out and shot 67.

Though the wind was blowing in the opposite direction to that in the practice rounds, the scoring was good. Norman and Michael Allen, winner of last year's Bell's Scottish Open, both shot 66 to take the first round lead. Behind them came Nick Faldo and Peter Jacobsen on five under par, and Christy O'Connor Jnr, Ian Woosnam, Baker-Finch, Martin Poxon and Craig Parry on four under.

'The course is tough,' observed Norman, 'and you've got to take advantage of any situation you get given and accept that you're going to get into trouble.'

'The elements are what make this golf course so difficult,' said Trevino, who shot a first round 69. Diet Coke in one hand, cigarette in the other, he gesticulates to the press. 'In my opinion, the pin placements were very difficult today, and rightly so because the R&A knew it wouldn't blow.'

Trevino maintains he hit his best shot of the day at the seventeenth, a three-iron which rolled off the green and on to the road. He managed to get up and down for par. 'It's just a very difficult green to land the ball on,' says Trevino. 'That green is a seven-iron green. It's not built to take a five-iron or a four-iron.'

'It doesn't reward intelligent golf,' said Palmer. 'It rewards poor shots and penalises good shots.'

'Do you think it should be changed?' someone asked Trevino.

'Don't ever change anything at the Old Course,' shouts the Mexican, horrified. 'Please don't touch it.'

'Are you pleased to be on the leaderboard at this stage of the tournament?'

'Always, always. You always want to start fast. You always want a good first round in a major.'

Friday, 20 July

One of the reasons why golf is the greatest game ever invented is that anyone can win at any time. Even in a field such as this, where 156 of the best players in the world are competing for a total purse of £825,0000, unfamiliar names from the lower rungs of tournament golf keep appearing with delightful incongruity at the top of the leaderboard. Jamie Spence, an unknown Englishman from Tonbridge, Kent, playing in his first Open, went out this morning and shot 65. His round of eight birdies included one at the Road Hole – the equivalent of an eagle on any other. Walking down the eighteenth, he looked up to find himself at the summit of the leaderboard with Payne Stewart.

At 27, Spence has visited the Tour School five times. His best finish ever in a tournament was ninth in the Belgian Open earlier this year. He has missed the last four cuts.

'First and foremost, I just want to say that this round is for my father,' says Spence, a slender young man with a boyish face and a shy smile.

Last Christmas his father had a heart attack. 'That was a bad time,' says Spence quietly, 'and it stuck in my mind. It changed my attitude to the game. You get so wrapped up in your own little world. Golf was so important. It still is, but it made me realise that golf is not everything, and making a bogey or three-putting doesn't matter in the long run. I just go out and enjoy it now.'

'Do you think you can win the Open?' he is asked.

Spence gives a short laugh. He's more of a realist than that. 'Well,' he says, 'it's a dream, isn't it?'

Meanwhile, the Shark is on the warpath. The candy-striped figure of Payne Stewart was an early casualty; Norman ate his lead for lunch. He reached the turn in 33, with birdies at the fourth, seventh, eighth and ninth. Behind him came Faldo, and behind them both came the diminutive figures of Parry and Ian Woosnam, each chasing his first major victory.

For several holes the four matched each other birdie for birdie, then Norman and Faldo began to draw away, ending the day joint leaders on 12 under par for the tournament. Parry slipped slowly down the leaderboard, eventually coming to rest on eight under par. Woosnam, who came to grief at the seventeenth where he took a double-bogey six, was a stroke behind.

After his round, Norman looked invincible. 'I'm playing well and putting well right now,' he says. 'When I get to the green I feel I am going to make the putt.'

'He can overpower a course like this,' says Nick Price, who is lying seven under par for the tournament. 'There are bunkers that come into play for the rest of us that he doesn't even see. He's going to be a hard man to beat. We're all going to be chasing him.'

'I definitely feel I can win this week,' says Norman. 'That will be my approach, to go for it tomorrow. I am enjoying the game, I'm not really charged up or excited. Right now I'm in a good position. If I don't come out and do something spectacular tomorrow, I'll still be in a good position come Sunday.'

Nicklaus, it was put to Norman, believes that in order to dominate golf a player has to be dominant.

'What is dominant?' asks the Shark, considering the point. 'Is dominant going out every week believing you can win? Well, I do that anyway. That's just the way I am. I'm a very confident, positive person.'

One thing is for certain, the outcome of the Open battle between the giants of world golf will prove – at least in the collective mind of observers of the game – who really is the number one player in the world.

The cut fell at 143 – one under par, three shots lower than that of the 1989 Open at Troon, which was the lowest cut on record at the time. The list of the guillotined read like a *Who's Who* of golf: Seve Ballesteros; defending champion Mark Calca-vecchia; Tom Watson, winner of five Open Championships; Gary Player and Arnold Palmer, who have won 16 major championships between them.

SATURDAY, 21 JULY

Two years ago Greg Norman went up in an F14 jet over St Andrews. 'Have you ever been in a dog-fight?' asked the pilot during the course of the flight. When Norman replied in the negative, the pilot called up a colleague on the radio and a mock dog-fight ensued. They hunted one another through the skies. 'Keep a lookout for him,' requested the pilot, 'and tell me when you see him.' Norman gazed out into the blue. 'There he is,' he cried suddenly, spotting the other jet. Without warning, the pilot dived, the ground came up and the G-force hit Norman like a brick wall. He was copiously sick.

Sometimes golf's maxim is wrong. Sometimes it's not how many, it's how. In years to come, the annals of golf will only record one outcome that third day. Faldo's and Norman's respective scores of 67 and 76 will be nothing more than numbers on a page. Historians who may never have walked the course that day will write that Faldo struck a psychological blow at the first when he birdied from 11 feet, while Norman, who had hit his approach shot inside Faldo's, made par. They will note that Faldo turned in 33, leaving Norman three shots adrift; that the Englishman salvaged par from a near unplayable lie in the gorse at the twelfth, but that the Australian could do no better than bogey from the fairway; that Norman missed from short range at the thirteenth, fourteenth and fifteenth holes; and that the two players, level at the start of play, were separated at the end by nine strokes.

Golf is not a fair game. It does not reward proportionately that which is put into it. To some people, it will give more, others less. It has no favourites and makes no concession to greatness. Today, it was Faldo who got the breaks, another, it might have been Norman on whose head those blessings were heaped.

Only Norman knows what really happened that day. Only

he knows where the magic went. But in the absence of any such explanation there was nothing left to do but listen to the opinions of other players.

'Greg didn't have the run of the ball,' commented Faldo. 'His putting hurt him. Every time he didn't get a break or didn't get the ball close, three-putting killed him.' Norman had five three-putts during the course of the round. That's *five*.

'He was cruising along very nicely,' said ex-European Tour player Simon Hobday. 'He should have just kept cruising. I think he tried to either beat Faldo, or to beat the golf course. You cannot push golf courses like that. He tried to overpower the golf course and the old bitch bit him. And, of course, the more it bit him, the more he tried to push. He tried to carry the bunker here and take a chance there.'

The comments written on the bottom of Norman's score sheet were terse: 'Just putted terrible . . . Had a couple of bad breaks on the twelfth and thirteenth and that was the end of my day.'

While Faldo and Norman locked horns at the top of the leaderboard, a 24-year-old Midlander by the name of Paul Broadhurst went out and shot a record-breaking 63. His outward half of 29 was matched in the afternoon by Baker-Finch who, having begun the day a distant eight shots behind the leaders, collected five birdies and an eagle for a 64. He ended the day tied with Stewart in second place.

Sunday, 22 July

Only two players on the course today were applauded as loudly as the winner was: Sandy Lyle and Greg Norman. Lyle was so proud to be standing on the first tee on the final day with a chance at a top-ten finish, anyone would have thought he'd won the tournament.

The Shark, too, walking down the first, was given a rousing reception. His face split into an ear-to-ear grin. But to his more cynical followers, his final round of 66 to finish fifth proved nothing. Sure he was going to do all right in the last round – there was no pressure on him. As far as they were concerned, Norman had choked once too often.

In the weeks before the 119th Open Championship, Nick Faldo had two dreams. In the first, he dreamt that on the fourth day of play he would lead the tournament by five shots after three rounds, and in the second he dreamt that he would play the final hole of the Championship leading by four shots.

Call it a premonition, call it what you will, Faldo had no intention of leaving anything to chance. Most of his life has been spent in preparation for days such as these. Early this morning he was out with David Leadbetter working on his putting in jeans and a T-shirt. When he felt the nerves begin to take hold of him, he went back to his hotel and slept until it was time to warm up for his round.

I went out with Faldo and Baker-Finch in the cool of the afternoon, walking alongside bright banks of spectators. Stewart was just ahead of us, bizarrely resplendent in stars and stripes – the colours of America's National Football League – and gold-tipped shoes.

Faldo entered the final round with a five-stroke lead, and no one since McDonald Smith in 1925 at Prestwick had failed to defend so great an advantage. It was Faldo's hour of glory and he enjoyed it. All his work had been done in the first three days: his 54-hole total of 199 beat Tom Watson's Muirfield record by three strokes. He played steadily, cautiously even, but always poised for flight.

On a day when the wind blew strongly from the east and the pins were placed in the toughest positions of the week, Zimbabwean Mark McNulty shot a flawless 65. Earlier in the week he had echoed Strange's comment that strength was an advantage at St Andrews. 'I disagree,' said Paul Stephens, his caddie, at the time. 'I think it is a straight-hitter's golf course.' Stephens's theory would seem to have been borne out. Birdies have been scarce today, but McNulty had seven and never dropped a single shot.

I left Faldo and the forlorn Baker-Finch at the fourteenth and went ahead to the Road Hole, where I sat on the cold stone wall and watched the final act in the drama unfold. Woosnam disappeared into the depths of the Road bunker. When he re-emerged, his late charge for his third successive tournament victory and his first Open title had ended. He finished tied third with the American Jodie Mudd.

Next came Stewart, who had drawn within two shots of Faldo with six holes to play. He sent his approach sailing over the road on to the greasy verge beside the wall and came distraught to weigh up the consequences, chewing gum furiously all the while. A shot dropped there and a five from the Valley of Sin, and the American was left to share second place with McNulty.

In winning the Open Championship Nick Faldo became the first British golfer since Henry Cotton before the Second World War to win the title twice, and the first man since Watson in 1977 to win both the Masters and the Open in the same year. His last-round score of 71 for an aggregate of 270 surpassed Ballesteros's record by six strokes.

Some moments in golf are so precious that they stand apart from all others. Framed in our memories is a picture of the Golden Bear, putter raised heavenwards, as he claimed the US Masters title, aged 46; so, too, is that of Ballesteros striding gloriously to victory here at St Andrews, and Sandy Lyle's ecstatic dance across the eighteenth green at the US Masters.

Nick Faldo has earned his place among them. Breaking through the crowds in the brilliant light of evening, arms raised in a victory salute, he was hailed as the best golfer in the world.

As a child, Faldo had another dream. In generations to come, he wanted people to say: 'Did you see Nick Faldo play? I did and he was quite something.'

I did, and he was. Quite something.

6

LEGENDS

York, 7 August 1990. Into York's trendiest restaurant walks Simon Hobday clad in red trousers and a stiff-collared golf shirt (from the previous day). In a room made up almost entirely of Levi 501 wearers, Hobday looks about as fashionable as a dinner jacket at an acid party. But he is in his element. He is as comfortable in this environment as he has been holding court on the putting green for the best part of the day; as equal to the occasion as he is on the range, swinging as beautifully as Ben Hogan under the admiring gaze of a dozen players. On the European Tour, Simon Hobday is a legend.

In a sport full of drudges, of conformists, of players whose lives have been devoted to the strict adherence of rules and regimens, Hobday is that rare jewel: a rebel. Tales of his exploits are quintessential Tour lore; ten years after he quit the European circuit, they are still as fresh as this morning's news. Nothing you hear these days is in quite the same league. There's no comparison, for instance, between a story about Mark Roe taking an air rifle from the boot of his car and using the sign behind the fourteenth tee at Moor Park for target practice, and one about the events preceding Hobday's night in a Mexican jail.

Hobday is one of the last remaining symbols of a bygone era when players took neither themselves nor the game too seriously. All of that has changed. It's becoming increasingly obvious that unless a new generation of personalities is introduced into the game without further delay, all humour will be lost from professional golf. As it is, characters on Tour are becoming as rare as albatrosses.

Having said that, I am a fierce critic of articles which state categorically that there are no longer any amusing or entertaining players in the game. But after giving the matter some thought, I have decided that, although any person closely involved with the Tour could name you at least 30 pro golfers who are renowned pranksters and practical jokers (Mark Roe, Robert Lee, Roger Chapman and Gordon Brand Jnr, etc.) or have wonderful senses of humour – Mark James, Gordon J. Brand, David Feherty, Tony Johnstone and some of the Australians, for example – not one of them would appear so to the spectator public.

And as for real characters, well, you'd be hard pressed to think of more than one or two. There'll never be another Max Faulkner, or a Trevino, a Doug Sanders, a Gary Player, or a Brian Barnes. But then that, of course, depends on whether your definition of a character is someone whose escapades tend to be drunken ones, or a wise-cracking showman like Trevino.

'I think when they say the characters have gone out of the game, they mean there's none of this staying out till three in the morning and getting drunk like there used to be,' said Mark Roe when I asked him about it. 'You're just playing for too much money. It's too serious a business . . . They were great characters, but they used to drink like fish those boys. You shouldn't have to become a character by going out drinking all hours, or womanising, or whatever.'

Mark James came by while we were talking.

'Do you think there are no characters left on the Tour?' Roe asked him.

'There are more characters now than there ever have been,' said James.

'But there's no one like Trevino, is there?'

'Trevino?' said James, with a snort of disgust. 'You call that a character? He doesn't say a word for 15 holes, and then he sees the cameras and he comes out with all these one-liners.'

Right now I'm watching one of the first category of characters pour himself a Carlsberg Special, and idly wondering whether the US Seniors Tour is ready for him. Hobday confesses to being nervous and looks horrified when I produce a tape recorder. 'What kind of stories do you want to know?' he keeps asking. We embark on several safe subjects, beginning with a discussion on the merits of tournament professionals as people.

'This is a gentlemen's game played by gentlemen,' shouts Hobday, since the din is rapidly approaching a crescendo. 'And if they aren't gentlemen, they bloody soon will be.'

Several people look up, startled. Hobday takes not one iota of notice. He has been attracting attention for most of his 50 years. Born in Mafeking to veterinarian parents – one of whom was awarded an MBE and the other an OBE, he can't remember which – he moved to Zambia at the age of two when his father was called in to deal with an outbreak of foot-and-mouth disease. He played golf from an early age and continued a successful amateur career long after he became a farmer.

In 1970 disaster struck. The Zambian government deported him for playing golf in South Africa and took away his farm. He was given two options by the British High Commission when he appealed to them: he could move to Britain and live on the dole, or he could move to Rhodesia. He chose the latter. With no alternative means of making a living, he turned professional and came to Europe. He was 28 years of age at the time.

Nine years ago he took a year off the Tour to move his family to South Africa and never returned. The Tour became all-exempt and Hobday refused categorically to go to the Qualifying School. Instead, he amassed a small fortune in the car alarm business and continued to play the Sunshine circuit. But now, prompted by the creeping advance of old age, Hobday has decided to 'take up the cudgel' and try his luck on the Seniors Tour. 'They had two Seniors events in South Africa. I went to watch and I thought, "Shit, I can beat those guys." So I got keen again. It's not often in life you get an over.'

I bring up a recent conversation I had with John Bland, who said that he doesn't think that the European Tour Qualifying School breeds winners in the way that the old system of pre-qualifying did.

'I agree with that,' says Hobday immediately. 'Because you might have a player that's exceptional like Olazabal, but before he gets on Tour he has to go to the School. So he goes to the School and he has one bad week and he's gone for the rest of the season. Now what does he do? He goes back to selling cars or training shoes or whatever. Then he goes back to the School the following year and has another bad week. His heart's broken. He doesn't come out again.

'Whereas, in the old days when they pre-qualified, they would have about 30 spots and the guys that could play got in. If he played four rounds he'd play the next week . . . and eventually he worked his way up to winning tournaments. I don't know how many people are out there that could win tournaments that aren't actually playing . . .'

'So I agree with John,' says Hobday finally. He has to go to the Seniors Qualifying School in America later on in the year. 'I didn't know he had that much brains to actually work a thing like that out!' he says with a grin, knowing perfectly well that Bland is anything but unintelligent. Swirling the amber liquid in his glass, he turns his attention to Bland.

'Do you know the difference between Bland and a coconut? You can get a drink out of a coconut.'

Hobday laughs delightedly at his joke, but not maliciously. He's the kind of person who could insult people's babies without causing offence.

'He's actually got quite a capacity for practical jokes, John. We've a fellow in South Africa called Phil Simmons who's a big strong bloke – one of the longest hitters in the world – and Blandy started this thing going quietly around the Tour where everybody called him Phyllis. You'd get the guys on the scoreboard putting up Phyllis instead of P. Simmons. And John would send him [flowers and] telegrams from overseas saying things like: "We had a wonderful night together, Love Bruce." The man went crazy.'

Last year Bland started everyone on Tour calling Hugh Baiocchi Cliff (Richard) since Baiocchi has the same kind of ageless face as the singer. Baiocchi got his own back. At the 1989 Murphy's Cup he and one or two other players organised a first-aid buggy and a nurse to fetch Bland from the practice ground and carry him to the first tee. A dozen players had formed a reception committee and were all falling about when he arrived. Bland was livid.

'Right, Baiocchi,' he said to the South African, who was laughing loudest. 'When customs hold you up for four hours at

Jan Smuts [Johannesburg airport], don't come crying to me.'
Bland, you see, has friends in high places.

Hobday listens. 'Thank God there's just a little bit of fun
left. Those things used to happen all the time when I was out
here. Nowadays the boys are very serious . . . They can't release
themselves they're playing for so much money. I mean, they've
got to have a few beers and they've got to relax. The boys aren't
relaxed at all. Take a guy like Martin Poxon, for example. I
mean, hell, he doesn't know anything other than the golf club.
There's nothing else in the world other than hitting golf balls.
Sam Torrance and Noel Ratcliffe – they used to go out and
have a pint. Now they're all dedicated, the lot of them. In the
old days, if we missed the cut that was the signal to blow the
brains out! That was it. Take the town apart! Now they miss the
cut, they go to the next tournament, they practice.'

'The money's done that but it's also improved the standard
of golf unbelievably, particularly from the bottom. The winning
scores aren't that much different, but if you think you can make
the cut by shooting level par or one over out there today, you
are living in a dream world.'

The other big change in tournament golf since Hobday
played is the way the golfers are looked after. The Tour
sponsors, Volvo, provide courtesy cars, players' lounges, catering
facilities, superb practice ground facilities, and so on ad
infinitum. At the start of every tournament players are given
four dozen balls and a handful of gloves, and are kept regularly
supplied with shoes, sweaters, shirts and visors. In Hobday's
day, players received six balls on arrival at a tournament and six
if they made the cut. Gloves and shoes were luxuries only given
out at the Open.

'I tell you, I hear stories about players saying, "If you don't
give me a couple of hotel rooms, I'm not going to play",' says
Hobday. 'To me, they should be burned at the stake. They
should be putting things back into the game.'

Hobday might feel strongly about that, but he doesn't think
there is anything wrong with Tour players taking advantage of
the comfort zone created by the increase of prize-money, and
merely playing to make a living. 'If they're good enough to
make £50,000 or £60,000 then it's a good job, isn't it? So I take

my hat off to them. They still have to work bloody hard because it's the toughest job in the world, in my opinion. If they can make £60,000 a year playing golf, then they deserve everything they can get.'

We picked up our drinks and negotiated bar stools, exuberant locals, Ross McFarlane and Vijay Singh, who were engaged in a battle to the death on a space invader machine, and the wooden trellis-work that separated the bar from the restaurant. A hen party of seven monopolised one corner of the room and assorted pro golfers occupied the rest.

'That thing makes me very nervous,' said Hobday, eyeing my tape recorder with deep suspicion, once we had found our table. But on the table it stays. I decide that it's high time he dispensed with the small talk and opened up about his chequered past. 'First,' says Hobday guardedly, 'tell me what you've heard.'

Well, among the more infamous Hobday-abroad stories is one which took place in Crans-sur-Sierre, Switzerland, venue of the European Masters.

It was a bitterly cold night in the mountains. Hobday had made every possible attempt to warm himself, even resorting to gathering his week's supply of clean and used golf clothes from their piles on the floor (he has an aversion to doing laundry) and putting them on. Finally he decided that the only hope he had of warding off rigor mortis was to go down to the village and fortify himself with several brandies. This he did. But once in the bar Hobday, who was wearing more layers of protective clothing than the average American footballer, began to sweat. At intervals he peeled off individual garments.

Sam Torrance observed this with amusement. 'I'll bet you £5,' he said, as Hobday divested himself of a sweatshirt, 'that you won't take off everything.'

Now, apart from the fact that he was four sheets to the wind by this stage, Hobday is one of those people to whom a dare is an irresistible challenge. In a trice, he had stripped naked. He then continued to drink away the evening as though everything was perfectly normal. Of course, the news spread like wildfire and eventually half the village had converged upon the bar. Old ladies and assorted voyeurs gawped. Hobday couldn't have cared less. Clothes or no clothes, it mattered as much to him as it would to a five-year-old. When the management pleaded with him to at least wear his underpants, he put them over his head.

Mortified, the player who had accompanied Hobday fled the bar. Hobday ran after him, his clothes under one arm and his underpants still on his head. Rounding a street corner at speed, he came face to face with a policeman. Each did a double-take. 'Good evening,' Hobday cried gaily, deciding that courtesy was his best line of defence. But the policeman just nodded an acknowledgement.

The following morning the Tour committee tried to fine Hobday, but without success. He told them firmly and succinctly that what he did in his private life was his own business.

The stories get worse.

There was that long flight to Australia, for instance. The back of the plane was full of bored, under-occupied Tour players. At breakfast-time, Hobday's neighbour came up with a plan to entertain them. He cut a hole in the bottom of his breakfast tray, unzipped his trousers and carefully inserted his member. Then he rearranged his eggs and bacon around it and garnished it with a sprig of parsley. He pressed the orange call button. The stewardess arrived, all smiles and what-can-I-do-to-help-you-sirs.

'I think there's something wrong with my mushroom!' said the wicked Australian.

Such horrendous activities must have slipped Ken Schofield's mind because he came up to Hobday yesterday and asked why he didn't try for his player's card. He said the European Tour needed more characters.

'I knew Ken Schofield when he was a virgin,' announces Hobday irreverently. I blanch slightly. 'When I say virgin, I mean when he first came on Tour; I didn't mean virgin in the proper sense . . . But anyway, he's done a helluva job. I wish he had been tougher with the anti-apartheid thing, but other than that the Tour has taken off. But George O'Grady was there before Schofield. I remember O'Grady when he was a virgin. He used to come and say, "Uhh . . . uhh . . . Hobday . . . You've been swearing on the course and I've got to fine you £40," and he'd blush.

'There was one particular time in Sweden. I'm going like hell with an American bloke and I'm in contention. I get to the eighteenth hole in the third round, and as I hit the ball my driver shatters and the ball goes in the water. Of course, I let rip. But the [American's] wife was walking with us so he pulled me in. They had to fine me. Georgie had to come and find me on the putting green the next day and he was all blushes. I said to him, "What the hell was I supposed to say?" I mean, what would he say? "Tut, tut, tut?"'

In those days, Hobday had two main accomplices on Tour: Irishman John O'Leary, who is chairman of the European Tour tournament committee, and Australian Jack Newton. Now one can imagine Newton sowing a few wild oats in his time, but John O'Leary? No one more unlike Hobday could ever have graced the professional ranks. In all the times I have encountered him he has never been anything other than the absolute model of decorum. He is softly spoken, has a calm, deliberate bearing and the most impeccable manners.

'John was a wild man,' Hobday informs me, banishing this image in an instant. 'The situations you could get into with him! He'd drink, chase women and do all sorts of weird and wonderful things in those days. He was scared of nothing. He didn't care, John, at all. He was always a perfect gentleman but he had a sense of fun, which he hasn't got anymore. He has, as you say, gone quiet.'

'What was Jack Newton like?'

'Newts? He's a great guy. One of the best . . . You should have met Newton then,' says Hobday with a grin. 'I mean, you would have fallen in love with him. He was a good-looking boy and he was unbelievable with women. They'd just run at him from all angles . . . But he was a gentleman. I never saw him say no.'

But marriage caught up with Newton eventually. He and fellow Australian Bob Shearer met their wives at the same time. They were whiling away an afternoon in the tournament bar one day when they got chatting to a couple of Piccadilly girls (the old equivalent of today's Guinness girl). They decided to invite them out to dinner.

'Which one do you fancy?' said Newton to Shearer in a whispered aside.

'I can't make up my mind,' said Shearer. 'Which one do you like?'

Newton, too, was spoiled for choice. So they tossed a coin. But halfway through the ensuing evening, each realised they liked the other's partner better. They swapped over and are still married to the same girls today. 'Newton's wife, Jackie,' comments Hobday, 'is an absolute saint. I mean, she must have known he was a bad bastard.'

Hobday's wife must have married him knowing the same thing.

'Oh, no, my wife used to think I was a great bloke,' insists Hobday. Her opinion was revised when Newton, then single, arrived in Zimbabwe to play an exhibition match. 'He stayed with us for 12 days,' explains Hobday, 'and every morning at breakfast there was a new woman. A brand-new woman every single day! My wife thought that if I had mates like that, I must also be a crook. I've been in shit ever since.'

With some justification, I would imagine.

'What sort of things did you and Newton used to get up to on Tour?' I asked Hobday.

'Well, I can give you an example of madness. Tertius Klarssons, Newton and I were sharing a room in Germany one year. Klarssons had missed the pre-qualifying and Newton had missed the cut; I was lying third in the tournament. So those boys were on the tear. They said to me, "You can't stay here now, it's not even dark. You've got to come out until midnight at least." I thought that was a good idea. But at 12 o'clock I went back to the hotel and it was all locked up. I had forgotten the key. I tried throwing stones at the window to wake somebody up but I was unsuccessful. So I went and slept in the hedge.

'These two bastards rocked up at three in the morning, drunk as skunks. I said to Newton, "Thank God you've arrived because I forgot the key." He promptly threw the key away in fun and it skittered across the road and went down a sewer. He had to climb up a neon sign, break into a guy's room and let us in. Of course, I was gone the next day. I had no chance of playing any good after that.'

And Hobday wonders why everybody thinks he's crazy.

'They don't,' I say soothingly, since the thought seems to annoy him.

'They do. I hear them at the bar. Why am I crazy? When I play I get angry sometimes. I get pissed sometimes. I chase women sometimes. Christ, what's so odd about that?'

The trouble is Hobday just doesn't do the things that normal people do. Only Hobday would think of putting a Viking hat in his golf bag in case he won the Irish Open; only he would think of wearing it to play his approach shot to the eighteenth green once he knew he wasn't going to, and only he would hole it. Hobday offered the hat ceremoniously to the victor, Des Smyth, before he putted out. Smyth refused and three-putted.

Many of his adventures involve naked or semi-naked romps (when I said this to George O'Grady, he muttered something which sounded suspiciously like, 'What do you expect from a sex maniac?'). One year he stripped down to his underpants and walked across a snake-infested lake in South Africa in the middle of a tournament. On another occasion, when a player bet him that he couldn't run naked around the eighteenth green at Vilamoura Golf Club in 15 seconds, Hobday did it in 14.5.

Some of the best Hobday stories have arisen out of his reactions to disasters on the golf course. He once struck himself so hard on the forehead after missing a putt that the blade broke off and slid down the back of his head and blood trickled down his face.

Leading a tournament at Wentworth, several seasons ago, he began to have nightmares on the greens. The more determined Hobday became to get the ball in the hole, the more the blade tormented him and the further the tournament slipped from his grasp. He ran the gamut of emotions. He was angry, he was despairing, he was outraged, he was hysterical. Eventually there was nothing else to do but laugh.

So when the putter failed him again it got the yellow card, and at the next hole it got the red. After he had finished his round and signed his card, having lost to Ballesteros, he tied the offending object to the bumper of his car and raced off down the road. Up and down he drove, with it leaping and bounding and spitting sparks behind him. When there was nothing left of it save the head, he took it to a pub and bought it a pint.

'I'm afraid,' says Hobday unrepentantly, 'I'm one of those people that lose their temper.'

He has made something of a study of the way that other players cope with the blows the game deals. 'For me, that's the highlight of the game every day I play, to watch how the other guy reacts.

'I love the delayed-action guys. Let's take a nice quiet guy like Faldo, for example. Ice cool. But you can see that the ball has decided that he's going to take a beating today, and it bounces this way and bounces that way. He's got everything under control but you know he's seething. And eventually he pops. I've seen guys walk up to a tree and just smash it with their fist, and they're the quietest guys in the world. Now that to me is funny. Most guys lose their temper straightaway and throw a club or hit the caddie or whatever, and that's bad manners. But these boys, you can see them go.'

Inevitably, Howard Clark's name comes up. Towering rages on the golf course and Clark are, unfortunately, synonymous.

'That means he's extremely competitive,' explains Hobday. 'But because this is a gentlemen's game played by gentlemen, you've got to' – he imitates a player mincing round the course minding his p's and q's – 'and I disagree with that. A player can break as many clubs as he likes when he's playing with me as long as it's not on my time. He can go in the trees and whine as much as he wants. But there are times when the course belongs to me. It's my turn and I don't want to hear him swearing and cursing and shouting and screaming. Then he must bugger off. He doesn't know when to get cross or when to throw a club, or even how to throw a club. Some guys get so angry they throw it like a javelin. You've got to learn to throw it sideways so it lands softly, face up.

'We all get cross, but you must get cross in your own time. I mean, if it's your drive and you hit it in the trees, you don't smash the marker to smithereens. That's not your time. Now the other guy's got to try and play. He can't, can he? Let him hit and then smash the thing. That's what you've got to learn.'

This morning, on the recommendation of several players, I went down to the range to watch Hobday practise. His swing is as classic as it ever was and his ball striking as pure. It is said that David Leadbetter, who was an assistant pro in Zimbabwe when Hobday was in his prime, based his method on Hobday's technique.

'Who told you that?' asks Hobday, embarrassed. But he admits it's true. 'All Leadbetter did was come overseas and teach them to swing like I did. But I didn't teach him how to teach.'

Like most people, he thinks that Nick Faldo would have been a good player without Leadbetter's help but not necessarily a great player. 'You must remember that the teacher is only 2 per cent of the player. No more than that. Leadbetter might have said, "Do that, and do it a million times." Faldo's the one who's done all the work. Leadbetter made him square at the top of the backswing and put him on a plane, and that's all he's ever done. I mean, you get a diamond, you polish it and it shines. That guy was a diamond to start off with. He's got magnificent rhythm. If you took a stopwatch and pressed it when he took the club away and pressed it again when he hit the ball, it would be exactly the same with every swing. The driver would take the same amount of time as the wedge, and that's the best thing you can have in the swing.'

But the best swing in the world is no use to a man with no magic on the greens. Hobday was nearly brought to his knees by the yips. That, far more than drink, kept him from reaching the heights.

'What do the yips feel like? Well, I'll describe how it feels when you've got a putt from four or five feet. You take the putter back and then it's like somebody hits you on the back. It's like an electric shock. You're afraid you're going to miss the ball. You think you're going to hit it ten feet past. Or you can hit it short. Your arms just seize up. Sometimes they hit and sometimes they don't. You can miss from anywhere. It's a terrible bloody affliction.'

'How does it start?'

'Well, to begin with you'll yip one putt in a tournament and not yip another. Then you'll yip every tournament once, then once every nine holes, then three times in every 18 holes and, eventually, you don't know when it's going to happen. The worst thing you can do is yip one at the first. Then you know you're going to have a bad day. Your feet hurt when you walk on the green. It's like walking on coals. You want to get on and get the hell off as quick as possible.'

Once, at his wits' end, Hobday went to see a hypnotist, convinced that if he could only believe he was a good putter, he'd be the best putter in the world.

'The hypnotist turned out to be a woman. She put me under and when I walked out of there, I swear to God, I thought I was the best putter in the world. There was no question. Did I ever charge at those putts? I had 42 putts that day. Forty-two. And I still thought I was the best putter in the world. It wore off after two or three days . . . Terrifying. Now that didn't work.'

Hobday is concerned about my well-being. He worries that I haven't eaten enough, laughed enough, and that his stories aren't funny enough. At intervals he glowers at my tape recorder as if he might bewitch it into not participating in the conversation. His anecdotal repertoire is inexhaustible. All it needs is a key word to trigger his memory and he's off. I try 'pre-qualifying'. It turns out to be a good choice. Open Championship pre-qualifying in particular and Simon Hobday appear to be incompatible.

The jinx began at his very first Open. Hobday, who was on the putting green waiting for his tee-off time, heard the starter call his name and began to walk over to the first. In the space of some 25 yards he slipped on a rabbit scraping and snapped all the tendons in his ankle. He never hit another shot all that season.

A succession of last-ditch misadventures followed, but after several years Hobday managed to arrive at the twelfth hole at St Andrews leading the pre-qualifying. Confident that he was home and dry, Hobday began relaying stories of past near-misses to his playing partner, Klarssons. On the next hole he drove out of bounds. His approach finished in a cavernous bunker. At the sixteenth his ball hit a cigarette box by the side of the green and ricocheted out of bounds.

'At the seventeenth, I made five,' remembers Hobday. 'But

by now the stories have stopped. I've got to make four up the last to get in. So I drive it up the fairway. I've got the club halfway back to hit my second shot and a man in a motorcar knocks over a kid [on the road that runs alongside the eighteenth]. Right next to me. Hooters and screaming and brakes. So, of course, I mishit it right on the back edge of the green. I've got a 50-foot putt. I putted down like Doug Sanders. I thought: "Shit, I'd better hole this [next] putt to get into the play-off." I missed it by a yard but I still got into the play-off and we went round one, two, seventeen and eighteen three times before I got in.'

The evening wears on and the restaurant slowly empties. Only the hen party in the corner shows little sign of abating. They shriek and cackle on relentlessly. The dregs of Hobday's second lager of the evening are untouched. He has decided that if he is going to make a serious attempt at the Seniors Tour, he is going to have to stop all drinking, womanising and other forms of revelry. And once he has made up his mind about something, he is not easily swayed.

He waves for the bill. I plead for one last story.

'What about?'

'Caddies?'

Hobday acquiesces. 'I know the worst caddie I ever had . . .' he begins. He lights another cigarette, settles himself more comfortably in his chair, and prepares to do the story justice.

The tournament venue was Wentworth. Hobday had arrived on the first tee to find that all the caddies had been taken. Except one. Hobday found him skulking round the back of the caddie shack, a hippie-like character with waist-long hair.

'He was as scruffy as hell,' recalls Hobday. 'I thought he was a wino. I said, "Are you pissed?" He said, no, he's perfect. And he talked like you and I are talking now. So we set off. I've already hit my drive so we're running. We go down this mound on the first and he falls and rolls all the way to the bottom. That's where it started. He must have been on drugs. Uphill he was perfect, but downhill he just went faster and faster and faster, then his angle would change and the clubs would pull him down.

'He'd fallen over thirteen times by the time we got to the seventeenth. By now he's got sand on his face, his hair is thick with it, the bag must weigh 30 pounds it's so full of sand. Every club you took out you had to wipe off. He was in terrible trouble, this boy. Now the back of the seventeenth green slopes steeply down to the tee. So I took him over to the side of the green while the other guys were putting out and I said. "Do me a favour, please. Do not under any circumstances come over the back of the green. Go down the pathway where the slope is nice and gentle and I'll see you on the tee." And I took my driver.

'When they finished putting out, we all went over the back of the green. We're going down the hill and the clattering starts at the back of the green. We look up and he's at the top of the hill. You had to see this guy's stride. He was doing 60 miles an hour. But every time he put his foot down the bag would come forward and hit him on the shoulder. It was giving him a terrible hiding. But the weird part was he still had the pin. He'd forgotten to put it back in the hole.

'So now he decides he's going to take a tumble and the only way he can stop himself is by putting the pin in the ground and doing a kind of pole vault. Of course, it snaps. How he didn't kill himself, I've no idea. He did a belly-flop and landed on the pathway on his nose. He's got his feet on either side of the bag. I never even picked him up. I just thought: "I told him."

'He comes hobbling along to the tee, but the clubs have given him a smack on the back of the head and he is pumping blood everywhere. Oh God, he was a horror story. He had denim dungarees which were broken by the time he was finished, absolutely broken. Torn to ribbons. The buttons were missing and there was grass hanging out the pockets. I gave him his £10 at the end and told him to go and take a shower. I said to him: "Go away and for God's sake get another bag. Don't come anywhere near me tomorrow."

'But now I'm sitting in the bar afterwards and every guy that comes in – because they didn't have yardages in those days – says, "Bloody incredible that seventeenth hole. I thought it was an eight-iron and I hit it straight over the back of the green." Because the pin is only half-height so it looks further away.'

Hobday grins. 'I kept quiet. It wasn't me.'

7

TO BE THE BEST

Dunhill Cup, Scotland, October 1990. This afternoon a white ball split the blue at St Andrews, took two bounces on the out-of-bounds tarmac road, parting unwitting passers-by and spectators like chaff, and landed 15 feet from the pin.

The unluckiest player in golf just got lucky.

'Is that my ball?' The tone was one of amused disbelief, a rich Australian twang which I heard before I saw the broad smile, red sweater and blond head of Greg Norman looming above the gallery beside the eighteenth green. On a day like today, with a strong wind behind, this short par four is easily drivable for prodigious hitters like the Shark, even without the use of artificial aids. And without luck. I thought to myself: where is good fortune when you really need it? Coming down the 72nd hole of a major championship, for instance.

Holing out for birdie in the pro-am where it couldn't matter less, something similar must have crossed Norman's mind.

It used to be that the nickname Great White Shark was one of endearment and a tribute to Greg Norman's aggression on the golf course, his fearlessness, and the ruthless manner in which he hunted down his opponents and went in for the kill. No more. Now, as these things often do, it has become a term of derision. Switch Shark for Carp: the fish that let all the big ones (the majors – golf's indisputable measures of greatness) get away.

That's what happens when a man fails to live up to other people's expectations of him.

Within two years of turning professional in 1976 at the age of 21, Greg Norman came to be regarded as the brightest, most incandescent manifestation of Australian genius since the Sydney Opera House. Not since Arnold Palmer had a player combined such power and flair on the golf course with such charisma and charm off it. In the first year of his career, Norman overcame Jack Nicklaus, his hero, in the West Lakes Classic. In his second, he won two tournaments; in his third, he won four. Since 1977 he has only once had less than three victories in a year, and on five occasions he has had five or more, his best season being 1986, when he notched up an incredible ten titles.

Who could have guessed that 14 years down the road, Norman would have won just one Open Championship, the 1986 Open at Turnberry, and not a single Masters, US Open or US PGA championship. His 61 other tournament titles, which – most damningly in the eyes of the Americans – only include nine of the US Tour, mean little in a sport where a champion's worth is assessed by one method and one method only. The majors. All the near-misses in the world don't count.

Just to reiterate, Norman:

1986	Bogeyed the final hole of the Masters to lose to Jack Nicklaus.
1986	Lost to Bob Tway in the US PGA after the American holed his bunker shot on the last.
1987	Was beaten by Larry Mize on the second extra hole of a play-off for the Masters when Mize holed his chip shot.
1988	Bunkered his drive on the eighteenth in the play-off for the Open Championship at Troon to lose to Mark Calcavecchia.

Cynics would add that he also lost an 18-hole play-off for the 1984 US Open to Fuzzy Zoeller; that David Frost holed a 50-foot bunker shot to beat him in the 1990 USF&G Classic; and that Robert Gamez holed an improbable seven-iron on the final hole to win the 1990 Nestlé Invitational.

When a player comes within a hair's breadth of victory that

many times and doesn't win, you've got to start looking for reasons. Either he isn't destined to win another major, or he doesn't have another major left in him.

'Do you think fate owes you a major?' Norman was asked after the play-off at Troon.

'Shit,' replied Norman with feeling, 'it owes me four.'

In direct defiance of the above statistics, given the importance of major championships in the game of golf, Norman rose to the top of the Sony world rankings – an elaborate system of points instituted in 1986 – and took up an unassailable position there. He was briefly deposed by Seve Ballesteros in 1988, but Nick Faldo, who accumulated four major championship victories during the course of Norman's reign, failed to dislodge the Shark until August 1990 (and then for only six weeks).

In light of this, the credibility of the world rankings has come under close scrutiny. Administered by IMG, they are calculated on a scale whereby all four majors, plus the Players Championship in America and the PGA Championship in Britain guarantee a player a minimum number of points. In the 60 other tournaments included in the ranking system, the number of points awarded depends on the strength of the field, which is based against the world rankings. This means that the top players (in 1990, eight in the top 20 in the rankings and 16 in the top 50 are managed by IMG) can inflate the points value of a tournament simply by competing in it, thus perpetuating a kind of chain effect whereby they are the only ones able to make realistic advances in the rankings.

When it was felt that Norman had outstayed his welcome at the top of the world rankings, a peculiar trend started among observers of the game almost to hold him personally responsible for monopolising the number one spot. Part of this was resentment that a player who only had one major victory to his name should be rated above a man with four, and part of it was because, as an IMG client, Norman was the golfer most obviously reaping vast financial rewards as a result of being 'the best player in the world'.

Paradoxically, the world rankings don't even mean very much to the Australian.

'Never have done,' says Greg Norman positively.

The reason? Because unlike other professional sports which have a world ranking system, i.e. tennis and motor-racing, golf has no world Tour. '[The ranking system] doesn't work and never will work until we have a world Tour; until we have all 120 players playing in different tournaments round the world under various conditions all the time.'

'Do you think it would ever be possible to have a world Tour?'

'I would love to see it, personally. Whether you could ever get the Schofields, the Bemans, Japan and Australia, to all sit down and be sensible, and not be self-centred and selfish towards their own Tours . . .'

But until such a time as there is a world Tour in golf, he feels very strongly the Sony rankings are an unacceptable method of assessing the rating of players, particularly when there are bonus schemes and contractual benefits resulting from them. 'Ever since the inception of the world rankings, I've been fortunate enough to have been at the top of it to be able to voice my opinion,' says Norman, who has always been their most outspoken critic in spite of the fact that he has most to gain from them. 'But it's amazing when I'm number two now people are writing differently about it. I won't say very much about it anymore because it sounds like sour grapes.'

Tall, golden and larger than life, Greg Norman makes himself at home in his suite at the Old Course hotel. In the short space of time since he found me sitting forlornly in the foyer (dwelling on luck and the general unreliability of professional golfers), he has made dinner arrangements with a friend, read a fan letter on the way up in the lift, divested himself of shoes, waterproofs and sweater, answered two questions and dispatched his caddie, Bruce Edwards, to fetch a couple of lagers. At last he settles down, the picture of relaxed contentment.

It is 6 p.m. Twilight is falling over St Andrews. Norman has just completed a five-hour round in a gale-force wind, and satisfied the demands of his pro-am partners, a crowd of pen-wielding autograph hunters and several reporters, but he couldn't look less harassed if he was lying undisturbed on a beach in the Bahamas. On the contrary, he seems to be enjoying himself thoroughly. Nothing is too much trouble for him, no phone call a nuisance, no question too direct.

'What is your feeling about appearance money?' I ask, with the latter in mind.

'Well, you see, appearance money as far as I'm concerned is totally up to the sponsor,' says Norman immediately. 'It's his money. And I get offended when somebody tells me what to do with my money and how I should spend it. Dunhill, for example. If they wanted to go out and pay a million dollars to get Faldo and Ballesteros or whoever to play, that's their money. They feel they can justify it . . . that they'll get exposure from those players . . . So it's not an issue for the Tour administration to handle. It's an issue for the sponsors. Now if the sponsors all get together and say, "Hey, we're not going to pay appearance money", now it might be a different deal.'

Appearance money has been a contentious issue for over a decade since it was first paid to players such as Seve Ballesteros. A criterion was established for the giving of it: a player had to have won a major, or have topped the Order of Merit. What it basically means is that a golfer is paid to play in a tournament regardless of how he subsequently performs. How much he is paid depends on his perceived value in terms of how much media coverage, gate entrance money and brand or product awareness he will bring the sponsor. In 1990, a player like Ronan Rafferty might get £20,000, José Maria Olazabal was paid in the region of £30,000, Ian Woosnam, £40,000 to £50,000 and Nick Faldo and Ballesteros around £60,000. The Spaniard, who was unquestionably a European sponsor's biggest draw card, had received over £750,000 in appearance money in 14 started that season as compared to £148,000 in prize-money.

The situation was fast approaching the stage where players were effectively holding sponsors to ransom by refusing to play unless they were given appearance money. At the time of writing, the PGA European Tour were forming a subcommittee to deal with the problem and appearance money was to be outlawed. Sponsors would be notified that they faced elimination from the 1992 Tour schedule if they were caught paying appearance money to a player.

'The people who pay are the problem,' said Ken Schofield in his press conference on the issue, 'not the player. He just takes the cheque.'

'It'll never happen,' says Norman with certainty. 'I mean, as tough as the US Tour is about appearance money, it still happens over there. You know, if a sponsor wants you to go and do an outing for him in another city away from the tournament, and he says, "Hey, here it is [appearance money], go and do it on Monday." He's happy and you're happy. So whether it's blatant or whether it's behind someone's back, it still goes on.'

The principal argument against appearance money in whatever guise has always been that once paid, a player is not necessarily going to be driven to do his best. In his own case, Norman refutes this emphatically.

'I think – I know this is a fact – I play better when I get paid because I don't want to let the person down who paid me. If I get to a tournament in the States and I think I'm not really playing that great, you know, my system's not ready to play, I don't play. But if I feel the same way going into a tournament in Japan and Australia, I get up and I grind my arse off, because I don't want the sponsor to think: "Look at that Norman! Come over here, takes all the money and runs."'

It's a shame there aren't more players with Norman's values. Mark Calcavecchia, for example. He was paid to play at the Dutch Open earlier this season, but when he missed the cut after having played two atrocious rounds of golf, he lashed out like a spoilt child and broke a sponsor's advertising board. Cursing and shouting, he left the course and country, appearance money in hand, never – if justice is done – to return again.

That kind of behaviour incenses Norman.

'I don't want to do that because it ruins it for somebody else coming behind me in ten years' time, and it ruins the image of the game. And I'm not that type of person,' he adds.

It is this conscientiousness in honouring his commitments, combined with rugged good looks, a down-to-earth manner and excellent business acumen, which has helped Norman become the second-richest player in the world. Arnold Palmer is the first. According to a survey done by *Golf World* (November 1989), Palmer's off-course income, including endorsements and appearance money but excluding prize-money, media fees, course design fees and non-golf business investments, totals $9 million, while Norman's is in the vicinity of $8 million. The Shark's worldwide published earnings prior to the 1990 Open Championship were $7,296,921.

When your own annual income is barely more than the last four figures in that number, it can be hard to imagine what would motivate a sportsman to keep going when he has scaled the financial and physical heights that Norman has. Where does the desire come from?

'I honestly believe that I have not achieved what I want to achieve in the game,' says Norman, instantly dismissing the idea that he has reached a sporting peak. 'I think once you reach your pinnacle, there's only one way to go and that's downhill.'

But a decade and a half on the road is a long time. The pressures which accompany professional golf at world-class level don't lessen with age. They increase. The travelling becomes tougher and lonelier. Playing a tournament schedule which criss-crosses four continents becomes more of a drain on a golfer's mental and physical resources.

'It's just a fact of growing up, I s'pose,' says Norman resignedly. 'When you were 25, you really didn't care. You just went out there with one objective: to play golf. Ten years down the line, so much more has happened, so much is happening around you, that you have to pay a little bit more attention to it. I mean, you have to watch what's going through your own office now. You really can't just say, "Okay, go ahead and look after it, guys", and let it go.'

For Norman that means that every day he is in the country he leaves his home in Lost Tree Village, Florida, and goes straight to the office, where he will take the time to understand the complexities of his business empire. Golf is the next priority. Norman plays and practises out of Grand Cypress, Orlando. Only when he has fulfilled all of his obligations can Norman go home and relax with his wife, Laura, and his children, Morgan-Leigh and Gregory.

Is it any wonder that a laid-back pro-am day like today seems a comparative stroll in the park.

'You wake up every morning and go through the same routine so it gets kind of monotonous and boring. Sometimes you just want to say, "I'd love to walk away from it for three months." But you can't. So you're always walking this fine line. And that's what the unfortunate thing about it is. A lot of the media don't see that. Because you can see it in the articles they write, and a lot of the spectators believe what the media write. So the person who gets hurt in the long run is the player, and then the game eventually.'

There is a knock at the door. Norman bounced up in mid-flow and lets Edwards in with the lagers.

'What time shall I come in the morning?' asks Edwards when he can get a word in edgeways. A dark-haired young American with designer stubble and the same friendly manner and easy smile as Norman's, he declines Norman's invitation to stay for a drink.

'Come around eleven,' says his boss. 'Come and have lunch or a snack, if you like.'

'It's sad,' says Norman, resuming the conversation without a pause, 'because we're not all as bad as what a minority of the press would like to make us out to be . . . I read articles, not only about myself but about other players too, and you think, "Well, I know this guy and I know he's not like that" . . . But that's what happens and it disappoints you.'

It turns out that he had this identical conversation with some friends of his last night. Norman's friends said to him that the press couldn't see how sincere he was or how much he did for the game behind the scenes. When Norman does something – like dedicating his 1988 Heritage Classic victory to Jamie Hutton, a young fan desperately ill with leukaemia – it is because he wants to do it and not because he thinks it will make him look like a hero in the press.

'Success is wonderful,' says the gregarious Australian who, until recently, had always taken fame in his stride, adding, 'but it can also be very painful.' Norman copes with it in the best way he knows how. By being himself. 'I've been pretty good with it,' he says, 'but, I guess, in the last twelve months it's been a lot harder to take . . . People have been a lot more critical.'

There comes a time when being a nice guy behaving like a good sport when the chips are down is no longer enough. A sportsman who is the best in the world at what he does is expected to win the championships to prove it. If he doesn't – if he continually stumbles at the last or loses tournaments through outrageous streaks of misfortune – then sooner or later he's going to have to pay a price for that. He's going to be pilloried by the media and criticised by spectators.

Norman tried to turn his back on it. He stopped reading newspapers. He cancelled the golf magazines which he had sent to his house from all around the world. This morning, going out for his round, he said to Edwards: 'You know, I'm fed up. I'm just going to mind my own business from now on. I'm not going to try and help anyone' – which is not true because he will because he's that type of guy. 'But you get to a point where you think, "What the heck's the point? Why am I banging my head against the wall?"'

He sighs with frustration.

'I love the game with a passion. And that passion sometimes gets to a point where you wish other people would realise what the game is all about and do the same thing. Put a little back into the game.'

Unlike most of our games, golf is not played on a regulated pitch or field, rolled flat and measured identically from Kidderminster to Timbuktoo. It is played on golf courses as diverse as St Andrews and Shoal Creek, it is influenced by, and is at the mercy of, all weathers, and it involves a stationary ball. This last once caused Ted Williams, a ball player, to remark to Sam Snead: 'Golf's not that hard. The ball doesn't move.'

'Yes,' retorted Sam drily, 'but we have to play our foul balls.'

These three factors, when taking into account the enigma that is the golf swing, combine to make golf a capricious and unpredictable game which requires at least as much good fortune as a chihuahua would need in a pen full of crocodiles. But the question regarding the plight of Greg Norman in the majors is whether ill-luck has always played a part in his downfall, or whether he has made serious errors of judgement when it has mattered most.

'You can always say you made a mistake,' says Norman frankly. 'Everybody focuses their attention on the dramatic last two shots, or whatever, and if you go back one or two holes, you think, "That's what I did wrong." Some people call it unlucky. Some people call it fate.'

There is a pause. A slight tightening of his mouth is the only visible sign of tension. He says suddenly: 'I mean, it's kind of tough because I'm the only one it's ever happened to – and had it happened twice back to back. And you think, 'Well, the law of averages says you win 50 percent of the time, not lose 100 percent of the time.' But you know, I really don't call it bad luck because I really don't think of it that way.'

'Well,' I said, 'it doesn't necessarily have to have been bad luck on your part. It could have been good luck on theirs.'

'True,' says Norman, surprised. 'That's true.'

And he laughs, revealing a perfect row of white teeth, and the moment of unease passes.

'Oh, yeah, anytime you reflect on something, you say, "Well, if I'd done this or I'd done that." I really don't do that. Because you really can't change what's happened . . . Sometimes it's beyond your control – like what those guys did to me. So when it's beyond my control, then I feel a little better about it because I had nothing to do with it. The only way I can control my own destiny is the way I execute the game of golf. And I play the way I feel like I should play, not the way some other guy in a magazine or newspaper tells me I should play.

'I mean, the eighteenth at Troon, for example. I still believe to this day, if that had landed six or eight feet left or short of where it landed, it would never have reached that bunker because that bunker wasn't in play all week. Now you'll sit back and read where people say that bunker was in play; it's always been in play. I know exactly how far I hit the golf ball, but it was just one of those things. I've watched the replay and slowed it down. It landed right on top of a hard mound and skidded. But, you know, that's seaside golf. That's the way the game crumbles.'

Norman's graciousness in defeat and perpetual good humour in the face of disaster has been the reason for his perennial popularity, and has earned him the admiration of his friends and rivals. After the Open Championship, it prompted Sandy Lyle to remark in his artless fashion, 'I think a lot of people respect Greg an awful lot.'

Norman says that he believes you have to take the blows golf delivers on the chin. Ostensibly, he has done that. Only he will ever know how deep the cuts still run, how complete the mental healing.

'You go off and try to resurrect it and start all over again. But the whole crux of the deal is as long as you believe in yourself and don't believe fate's against you and don't believe in bad luck . . . If you believe in your own ability and you love the game with enough heart to say "I can bounce back from whatever they throw at me", I can come back. I know I'll be back. Whether it be next year; whether it be the year after that. I know somewhere down the line I'll be able to do it. And things'll turn around and maybe I'll hole my second shot, or something like that.

'If I didn't believe in my ability to be able to say, "Yes, I'm going to play for another ten years and do what I want to do, then I'd probably walk away from the game tomorrow," says Norman, blue eyes determined. 'It's my belief in myself and how much I love the game that is why I keep playing it. I mean, the money's great, sure, but I don't play for the money. I play for wanting to win and the winning makes you successful . . . That to me is the test of the true character of an individual, how you win and how you lose. Probably more, how to lose.'

Are such characteristics intrinsic or learned?

As a child Norman says he was introvert and shy. I look at him now, the absolute epitome of confidence and self-possession, and my imagination fails to make the necessary mental leap between the two extremes. 'Even when I came on Tour in '76, I was very introvert and shy,' insists Norman. I think the disbelief was showing on my face. 'But I could see that it wasn't going to do me any good being that way, because you're going to miss the boat in a lot of things. I actually had to change my whole personality and attitude to become successful. And so one thing leads to another; if you do it off the golf course, then it happens on the golf course.'

There is another knock at the door. Norman springs up to answer it and he and his manager, Hughes Norton, greet each other with delighted cries.

'How ya doing?' shouts Norman exuberantly.

'Great, great, great,' responds Hughes with equal excitement, followed by, 'I've been better, I s'pose.'

Having introduced us, Norman sits back down and picks up the threads of what he was saying with barely a pause.

As long as he can remember, he has always had a competitive nature. 'I've always wanted to be the best. Always wanted to be the first off at the traffic lights, stuff like that.' The Shark laughs wryly. 'Everything I do is exactly like that. Having a talk with Hughes' – he glances over at his manager, merriment dancing in his eyes – 'I always want to have the final say.'

'What d'ya mean, you want to,' says Norton indignantly. 'You do.'

'That's the way I am,' confesses Norman with a grin.

When Greg Norman walks on to the first tee in the morning, he wants to feel one overriding emotion: nervousness.

If he can feel the adrenalin pumping through his veins, if he is filled with the desire to play well, he knows he is in for a good day. That is his barometer. But if he walks on to the first tee and those butterflies are missing, invariably it means he is going to struggle to concentrate and get himself motivated.

'If you're already down,' explains Norman, 'it's hard to bring yourself up. How do you get yourself over it? Do you talk to yourself or be really hard on yourself? But when you're up, you can bring yourself down and then you automatically get up again because it comes to crunch time and you've got a score to post. When you're flat . . . you're only hoping for one or two birdies. But when you're flying, you're looking at six or eight birdies. It's an amazing feeling to have. It's very difficult to explain to anybody unless they've really experienced it . . . It's something way beyond anybody's comprehension. I've felt it outside golf, but that's just the way I am.'

'Doing what?'

'Well, I've felt it driving a car – you put yourself on edge.

Anytime you go beyond your limitations, right, your comfort zone – everybody has a comfort zone, no matter what you do – now you really feel like you're naked in the street. And now you don't know where to go because you've got no control. You've never done it before. It's like winning your first golf tournament. Once you learn to win, you're comfortable with it. You think, "Let's go ahead and do it." But if you haven't won it's like walking into a dark room; you don't know where all the obstacles are. You walk in there and you kick the table and you stumble and make a couple of bogeys . . . That's what happens when you lose your comfort zone.'

According to Norman's theory, the best players are the players with the widest comfort zone parameters. They are players who can adapt to situations to such an extent that they can play badly and still win. As an example, he cites his own victory in the Memorial tournament at Muirfield Village earlier this year.

'I played horrible golf. Probably the worst golf I've ever played, but I won the golf tournament. I figured out a way to win the golf tournament. Yet there's times when you've played great – the Masters and tournaments I've been beaten in – and you've lost. Now which way would you rather have it? That's the final argument.'

Walking this tightrope between triumph and adversity, engaging in bloody head-to-head battles, and challenging himself to win the tournament when he might be ten shots in arrears, these are the reason why the Shark is inextricably hooked on golf.

'I couldn't give up this game,' says Norman with conviction. 'Even though I could, I couldn't. That's what you would miss after a period of time, that feeling of getting in there and coming back, or playing just one [perfect] shot.'

This is testimony to golf's addictive powers, of how the love of the game is never really destroyed by its cruelty. Not even when it breaks his heart and steals his dignity. I find myself thinking back to that grey day at the Open Championship when Norman shot a 76 to Faldo's 67.

'What really happened in the third round of the Open?'

Norman doesn't hesitate. 'I lost my rhythm with my putter,'

he says. No excuses given or sympathy asked for. 'The putt I missed on the second hole, I guess, was a very makeable putt, but I just hit it too hard and hit through the break. And the next putt I missed a couple of holes later, I hit too soft. So now I'm second-guessing myself on the line and speed, and as time goes by I'm getting myself worse and worse in a hole in the way I feel about my putting. Then I hit a good drive on twelve, which I thought was perfect and it trickles into the bunker, and I hit a drive on thirteen, which I thought was perfect and it rolls into the bunker.

'And that's where, to me, the whole tournament changed – the tee shot on twelve that fell in the bunker. I lost my momentum. I lost it even though I was only a couple behind Nick . . . Nick putted extremely well the whole week, there's not question about it. He was making everything that he looked at and he had a lot of confidence. And he kept the momentum going. So that's what happened: it was the ebb and flow of momentum.

'I've seen so much of it in negative terms,' says Norman. He is speaking of losing. 'It saddens me. If somebody beats you, heck, he beats you. He's better than you on the week. You've got to say to yourself, "Well, I'll go out there and work harder and beat him next week."

'Sure, your confidence can go down very quickly. It's happened to me over the years. But you know deep down in your gut it's just a superficial deal. Three months will go by and you'll be bouncing right back into the game. You'll think: "What went wrong for three months?" But that's always going to happen because of the mental and physical parts of your game. Your mental fits your physical and vice versa. So it's an amazing contrast of passions because your mind is so strong. And if it's strong in the negative side then you'll never play great golf, but if it's strong in the positive side then you're going to be around for a long time, no matter what people say or do to you.'

Yesterday, in driving rain and a force-nine gale, Norman worked for two hours on his game on the practice range at St Andrews. For only the second time in his career, he has flown his coach of 18 years, Charlie Earp, over from Australia. Norman is a self-taught player and if his swing is in the groove it rarely alters. But lack of practice caused him to lose his swing plane. 'I got my hands too high and that meant I wasn't swinging down the line. I was dropping too far inside the line and the club was going out.'

One day of working with Earp and Norman is swinging the best he has in a long time. 'You know, if you're going to maintain a level of golf, you have to practise every day. No question about it. Whether you're playing good or playing bad you have to practise. And I didn't. I kind of took it easy. I didn't really hit the full six hundred balls a day that you need to groove your swing. I've hit about three thousand in the last week.

'See, that's what I love to do,' explains Norman with a grin. 'I love staying out and hitting balls because I'm in my zone, you know, I'm in my element. I can control what I'm doing. I don't have anybody out there saying, "Come, we've got to go and do this, we've got to do that." I'm there. I'm locked in for three or four hours and I love it.'

'What are your biggest strengths in life and in golf?'

'In golf, I would say my biggest strength is driving the ball. I'm long and I'm fairly straight so I have an advantage there. As a person, I guess, my self-belief. I won't do something unless I believe I can do it. I think I'm a very, very honest person. If somebody asks me a question, I'll give them my honest answer. Now whether the truth hurts somebody, that's their problem, not mine. I always stand up for my own beliefs. If somebody challenges me and I know I'm right and they're wrong, then I'll go and talk to them about it. I won't let it stew, I'll get it off my chest. And I never hold a grudge.

'That's the way I am,' says Norman quietly after these frank admissions. 'I mean, I'm not putting on any pseudo face here.'

I have never been more certain that someone was being absolutely straight with me.

His inability to say no, he admits is a big weakness. Most other top players wouldn't think twice about refusing to do an interview, for example. 'I won't do that,' insists Norman, 'because I've always believed that life's a two-way street. If somebody wants to ask you to do something, then that's a reflection on you and your ability . . . And, you know, it's time, but heck, what's time? Time's something you can use for you and you can use against you.'

'How do you manage not to spread yourself too thin, to still have enough time to concentrate on your golf game?'

'Well, you see, the down side to it is that these people, when you do say no, sorry, I can't, I've got another commitment, they see that you've done it forever. You've always been willing to give an interview and when you say no, they get kind of pissed off. I had it today with some guy on the putting green. I wanted to go and get ready for my game. I've got things to work on, and here he is asking me questions. I felt like saying, "Hey, goddammit, imagine if I walked in when you were writing and deep in your concentration." But I didn't. But I was short enough with him that he knew and he walked away. Now when I see him again it'll be interesting to see what kind of reaction I get.'

The psychology of the media is a complex one. Being continually affable and amenable as Norman is no guarantee of good press, just as – perversely – behaving like a prima donna doesn't necessarily means that a player will receive more than his share of bad press.

Immediately after his round with Faldo at the Open Championship, Norman went to the putting green to work on his stroke. There he was approached by the Championship press officer who said that there was no time for Norman to give a press conference, and that a few quotes from him would suffice. Norman willingly complied. But due to a general lack of communication in the press centre the situation was misconstrued and Norman was reported as having refused to be interviewed. It wouldn't have occurred to many journalists to double-check for the simple reason that players flouncing off after bad rounds and refusing to be interviewed is commonplace.

'Yes, well, I'm not Seve,' says Norman tersely when I point this out. He has never refused to go into a press conference in his life. 'I'm not a Faldo – because I know Nick has done that a few times. If things don't go their way they're not acceptable. And I'm not that way. I mean, I bite the bullet and accept that you have your good days and your bad days.'

Norton rang Norman immediately after the 1990 Open Championship.

'Look,' he said to his client, 'you've got to get rid of this image.'

'What image are you talking about?' said Norman in astonishment.

'What are you doing turning down press conferences?' demanded Norton, and faxed Norman an article out of the Wall Street Journal.

'You know, I've even sat down in the press room and waited for 30 minutes for somebody to finish, and I've thought, "What the hell, I'd rather be out there practising,"' says Norman bitterly. 'But you have to do it. It's an obligation you have to fulfil, and if you don't fulfil that obligation, then you're missing a lot of steps on the way to doing the right thing.'

The phone rings for about the fifth time in the last hour. Norman hops up and answers it without a murmur. It's Nigel Mansell, the racing driver.

'You win a race, you come second, you sign a deal and then you call me!' chides Norman, his voice deep with affection. He reclines in one chair and hooks his feet over the back of another. He is going to be there for a while.

Norton has returned to his chair and we talk sporadically. He is the overall client manager for IMG in the States. He shows me a newspaper advertisement for a tournament organised by Norman in the States, in which about 20 golfers play for a million dollars with as much going to charity.

Snatches of Norman's discourse with Mansell drift over. It seems that the Australian has been plagued by reporters asking for his theory on Mansell's decision to postpone his early retirement and sign with Williams. 'What am I? Your press agent?' demands Norman.

Norton tells me about a book on Norman's mental approach to golf which is soon to be published.

'Oh shit!' laughs Norman, recovering from one of Mansell's quips. 'Don't give me that. I know you too well . . . How's the family?'

His manager, meanwhile, is explaining to me how in-depth interviews like this one, given gratuitously by Norman, can devalue his worth in the book publishing trade. Potential publishers might begrudge paying him to do what he has previously done for nothing.

'Do you know what the problem is with you?' Norman is asking Mansell teasingly down the phone. 'Nobody gives you a fucking hard time. So I've got to sit back here and do it.'

At length he rings off and settles down once more. He and Mansell have been best of friends for years. They share a love of fast cars and golf. At the 1988 Italian Open at Monticello (which he won), Norman, who collects cars, bought two Ferraris: a limited edition F40 and a Testarossa.

'Golf and racing-car driving – there's a very good correlation between the two, believe it or not,' explains Norman. 'Hand-eye co-ordination and feel.'

'Do you think that is the key to a good swing?'

'Buy the book,' shouts Norton from the doorway of the bedroom where he is practising his putting. 'We also have a video.'

Norman laughs good-humouredly but ignores him. Fundamentals, he says simply. Basic fundamentals and natural hand–eye co-ordination. Most professional golfers have the ability to feel the distance between the ball and the pin. The best players – most notably, Ballesteros – are just people who have been endowed with more of that feel.

Norman's brown hands grip an imaginary club.

'A very good friend of mine in Australia,' he says slowly, 'once told me that when you play golf, it's like making love to your hands. You can feel it. It's just there. You can just feel the clubhead and you can go, "I'm going to put that clubhead on that ball and put it to within a foot of where I want it." And you're making love to your hands all the time when it's on the clubhead. That's when you're playing well.'

The twilight has turned to darkness. Norman seems oblivious to the inky blackness of the room, content not to turn on the light. The silence is heavy, the only sound being the muffled clock of balls as Norton putts tirelessly in the glow of a bedroom lamp. I look at my watch and start guiltily. Two hours have gone by, Norman doesn't look in the least bit perturbed, or if he is, is too polite to show it.

So I ask one last question.

'What goals can be left for a player that has done everything short of win the Grand Slam?'

'To be the best I can be,' says Norman, smiling his easy smile. 'As simple as that. Now how good that'll be, time will only tell. You know, you can set yourself goals and go about trying to attain them, but you can also just say to yourself: "I want to be the best I can be. I don't want to settle for anything less."'

'If you settle for second best, then you're a loser.'

OUT OF BOUNDS

8

THE KING OF SWING

'The most maddening thing about golf is the
perversity with which the body refuses to obey the
mind.'

PAT WARD-THOMAS, *THE LONG GREEN FAIRWAY*

On the wall of David Leadbetter's Lake Nona academy
is a *Golf World* cover, its scarlet banner headline
proclaiming him 'the king of swing'. Framed
photographs of his most famous pupils endorse the sentiment.
'Nice place for a walk with five shots in hand,' Nick Faldo has
scrawled across a picture of the eighteenth hole at St Andrews,
scene of his second Open victory in 1990, while a beaming
Nick Price adds, 'I think I peaked earlier than you thought!!!' as
he claims the 1992 US PGA Championship. David Frost, the
possessor of one of golf's finest swings, stares intently from the
cover of a 1988 edition of Golf World. 'Thanks for all the
interest and effort you have put into my game,' he has written
appreciatively. 'You're a great teacher.'

To the players he has helped become champions, Leadbetter
is a genius, nothing less. 'David Leadbetter is the best teacher
in the world,' Faldo states unequivocally. Others are uncertain
whether to describe him as a monster, a guru, a pretender, an
inventor or an opportunist; or simply the latest in a long line of
distinguished teachers and gurus, all of whom represented a
minute advance in our understanding of the swing but none of
whom solved the whole puzzle. 'He's not a god,' Denis Pugh, a
former coach at Leadbetter's academy, said. 'He's not anything
other than a very good golf teacher who's got the best pupil in
the world.'

Make that pupils. Over the past ten years, the greatest

names in golf have enrolled at Leadbetter's élite academy. Faldo, Price and Frost have been joined in their endeavours by Tom Watson, Bernhard Langer, Ernie Els, John Cook, Craig Parry, Peter Barker, Mark McNulty, Mark O'Meara, Per-Ulrik Johansson, Catrin Nilsmark and Florence Descampe, to name but a few. There have been books (*The Golf Swing* was printed in eight languages and became the second biggest selling sports book of all time), videos (*The Full Golf Swing*, *The Short Game* and *Taking it to the Course*), instruction aids, endorsements and new academies across the globe, and all have been the result of Leadbetter's controversial theories and what is broadly known as his method – a technique based on the premise that the key to consistency under pressure is using the big muscles in the body (those in the legs and torso) to control the little ones (the hands, wrists and arms). The dog wags the tail, so to speak.

'Basically, we try to keep the clubface square for as long as possible,' explained Dennis Sheehy, who worked with Leadbetter for eleven years. 'Whereas the old teachings used your legs for power and your hands for speed, we try to eliminate the variables by using the big muscles and de-emphasising the smaller ones.'

Pugh was sceptical. 'The method is a marketing toy,' he said disparagingly. 'Really, David Leadbetter teaches golf. He doesn't throw the book at anyone except Faldo, but then Nick's Nick. He probably knows how his television works. With Nick Price, he just says: "Move the ball back half an inch in your stance."'

The problem, as Pugh sees it, is that teaching is subjective, and that by writing books and endorsing aids, one is effectively saying that there is only one way to play golf. This did not concern the 500,000 who flocked to buy *The Golf Swing*, but it did worry some of the game's top teachers, including Eddie Birchenough, Royal Lytham's respected professional – not enough, however, to prevent Birchenough from becoming a fan of the guru and his method. 'I think Leadbetter is a superb teacher. His knowledge of the game is second to none. He's made golf teaching almost a cult.'

In 1979, when the air in Florida boiled with humidity and the sky was that intense, mercurial blue that sears the back of your eyes, an angular figure took up residence on the practice ground at Disneyworld where Phil Ritson was a teacher. An Englishman by birth, he had arrived in Orlando from southern Africa and was aiming to try his luck on the Florida mini-Tours. 'He was the guy always standing on the range, with nothing to do but watch Phil all the time and try to learn from Phil,' Pugh recalled. 'He was the tall, quiet guy, who everyone thought was a good guy, waiting for a break.'

Leadbetter was the son of a timber merchant, who had spent most of his youth in Zimbabwe. A four-handicapper by the age of 16, he had played junior golf with the likes of Price, McNulty, Dennis Watson and Tony Johnstone, before embarking on an accountancy degree at the bidding of his father. In the grey corridors of business college, everything in him had ached to quit. He loathed the regimented columns, the regimented class. When the sympathetic pro at a Harare golf club offered him a job as an assistant, he had made the break for freedom without a second thought, burning his books and running away to the sunshine, the lush grass on the range, and the sweet, sweet sound of a perfectly hit shot.

In those years Leadbetter did not harbour dreams about wealth and glory on the international circuit. Most young professionals do at one stage or another but Leadbetter was always pessimistic about his chances, even when he was performing well on South Africa's Sunshine Circuit. Until, that is, he met Phil Ritson, the country's top teacher. Ritson was charismatic; he was influential. 'He was a very inspirational person,' Pugh said. 'If he was a football coach, he'd be a Jack Charlton sort of character. He'd have players doing things you wouldn't have thought they could do.'

Ritson took the self-conscious youngster under his wing. 'He said to me: "David, you can go as far as you want in this game,"' Leadbetter recalled.

Leadbetter wasn't convinced. Aware of his limitations as a player, he spent hours poring over instruction articles and books, preparing for the day when he'd be teaching amateurs at some quiet suburban club. Hogan, Snead, Nelson, Nicklaus and Palmer were all scrutinised and analysed and by the time he arrived in America, where he had followed Ritson, he had distilled from them what he needed and drawn his own conclusions. In Florida, Leadbetter wrestled with the mini-Tours but gradually surrendered to the desire to teach rather than play. Word of his ability travelled. He graduated from a bit part at Disneyworld to his own range at Grenlefe Resort in Haines City. A one-man band with a secretary to manage his steady trickle of takings, he was giving three-hour group sessions, at $120 for six people, when an impoverished professional by the name of Dennis Sheehy presented himself for lessons.

Sheehy had come, in effect, on a pilgrimage. So revered was Leadbetter by his long-term pupils – Price, McNulty, Frost and Wayne Westner, who by now were hitting the big time – that Sheehy was prepared to offer his services as an assistant in any capacity whatsoever, and to sleep on Leadbetter's floor, or in the greenkeeper's hut, or some other available corner in return for watching David teach or being taught by him. Leadbetter just smiled, shrugged and took him on board. Easy-going and kindly, in a vague, unbusinesslike way, he was to do exactly the same in later years with several other youngsters without real futures as players, most notably Simon Holmes.

This was the relaxed, enjoyable, slightly precarious position the Grenlefe academy was in on the day that Nick Faldo called and announced his intention of putting his game and, by extension, his life, into Leadbetter's hands.

'He was very intense,' said Leadbetter, recalling Faldo's arrival in 1985. 'You could see he was just totally consumed with getting to the top and being the best. His work ethic was unbelievable. It wasn't an exaggeration that he'd hit a thousand balls a day. I mean, it was hot. It was the middle of June and it was awful. But he'd be hitting balls and just working and working. He didn't let anything interfere with what he was doing. He said: "Listen, I know it's going to take a while but I'm not worried about it. I don't care how I play for a while." I thought: "This guy has the potential to go really far."'

With hindsight, what seems amazing, given Faldo's perfectionist nature and not inconsiderable achievements at the time, is that he should choose Leadbetter – a man based in America, whose teachings and background were so far removed from his own world – over any coach, and, more particularly, that he should choose him on the strength of one or two casual meetings when his entire career was at stake.

'I didn't think about it at the time,' confessed Leadbetter. 'It was just a case of, here's another guy with a good reputation and I want to help him. At the time, I didn't realise the consequences of either making the guy great or failing. But if he had failed, I would have been held up as some bum who'd sort of messed up Nick Faldo.'

NOTES FROM A GURU

Extracts from Leadbetter's file on Faldo:

NICK FALDO

British Open 90
Pre open – shorter+ feel laid off/posture resistance in right shoulder – feel tall as he pulls shoulder forward, keep extension in right arm.

Valderrama 90
Drill – getting to link 6 and hit feeling a pull.

PGA 90
Keep left knee solid. Club coming from inside – resistance back. Not inside too quick.

Skins Game 90
Problem – posture sloppy, weight on heels+head too far behind ball and down. Left hip closing too early on trigger.
Correction – posture taller, weight forward on balls, head squarer and up, feel left hip move open – trigger left hip open not closed.

Problem – backswing – too much move off ball – set late + no resistance, right shoulder turns too early – face too open at the top . . . no torque (length good).
Correction – resistance with right shoulder – feel more tilt (not

flat as 1st day) – sense remaining on left side + no move off ball – head steady, keep angle at back of right hand.

Problem – downswing – club dropping too much from inside, bunchy, head droopy – arms down too quickly, left leg slidey – early release + arm trapped – steep plane on release + high finish.

Correction – down swing – keep arms up as left shoulder separates – feel right should stay up – no left knee slide – feel hands high throughout the downswing – after transition turn right side into ball – right bicep and chest together – pull butt-end past ball – late hit – feel tall – allow head to move forward not stay back.

General – keep arms up and not drop down quickly causing dip – need to hold angle through impact . . . plane of shaft flatter through impact.

Drills – to the top 1st move leaving arms up+ hold it+ hit from there, grasp right shoulder-blade to feel right-side release.
Right arm only – shaft only to feel release.
Hit SW holding angle through impact + butt-end past the ball.
Hit shots with ball outside right foot to feel release and high hands + level shoulders with head moving forward not hanging back.
Looks great – shallow angle with driver.

Sheehy, who watched their progress – saw Faldo's raw, bleeding hands and Leadbetter's commitment – felt then that it was impossible that two such driven men could fail. 'One thing about David, and people don't really talk about this, is that he's that good and he's got that much belief in himself, that it's almost like he's fearless. When Faldo came along, both of them had so much to lose and yet they were so positive about it. And I loved that. There was just no doubt.'

The first sign that their faith and industry were to be justified came when Faldo won the Spanish Open in May 1987. The second was when he shot 18 pars in the most violently inhospitable conditions the British Isles have to offer, two months later, to win his first Open Championship.

'The most special moment in my career was when Faldo won at Muirfield,' Leadbetter sighed. 'To me, it was the culmination of so much hard work. I mean, a lot of other things have been really great, like Nick Price winning the US PGA, but that '87 British Open was a special time because it was just like, "Wow!" I was away doing some clinic and I phoned him at Grey Walls from the airport. They said: "He's taking no phone calls." I said: "Listen, I'm sure if you tell him it's me, he'll speak to me." And he came right on the phone and he was shouting and screaming. He said: "Jeez, I can't believe this has happened!" He was in tears; so was I. That was really special. He doesn't show emotion that often, but when he does, he does – like at the Open in '92. But at Muirfield he just proved to himself – not to anybody else, but to himself – that he could actually do it.'

Not everyone was pleased that Leadbetter had, in a manner of speaking, struck gold. Ritson, for reasons of his own, ceased to speak to him at all. Nobody had yet put a copyright on method – golf's X-factor, that enigmatic, unpredictable quality in the swing, will forever defy analysis – but Ritson seemed to feel that Leadbetter had taken what he had been taught and somehow exploited it.

'Phil would probably be frustrated because David has established new heights in coaching, and he might have seen the fabulous wealth David had acquired,' Pugh explained. 'I mean, he engineered the break for David, and got him into the States. But to sort of say that David sat at his feet and slavishly learnt everything from him would not be fair to either of them.'

Leadbetter was in complete agreement. 'He influenced me a lot in my early years,' he admitted. 'I'm not saying he didn't. But he was just a stepping stone on a learning curve. I don't teach like Phil Ritson at all. I was grateful to him. In fact, he even helped me get into the country. The only reason we don't get on – as I say, it's not that I don't want to get on – is that you hear all sorts of reports: "Hey, I taught David everything he knows and now he's doing well, blah, blah, blah." To me, there's a slight amount of jealousy there. I remember him coming to me four or five years ago and saying: "I hate teaching. I'm never going to give another lesson again, and if I do I'm going to charge $1,000 an hour and I'm going to be involved in a golf course complex and design clubs . . ." And I said: "Hey, that's great. Super. All the best to you." And then two years later, it's: "Phil Ritson's making a comeback. All the teachers out there don't know what they're talking about." But, you know, that's just human nature.'

At Lake Nona, all of human life was on display. A procession of unlikely characters through the igloo that was our press tent added an exotic flavour to proceedings, and made an otherwise unendurable tournament – for no other reason than the fact that rounds commonly escalate to six and a half hours, sheer misery if one is working on British deadlines – rather enjoyable. The Zimbabwean team of McNulty and Price, friends since childhood, came in and talked about the sand greens (browns), rivalry and sun-filled days of their youth; the Jamaicans came in and explained with a resigned air how they had shot a combined 174; and the defending champions, Fred Couples and Davis Love III, came in and told us that they intended to make a clean sweep for America in the team events of 1994 – US players had already made off with the Ryder Cup, the Walker Cup and the Dunhill Cup; the World Cup would complete the picture.

Every year, uninformed local reporters and golf writers who should know better draw comparisons between the World Cup and the Ryder Cup. This is like comparing Chaucer and John Grisham. Indeed, the only similarity between the Ryder Cup and the World Cup in the word 'Cup'. This is not to say that the latter isn't a worthy event but the standard of many players, and the ludicrous format, leaves a lot to be desired.

To all intents and purposes, the World Cup at Lake Nona was David Leadbetter's party. A handful of patriotic spectators braved the humidity to witness first hand the histrionics of Ian Woosnam on the 94 shot by Jacob Avnaim of Israel, but for the most part the thin, cosmopolitan stream of gate entrants were goal-directed Leadbetter faithful, intent on wearing a path to golf's new Mecca.

Only one man seemed immune to the charms of the academy. He appeared on the practice ground on the afternoon of the third round, when the air was hot and damp and filled with that sweet, earthy smell that precedes enormous thunderstorms – Nick Price had spotted him in the car-park and pleaded with him to give an impromptu clinic – and before long had brought the range to a standstill, each new arrival abandoning his clubs and hurrying to join the gathered throng of disciples. 'That's Moe Norman,' one pro told a newcomer in reverential tones. 'The greatest ball-striker in the world.'

The man holding the assembled players in thrall was in his mid-60s and dressed in heavy brown trousers and a stiff-collared white shirt, his face flushed with the effort of hitting one after another of the most beautiful golf shots it is possible to see. 'Five years, 1200 balls a day,' Norman puffed in response to a question about how long his method had taken to perfect. He fired off 10 shots as straight and true as arrows. 'Watch this for purity . . .'

'Ohhh!' groaned the crowd appreciatively.

'Purer than the water you drink,' Norman cried, adding in his Canadian cadence: 'But I keep it so simple and precise. I'm the only golfer in history who had had his hands lower through the hitting area than he has at address.'

'How do you start down?' a South African asked respectfully. 'I'm setting the angle of my downswing as I go back.'

'What's the fastest part of the golf swing?'

'The follow-through. They think it's the backswing.'

'Talked to Hogan lately?'

'Four years ago.'

'Did you used to practise with him a lot?'

'Not a lot. He liked watching me and I liked watching him.'

It was then the penny dropped. Norman was the legend I'd heard players refer to, the brilliant ball-striker whose genius had been denied the world. Born in Kitchener, Canada, he was, for most of his chequered career, an eccentric recluse who was so suspicious of strangers he refused to give his money to a bank and so scared of crowds that he seldom attended prize-giving ceremonies. He habitually slept in his car. Away from the fanfare, his feats were scarcely credible. It was said that he had shot 59 three or more times. Golf was so easy to him that he would wager he could break a course record without ever having seen the course, and do exactly that. He would concede

10-foot putts in match-play and then casually roll in his own 15-footer. He would play holes backwards, taking a nine-iron off the tee and a driver off the fairway. Her would deliberately putt into a greenside bunker if he was playing the final hole of a tournament with a two-stroke lead, just to make life interesting. A Coca-Cola addict who drank up to 30 Cokes a day, he once teed off a Coke bottle in the Los Angeles Open. He made history by becoming the only player ever to walk out of the Masters. Having caused a sensation at the start of the week by sacking his allotted caddie before he had even picked up the bag, he then decided that the breeze was too strong for him to continue in the third round. He was lying fifth in the tournament at the time. 'Too windy for golf. Back to Canada, back to Canada,' he said and was gone.

Golf balls flew like sparks from Norman's clubhead; the shadows of the crowd slid across his shoes. As a young man, it was his fear of people that kept him from becoming great. 'Forty-one inches back and 22 inches in front,' Norman explained. 'Keeps the club on line as long as possible. Wide, tight, wide. You don't see that today. Nobody believes in action-reaction any more.'

At last he took reluctant leave, offering theories and explanations for a dozen dilemmas as he went.

'That's the hardest shot in golf?'

'The next one.'

'Excuse me, Mr Norman,' I said, 'but could you tell me the secret of the golf swing?'

Norman stopped abruptly; the crowd milled round. 'Hard work, sticking with the same thing every day you play and believing in yourself,' he replied instantly. 'People are afraid of themselves. People are afraid to win. They're too busy looking for obstacles. What were you thinking of when you were walking over here? Can you tell me how many steps you took? How high you lifted your feet? Were you aware of any obstruction – a car? A telephone post? No? Well treat trees and bunkers the same way.

'Look at this little fella!' cried Norman suddenly, opening his palm and revealing a golf ball with the air of a conjuror unveiling a golden egg. 'How many people is he laughing at?

The King of Swing

Forty million people. Forty million people and they're all trying to get him. They don't know how. I'm the only guy who does. I'm the only guy who does.'

On Sunday, I walked down to Leadbetter's academy, a cool wooden bungalow more reminiscent of the home of a great Southern writer than a state-of-the-art school of golf. Fans whirred lazily, visitors lolled about in armchairs, swing videos wound and rewound and Mike Henderson, a national junior champion who has been a regular at the academy since the age of 12, slapped balls into the net. That Leadbetter himself was nowhere to be seen came as no surprise. A notoriously bad time-keeper, he says that his tardiness is a standing joke with Faldo and Fanny. If he tells them he'll see them at the eighth hole, Faldo replies: 'I'll expect you at the twelfth.' 'They have bets about which hole I'll appear,' Leadbetter laughs.

To journalists with distant deadlines or players without pressing problems, a lax approach to appointments might indeed seem mildly amusing – particularly since it can be justified by a punishing schedule – but there is no doubt that it is the single biggest cause of disenchantment among Leadbetter's lesser-known pupils (hence Chris Moody's toungue-in-cheek advertisement). Players have described the unique torture that is standing on the practice ground, hitting balls poorly, while Leadbetter and Faldo analyse and strategise interminably in the distance. Half an hour ticks by, then an hour, as Leadbetter inches his way down the range, then just when he is almost with you, someone else grabs him. There have been golfers who have actually made scheduled trips to Grenlefe or Lake Nona and have hardly seen hide or hair of him. 'Six minutes in a year wasn't enough,' Howard Clark, a former pupil and Ryder Cup player, complained. Pugh sided with Leadbetter. 'Any player who knows David's travel schedule and who thinks that David's going to spend five hours a week with him, five months of the year, is deluding himself,' he said.

THE DAVID LEADBETTER GOLF ACADEMY

INTRODUCES THE

LEADBETTER BUDGET PLAN

There is now a plan to suit any pocket.
To make himself available to a wider audience
David Leadbetter
is proud to announce

THE DRIVE-BY GOLF LESSON

Yes, you pay by the minute.
Pay only for the time you use.
Choose from either the

ONE MINUTE LESSON

TWO MINUTE SCHOOL

THE THREE MINUTE RETREAT

All rates as fully inclusive except the one minute lesson.
There will be a supplement if David has to touch the
brake.
Obviously this is not usually necessary except in extreme
cases.

More fun than a drive-by shooting.
Less expensive than a drive-through McDonald's.

PHONE NOW FOR A RESERVATION.

1 800 BIG HOOK

THE KING OF SWING

Designed by Chris Moody, this spoof advertisement says as much about the unrealistic expectations of lesser players as it does about the demands of Leadbetter's time.

Nonetheless, it doesn't alter the fact that for a golf pro with a fragile ego, lack of supervision can have dire consequences. Take the case of Ove Sellberg, for example. A talented Swede with two European Tour victories behind him, he was, none the less, someone who needed a great deal of attention to see him through the swing changes that Leadbetter wanted him to make. When that attention was not forthcoming, he began a slow slide into oblivion.

Leadbetter's explanation is that he hadn't yet set up his European division, with Europe-based teachers to monitor the progress of players like Sellberg. 'It was unfortunate because he was one of those guys who really needs to be constantly fortified as far as confidence goes. He's a little up and down mentally, Ove. He needs a guy to give him a sort of pat on the back. He played well when we started off but he lost some confidence and then it was a case of, he tried this, that and the other and he obviously hasn't played well at all in the last three or four years. We still speak and we're still on good terms and what have you. It's just the nature of the business. You can't be successful with 100 per cent of the people you work with, there's just no way.'

Mark O'Meara, with whom I eventually found Leadbetter, was not among the discontented minority. He stood on the range beneath the vast canopy of blue sky and hit balls with a balanced, beautiful swing. Leadbetter hovered nearby in traditional pose, legs spread, arms folded, expression obscured by dark glasses. 'Does that feel any better?' he enquired of the 38-year-old Ryder Cup player.

'It really does,' admitted O'Meara, as contented as a cat on that balmy Florida day.

Applause crackled like rifle-fire in the distance. The war being waged between golfing nations amid the pines and jade valleys of Lake Nona seemed as remote as the moon. Henderson rolled up in a buggy. 'Are those guys doing any good out there?' O'Meara asked, referring to the US team of Couples and Love, who had led by five strokes from the Zimbabweans at the start of the final round. 'Freddie and Davis ripping it out there?'

'Freddie holed his sandwedge at the first hole,' Henderson told him.

'Come on!' exclaimed O'Meara, his open, friendly face expressing frank amazement. 'Unbelievable. For eagle?'

'Unreal,' agreed Leadbetter.

As if inspired, O'Meara resumed practice with renewed vigour.

'Well, the pattern is there,' Leadbetter said, studying the flight of the balls. 'I mean, I know not everything's perfect yet but . . .'

'No, that feels good,' O'Meara assured him. 'If I can keep hitting it like that . . .'

A pleased smile played around Leadbetter's lips. 'I like the height on those shots, too,' he said. 'You're really starting to show the true loft of the club.'

Even Leadbetter's detractors agree that this is his forte, his ability to communicate – to relax, reassure and instil perfect confidence in a way that makes his lessons less like those of a maths teacher, dispensing complex and indigestible theories, than a sort of intravenous transfusion of technique and positive thinking.

'I'm not saying there aren't people who know more than I do as far as mechanics are concerned,' said Leadbetter. 'I mean, I can speak physics and theory with the best of them, but there are people out there who can cite *The Golf Machine*, which to me is like the most boring book ever. There's some good stuff in there, but people can't relate to: "Your right arm is four degrees out and you've got the blade two degrees above parallel." I'm such a non-technical person . . . I've always maintained that it's not what you know as a teacher, it's how you say it. It's 25 per cent knowledge and 75 per cent communication, no doubt about it.'

There are two major criticisms of Leadbetter's teaching. One is the complexity of the method. 'It seems very simple in its most basic form, but when things start to go wrong it gets very complicated,' the English professional Roger Chapman said. 'You go to the first tee with two or three different swing thoughts when you should only be going with one.'

'I would tend to disagree,' said Leadbetter when I challenged him on this. 'I mean, yes, I'm known as being analytical because a lot of the players that I teach are that way. But as a teacher you've got to be like a chameleon. You've got to change according to who you work with, which I do – I change hats. My philosophy is, hey, the more versatile I am, the more I can teach any type of player. Because everybody's mind-set is different. With Ian Woosnam, it's very simple, you just stand up there and whack it. With David Frost we also have to keep it unbelievably simple – a lot different to players like Faldo or O'Meara who understand the technical aspects.'

The other criticism is that Leadbetter tends to impose his method on players, rather than working with what they have.

'I would say that when you work with a person for a period of time, that just happens naturally,' Leadbetter said. 'Yes, there probably is a degree of imposition there, if you will. But not to start off with. I mean, I'm careful with that. I never go out to solicit business, I promise. I'll never go up to someone like Olazabal and say, "Hey, Ollie, I can really help you." I mean, Bernhard Langer's asked me to work full time with him now. Bernhard's won two majors and he's had a great year, but he's a bit like Nick in that he wants to be the best he can be. And what we do is we sit down and we discuss things. I mean, my biggest thing working with players is to make sure they understand what they're trying to do and why they're trying to do it. I don't say: "You have to do this." I say: "With your build, this is what I suggest." And if you listen to me teach different players, my approach is totally different. That's what's fun to me, that's what's enjoyable. That's what enables me to come back and give clinics to high handicappers, because it's fun: it gets my mind working.'

Nobody can argue that, complicated or not, golf's favourite guru has a winning formula. Yet despite his illustrious stable, his million-pound product endorsements and his global reach, all is not rosy in the Leadbetter camp. A year or two ago, when the classroom of indigents and unknowns Leadbetter had nurtured into the game's top ranks expanded into a multi-million-dollar teaching industry, his self-confessed weaknesses as a businessman had begun to show. In December 1992, he did the sensible thing and put his financial affairs into the hands of International Management Group. Not everyone saw this as a positive move. Almost immediately, three of Leadbetter's right-hand men – Simon Holmes, Denis Pugh and Gary Smith, close friends as well as assistants – turned their backs on him. For a man who values friendship and loyalty above all else, it came as a devastating blow.

'He was absolutely shattered,' said Sheehy who, along with Mitchell Spearman, chose to stay. 'I've never seen him so upset about anything. You put your complete trust in somebody like that and basically they throw it back at you. You know, money was the governing factor in their decision; it's quite simple.'

'You feel a sense of disappointment,' Leadbetter admitted. 'But, as I say, ego's a big thing in this day and age and people think they can make more money. Somebody asked me the other day: "What do you think about Simon Holmes going?" And I said: "Well, I'll tell you. Without being egotistical, I might have taught him all he knows but I haven't taught him all I know."' He gave a dry laugh. 'Simon Holmes first came to me as a very so-so player . . . and he learnt everything he knows about anything, I feel, from me . . . I was sad in Simon's case because you think that there's some sort of loyalty factor. I mean, [he and Denis] were earning good salaries and they had the potential to earn a lot of money. They used the excuse, "Oh, with IMG involved you're cutting us out." Which is bullshit because I run this place . . . and I make sure that the good people who work with me do fine. And I'm thinking in the long term, because in two or three years' time we'll probably have ten or twelve academies around the world which will be generating a lot of income. When you're one person, it doesn't take long for Seve to say, "Oh, I'm not working with Simon any more", or Bernhard to say, "I'm working with David and not Simon now", and your popularity goes bump.'

I put it to him that there was a clause in the IMG contract that amounted to restriction of trade, to which Simon and Denis objected. Pugh said that although IMG had 'managed to turn the David Leadbetter disorganisation into an organisation, the IMG contract wasn't any good for anyone but David Leadbetter. I was changing status from being in partnership with David to being an employee, and I didn't want that.'

Leadbetter's eyes widened. 'That's absolute bull,' he said succinctly. 'I could even show you the contract. All we said was that they couldn't use the David Leadbetter name to promote themselves. There was nothing more sinister than that. They've used a number of excuses for why they left but, to me, it was just a case of feeling that a big organisation would cramp their style. They'd lose their individuality . . . But I just let people do their own thing, and maybe that was the problem with Simon who, when he started with us, was just picking up balls and earning a few dollars an hour in order to support himself in the odd mini-Tour event. And then he went on to a pretty huge salary for such a young guy, earning more than a lot of Tour players, and sometimes you can lose touch with reality. But life's like that.'

'I think there's a tendency at times for David to think, "I made them and therefore they should appreciate it,"' Pugh said, 'but in my case that wasn't true. There was a lot of dialogue and I would say that I had a lot of input into what he did.' He considered the current lukewarm state of their relationship. 'I think we're still friends,' he said without conviction. 'We're just not very good friends. But in the end, the only reason for signing would have been not to upset David, and that's the wrong reason. The negative side of it has been the politics and backbiting of coaching on Tour, but my biggest regret is just on a personal basis, that we don't phone each other up every week any more just to discuss the weather.'

Sheehy found the whole business nothing short of incredible. 'For me, a big part of why David is the best is because he's such a good guy. That is the bottom line. He's not up in the clouds, he's not pretentious, he's not egotistical. Obviously, his family keep his feet on the ground, but I think it's just being a decent, everyday, down-to-earth, normal person that is the key to him being a good communicator. There are no airs and graces; he just empathises with people.'

It is perhaps because Leadbetter is so well meaning and sincere that he feels betrayed by people when they fail to credit him. Other teachers chalk it up to experience; Leadbetter seems to take it personally.

'I'll remember till the day I die Seve coming back here at the start of '92,' Leadbetter began. 'We worked on some things and he left here hitting it really well. He went to New Orleans the next week – that was the week before Augusta – and finished twelfth. I went up to Augusta on the Monday and Billy [Foster, Ballesteros's caddie] said: "I tell you what, Seve could win this week, the way he's hitting it. It's unbelievable." I thought: "Jeez, this is great. I can't wait till this guy plays." I get there Tuesday morning, walk onto the practice tee and Billy comes over and [rolls his eyes]. I said: "What's the matter?" He said: "Watch."'

According to Leadbetter, it wasn't so much that Ballesteros was cutting the odd ball or hitting one fat; it's that they were flying so far out of bounds they were in danger of breaching air-traffic control regulations. Leadbetter didn't need to look far to find the probable cause. In between shots, Ballesteros was engaged in a passionate argument with his brother and sometime teacher, Manuel, with whom he was plainly at odds. Like a man in a dream, Leadbetter walked towards the Spaniard. He took a deep breath. 'What's going on?' he asked.

Ballesteros looked carefully past him. 'Manuel is here,' he said flatly.

'And from that point on, I promise – you look back at the records – from that point on, he has not played well,' said Leadbetter. 'I'm not talking about Switzerland [Ballesteros's best finish in 1993, second at the European Masters] – that was probably a fluke. I mean, he was very sheepish at the Masters. He sort of avoided me. He finished tied fifty-ninth. I saw him in Japan and he said: "David, what we did last year was good but it wasn't natural. I want to go back to my natural swing." I said: "Fine." And you just think, that's strange to do that. I mean, he's wasted the last eighteen months of his golfing career.'

What hurt Leadbetter most is that by denying that his teacher played any real role in the achievements of 1991, his great comeback season, Ballesteros also denied Leadbetter the source of his satisfaction as a teacher – 'feeling what a player would feel for that one moment in time'.

'When you say: "Is there an ego involved?" I suppose maybe there is an ego because you say, "Well, Jeez, maybe I did do something to help that person to get to that point,"' Leadbetter confessed. 'On the other hand, you also get slapped in the face because sometimes you can help somebody who you've worked really hard with and you don't get any sort of credit whatsoever. But you know yourself personally that you did. But that's the nature of the business. I've come to realise that now. I realised that, hey, these aren't people you can control. Golf is an individual sport and the reason these guys are great is because they're different. They're selfish, to a certain extent. You have to be. But, for the most part, they're a really good bunch of guys.'

The door of Leadbetter's office crashes open and his young son bursts in. He wants to take his golf clubs to show his friends. 'There's too many people around, Andy,' Leadbetter says indulgently, shooing him out. Returning to his chair, he remarked: 'He's really getting into the game. He's just turned nine and he shot 43 off the ladies' tees the other day.'

These are the positives: his wife Kelly, a professional on the LPGA Tour, and their two children, heirs to an awesome golfing heritage. When he's not helping Faldo or Price to victories in major championships, Leadbetter coaches his wife, does an aerobic activity four times a week, pushes weights and stretches three times a week, fishes, skis, plays golf and updates his instruction book collection. He also obsesses about his diet. When he travels to Japan, a suitcase full of bread, cereals and soya milk goes too. Chicken is on the Leadbetter menu, but not red meat, not junk food, not alcohol.

If his fitness fanaticism is mirrored in his strong, pale face and spare, sinewy frame, then his lackadaisical approach to time-keeping and business management ('My organisational abilities leave a lot to be desired') are reflected in his tiny chaotic office, with its autographed photographs, framed magazine covers, scattered golf clubs, and desk piled high with contracts, newspaper cuttings, golf balls, swing aids, instruction books, player files and crumpled correspondence.

Following my gaze, Leadbetter grinned: 'I didn't plan this

success,' he said, in case I was wondering how it could possibly have come about. 'I consider myself fortunate, I really do. I've never been one of these guys that's been goal-oriented. You get these psychologists that say, you've got to have a one-year plan, a three-year plan, a five-year plan. It's like, hey, whatever happens, happens. I couldn't tell you how much money I've got. I mean, I have no clue. I never sign a cheque. Kelly signs some and IMG do some. I'm not trying to sound big-headed. What I'm trying to say is that because I enjoy it and I get so wrapped up in what I do, I sort of lose touch. Over here, everything is so fast – wham, bam, keep up with the Joneses. You're going at 150 m.p.h. There's nothing better that I can do than to sit in front of the TV and watch cricket. To me, that's totally relaxing. I sit there with my dad and we discuss things.'

In the early hours of the morning, before his one-year-old daughter gets up and starts demanding attention, Leadbetter will often lie awake and reflect upon the extraordinary chain of events that led him to become the most successful teacher in the history of the game. 'It is amazing what's happened. I sometimes actually think: "How come I got so lucky? Do I deserve all this?" Because a lot of it has been through what other people have done. It's not as if I've gone out and won the British Open. I don't know. I guess I just happened to be in the right place at the right time. A bit of luck, a bit of skill, mix it all together and' – Leadbetter laughs, swings back in his chair and raises his hands in a toast to the portrait gallery of champions – 'you've got this.'

9

A HEAVEN OF SORTS

'If there's a golf course like Augusta in heaven, I hope
I'm the head greenkeeper.'

GARY PLAYER, 1992

There are several things you need to know about Augusta,'
Robinson said, as we cruised down Washington Road
some time after 1 a.m. on Tuesday morning. 'The first
rule is: never, never lose your badge because you'll never even
get onto the premises to get another one. The second is: egg
salad is the only edible sandwich and they're gone by ten past
eleven. There are other sandwiches. There is the hot barbecued
pork sandwich, for example. That comes out of a can with a list
of ingredients 800 words long. Some people claim they've seen
a human being eat a pimento cheese; personally I never have.
The chocolate milk is the whole reason to go to Augusta, but if
there is a rain delay the photographers drink it all. That's all you
need to know to survive at Augusta.'

With that, we continued on our journey through the
moonlit streets, with the original innocent abroad, Graham
Spiers, a sports writer for *Scotland on Sunday*, wedged in the
back of the car. We were headed for the Super 8, a $23 motel
that had become an $89 motel for the week of the Masters.

Graham left his badge behind on the first morning. No
sooner had we crawled back through the traffic to Augusta
National and negotiated our way through five security
checkpoints, than Martha Gaye herself had lost Robinson's
badge. At Augusta, Martha Gaye has more influence than the
Queen. Indeed, the Queen would not even make it through the
gate. It matters not a jot to Martha Gaye whether one is an
award-winning writer of international repute in the game of

golf, whether one works for a publication that reaches two million people, or whether one is a freelance working for three golf magazines, two newspapers and a news agency; if Martha doesn't think you merit accreditation for Augusta, the Pope himself could not persuade her. There are journalists and editors who have spent small fortunes over the years courting her with flowers, trinkets and boxes of chocolates, but Martha Gaye cannot be bought.

Not that that stops the optimistic from trying. On 5 April, Martha's power centre at the entrance of the media room was a positive hothouse of floral tributes and saccharine bribes. Behind them, Martha Gaye was staring about her with murderous eyes for the culprit who had made off with Robinson's badge. A lackey incautiously mentioned to her that Bernhard Langer, the defending champion, was waiting alone in the interview room. 'I'm busy looking for Robinson's badge,' snapped Martha Gaye. As a point of principle, she continued searching for a couple of minutes longer. Then she leaned irritably into the microphone on her desk. 'Burn'd Langurr fur interview,' she intoned.

Augusta is golf's nearest realisation of heaven. There is nothing to compare with the vision that lies beyond Magnolia Lane: the rich, velvety lustre of the steep emerald fairways; the whispering pines; the vibrant splash of red and white dogwood, fuchsia, azalea, juniper, redbud, wisteria and holly; and the smooth outlines of the traps, as glistening and powdery as fresh-fallen snow. There is no afternoon more enjoyable than to lounge beneath the umbrellas on the clubhouse lawn, where the likes of President Eisenhower and Alastair Cooke have enjoyed clam chowder and peach cobbler, with an eye on the first tee, where Tom Watson is launching his drive, and an ear cocked in the direction of the interviews taking place beneath the old oak tree, where Gary Player is holding court. And there is no feeling sweeter than to lie in the sunshine on the bank above the short sixteenth, drinking pink lemonade and gazing down on the black shining mirror of Rae's Creek as all the greats come walking up to the green – Palmer with his distinctive swagger, Norman with his long, confident stride, Faldo with his eager, slightly self-conscious march. A mile downtown, there might be joblessness and murder, and in Rwanda there might be genocide, but here at Augusta, time stands still for golf.

'I'll never forget how I was struck by Augusta that first year,' Norman has said. 'This was what golf was meant to be, pure golf. This was the purest form of golf tournament. Everything about it was first rate. That drive up Magnolia Lane, with the clubhouse ahead, the practice ranges on either side, it just gets you in the perfect frame of mind for a tournament.'

There is something about Bobby Jones's Cathedral in the Pines, a tangible sense of joys and sorrows past, that makes history as weighty a presence here as it is at St Andrews or Muirfield.

Even Palmer wasn't immune. 'I walk this course and suddenly I feel like I'm 23 again,' he said, his brown face creasing into a smile. 'Only, I'm walking considerably slower.'

'Augusta,' observed Ben Crenshaw, the 1984 Masters champion, 'is the most tempting golf course I've ever seen. It goads you into trying different shots because there's so much to gain.

If you're right on your game and you live dangerously for a day and you can just skirt the trouble here and there, you can come off with a brilliant score. But if you're not, that's when it's really punishing.'

Herein lies the secret of Bobby Jones's masterpiece; at Augusta, even disaster comes wrapped in an aesthetically pleasing package. They key to survival is remembering that behind every graceful curve, every sparkling stream and every smiling azalea bush lurks a double-bogey – or worse. The real test is psychological. It's not enough to strike the ball well at Augusta. You have to be calculating enough to outsmart the swirling wind and outwit the enigmatic greens. And even then you might lose. Twenty-five years ago, on his 45th birthday, Roberto De Vicenzo scored a magical 65 for a 277 total, 11 under par. It seemed certain he had won. Pressured by a television crew for an instant interview, the gregarious Argentinian signed his scorecard and departed to the press room just as Bob Goalby, a little-known Midwesterner, began eagling and birdying to take the lead. Goalby had three-putted the seventeenth to fall back into a tie when De Vicenzo was told to go back to the scorer's tent. Something was wrong. 'At that moment,' De Vicenzo said, 'my feet went to my head.'

Tommy Aaron, his playing partner, was waiting solemnly by the eighteenth. 'He be very quiet,' De Vicenzo recalled. 'There were so many people around the table and someone said to me, "Roberto, check again. You make a mistake on your scorecard – it's not 65, it's a 66." I told them I think it was 65, but when I check again I saw that for 17, where I made three, Tommy Aaron had written four.'

When the full horror of what had occurred first hit the Masters committee, they had consulted Jones himself, who was in agony at the time with the degenerative central nervous system disease syringomyelia that eventually took his life. To Jones, who had once called a penalty on himself that cost him the US Open – saying afterwards when his honesty was admired: 'You might as well praise a man for not robbing a bank' – the matter was cut and dried. The rules were unequivocal: if a player signs for a score lower than he shot, then he is automatically disqualified; if, on the other hand, he signs for a higher score, then that is the figure he is stuck with. Thus, the much loved De Vicenzo, who had won 200 events round the world, including the British Open nine months earlier, had to be told that Goalby was the new Masters Champion.

Under the cruellest of all possible blows, his courage and sportsmanship were incredible to behold. He simply said sadly: 'I play golf all over the world for 30 years and all I can think of is what a stupid I am to be wrong in this wonderful tournament.'

We had come to Augusta via New Orleans, where I'd found a different kind of paradise. After the purgatory of Jacksonville, a benign twist of fate had ensured that, along with the other British golf writers, I had ended up in a suite in the divine Windsor Court Hotel. The only drawback was having to cover the New Orleans Classic, which is held at English Turn, half an hour out of town. The press centre is (I suspect) a converted greenkeeper's shed, the scoring is done by quaint old ladies who keep life interesting by making sure that the scores posted on the leaderboard, the scoreboard and the computer bear not the slightest resemblance to one another, and the whole thing is run, if that's not too strong a term, by a press officer who makes one think of a panic-stricken John Major on acid.

Naturally, there was no transport to the course. Michael McDonnell and Michael Williams, respectively of the *Daily Mail* and the *Telegraph*, found themselves being ferried to English Turn one morning by an Eritrean cab driver who told them he was a civil engineer by trade. Presently it became clear that map-reading had not been included in his training. Not only was he unable to find the Mississippi River Bridge, he was unable to cross the river at all. An element of desperation entered his driving. He raced down a motorway slip road, decided he was going in the wrong direction, did a U-turn and went back up again. Beads of sweat broke out on his neck. McDonnell and Williams gripped the seat covers. The final straw came when he took a charge at a red light from 150 metres away. 'Why didn't you say something?' an ashen-faced Williams asked McDonnell after the one-time civil engineer had admitted defeat and, unable to find his way back to the hotel, dropped them at a taxi rank half an hour after they set off. 'I did,' replied McDonnell. 'I said, "Bloody hell!"'

At Augusta, another type of insanity had strolled unmolested up Magnolia Lane. It was currently residing under the bows of the oak tree on the clubhouse lawn. 'There are at least seven players in the world's top 30, some from Europe, who are taking beta-blockers,' Mac O'Grady, Seve Ballesteros's eccentric coach, was telling reporters. 'By reducing anxiety, which is the effect of these beta-blockers, some players have improved their putting and they have been winning tournaments, including majors. Guys are suddenly making putts they never used to because they're taking the drug. Just look at some players who have been meandering over the past four or five years, not quite making it. All of a sudden their putts are going in and they are making a name for themselves.'

Unsurprisingly, all hell broke loose. At the Ryder Cup and the four majors, when there are a lot of newshounds about, a media silly season tends to result and you have relatively minor incidents, such as the Watson autograph saga, blown completely out of proportion. Now we had *The Star* screaming 'Golf Drug Storm!', the *Mirror* wailing 'Drugs Slur Rocks Golf', and the *Daily Record* revealing, 'I Popped Pills Says Sam', when anybody could have told you that beta-blockers and pot have been around golf for years, and neither have been shown to improve performance on the course.

When Nick Price was told of O'Grady's claims, he immediately volunteered the information that he had taken beta-blockers for seven years. 'It did more harm to my career than anything else,' he said. 'You don't seem to have any energy. You never seem to get tired and that means you can't sleep at night . . . My family has a long history of high blood pressure. My pressure is so high that without daily drugs I could die from a heart attack. I switched to another drug five years ago because beta-blockers wouldn't let me be myself. It was a terrible time in my life.' Price said that he didn't believe for a minute that what O'Grady said was true. 'We don't have that kind of thing in our sport.'

Sam Torrance admitted he had popped beta-blockers in 1992 after hearing that snooker players found they helped to steady their nerves. When he promptly fell to sixty-second in the money list, his worst position in 20 years, he stopped taking them. 'Last year, drug-free Sam won three times in Europe,' the *Daily Record* reported triumphantly.

Faldo thought O'Grady was talking nonsense. 'The only stuff that goes into me are vitamin pills – and the occasional whisky,' he insisted. Lyle, too, denied any knowledge of drugs in golf. He said the only white powder he sniffed was his baby daughter's talc.

But O'Grady stuck to his story. Beta-blockers are banned by the International Olympic Committee and by the Sports Council, even with a doctor's prescription, but they are not restricted in golf. 'The PGA Tour should introduce random urine testing to check for such substances and other prescription drugs that are used to help putting and any other aspect of the game,' said O'Grady, who claimed that he had taken beta-blockers for six months in 1988 and it had improved his putting. He had stopped for ethical reasons.

But as they say, there's nothing new under the sun. As long

ago as 1986, US Tour players were calling for drug-testing. 'I'm all for it,' Hubert Green had told reporters. 'I feel sorry for someone born in Ethiopia but I can't feel sorry for someone who puts a gun to his head by taking drugs.' Mac O'Grady, a self-styled voice of conscience for the narcotically challenged even then, had his own balanced view. 'Whenever you have leisure time there's going to be decadence,' he said. 'Once you've become successful it's easy to get involved in negative escapisms. You start to lose your basic chromosomes of integrity. Besides, what do people think this is, the 1950s? *The Donna Reed Show* or *Leave it to Beaver*? We've got to do something.'

Of the Europeans, Severiano Ballesteros did best in the first round, much to the astonishment of those who had collapsed in hysterics when he announced he was being coached by O'Grady. Prior to arriving at Augusta, he had missed three cuts in four starts, and his path to a 70 was by no means a smooth one. His missed five of the first nine greens and four more on the back nine. He also missed more fairways than he hit.

'His short game is fantastic,' enthused Raymond Floyd, his playing partner. 'There isn't anyone in the world even close to him. He hits a shot and you think, "Boy, that's lucky," but if it's lucky, he's lucky an awful lot.'

At the first hole, Ballesteros missed the green by 20 yards and needed two chips to get to two feet. At the second, he drove into the trees, but got up and down for a birdie. At the third, he missed both fairway and green, but chipped stone dead. At the fourth, his approach finished short of the green and right. He was now faced with a 20-yard shot over a bunker on to a lightning-fast downslope. Unfazed, he played a gentle lob to within six feet of the flag and holed his fourth successive single putt for a par.

'That was the most fabulous par I've ever seen,' exclaimed Floyd.

Ballesteros was more reserved. 'You can't win the Masters in the first round, but you can lose it,' he said. He was asked whether he thought he could triumph again in the event he had won in 1980 and '83 and so nearly won in 1985, '86 and '87. 'No, no, I'm just here for fun,' the Spaniard said with an attempt at lightheartedness, but he seemed dispirited and lacking in confidence. Beside him, the press officer had all but nodded off.

Ballesteros's 70 left him two strokes behind the leader, Larry Mize, at the end of the day. Tom Kite, the former US Open champion, and the South African Fulton Allem were in second place, with Watson, Norman and Tom Lehman a stroke further behind. Elsewhere, the foreign challenge had faltered. Faldo, who had recorded two of the seven European victories at Augusta in ten years, slumped to a four over par 76, as did Woosnam, while Langer, Price and Olazabal all scored 74.

For Mize, who had spent his childhood wishing and dreaming outside the gates of Augusta, it was a poignant homecoming. In 1987, after he had watched Ballesteros three-putt the first extra hole of the play-off and depart in tears along fairways striped with shadow, he and Norman, then world No. 1, had continued alone. At the eleventh hole, Mize's approach veered away. Norman waited on the green, fit and dominant, his Masters jacket just a heartbeat or two away. Mize had chipped, and the ball had bounced and skipped, checked and gained momentum until finally it toppled into the hole.

'For the most part, people just remember it as a great shot,' Mize said of the 105-foot chip that cut Norman's soul to ribbons. 'I think you have some who remember it as the lucky chip-in or whatever, and I'm sure at times that got under my skin a little bit, but it doesn't any more because I won the tournament and it's as simple as that. It isn't a one-hole golf tournament. I hit a heck of a chip to win.

'I've always felt that the timing of the shot is the incredible thing. If I chip in there on the eleventh hole in regulation and win it by one . . . it's not a big deal. But to be on the second hole of a play-off with one of the best players in the world [Norman], and one of the other best players in the world [Ballesteros] has already been knocked out of the play-off, then to hit that shot to win the Masters – underdog local boy from Augusta – is just incredible.'

In explaining the differences between performing in a major championship and an ordinary event, Bobby Jones once used the analogy of a trapeze artist on a high wire. 'In a major they remove the net,' he said.

Jones, one of only four men to win the Grand Slam of majors, thrived on the electrifying atmosphere, the tension accompanying that live or die gamble. So did the Golden Bear. 'I guess we'll have to handicap Mr Nicklaus like a thoroughbred and put a couple of 100-lb weights in his pocket,' said Jones after Nicklaus won the 1965 Masters by nine shots. He might have made good his promise had he known then that Nicklaus would win his sixth Green Jacket in 1986, at the age of 46, and that by the time he teed up in his thirty-fourth Masters, he'd have accumulated more eagles (18) at Augusta than double-bogeys (17), and Sunday would have been his best scoring day (he averaged 70.84).

'Every time I went to Augusta, I played well,' Nicklaus recalled. 'I was the guy to beat. I always enjoyed that. Not only did I know that, the other players knew that. And the writers knew that. That made for a confrontation – me against the rest of them. That was true of a lot of golf tournaments, but really Augusta more than anywhere else.'

In his heyday, Nicklaus liked to say that the majors were the easiest tournaments to win because everyone is trying so hard they don't play their normal games. Dan Forsman knew what he meant. In 1993, he took a seven on the twelfth in the final round to effectively throw away the title. Walking the high wire between glory and ignominious failure, he had suffered from vertigo. 'I've often tried to describe it to somebody by saying: "Put a two by four plank over a couple of cinder blocks and walk six feet – no problem. Well, put it over the World Trade Center, and have the wind blowing and people waiting for your demise and roaring here and there, and think about what you've read about the ones that have gone through there and have fallen to their death. That gives you an idea what it's all about."'

This year, Forsman had a chance to relive that experience, to make amends for his mistake. He made seven birdies in a round of 66 to lie a stroke behind Mize on four under par, level with Norman and Lehman. José Maria Olazabal, Hale Irwin, Tom Watson, Tom Kite and Ernie Els were in third place on

141. 'Now everyone is telling me if I can just get by 12 on Sunday, I might be able to win the tournament,' Forsman said in annoyance. 'It isn't life and death here, even if some players, including myself, think it is. Other things are far more important than what I did on the twelfth hole here.'

He stopped, realising he was kidding nobody but himself. A small spasm passed across his face as the agony of the quadruple bogey seeped back into his mind.

'I walk across that bridge [to the green] a little softer,' Forsman admitted. 'I turn the corner on that bridge a little bit quieter. I sort of bow and pay homage to that great hole, the twelfth. It sounds corny but anybody who has been through the same situation would say the same thing.'

On the three practice days preceding the Masters, some 50,000 people poured onto Augusta's sea of green. On Saturday, only the élite and the privileged dared come, and their passes were scrutinised by a scanner as they entered. At Augusta, tournament tickets are not sold, they are handed down like family heirlooms, so ticket touts do a roaring trade. The *Augusta Chronicle* revealed that patrons were asking for as much as $3,200 per badge, with one woman, a Mrs Ezell, buying a Masters badge for her husband for $600 a day. What's more, the committee had issued a statement to say that, as from next season, practice-day passes would no longer be on public sale.

Augusta's rules and regulations are as arcane as the club itself. Along with forged tickets, one is forbidden to bring any drink not transported in a Masters green cup on to the premises (there are no commercial logos other than Augusta's own on the course). Lewine Mair's *Telegraph* diary reported that one spectator, having paid his $20 practice-day fee, realised he had forgotten his binoculars. He pointed to a white car in the nearby parking lot, and asked the man at the gate if he might nip back and fetch them. 'Certainly,' said the guard, 'but it will cost you $7 to get back in again.'

Political correctness has never strayed onto the jewel-like turf of Augusta National. It could have held its head high in the days of the Civil War; on its 60th anniversary, only one black member among 310 besmirches its reputation as a white stronghold. 'I don't know if they voted on it,' Ron Townsend told a journalist, 'I just know I've become a member. But this is the South here, and let's face the fact.'

'One of the great disillusionments in my life is the way the Masters has become such a revered tournament,' former US Tour player Charlie Sifford said bitterly. 'As far as I'm concerned, it is one of the most racist and hateful spots on golf's globe.'

Nevertheless, African-Americans continued to spear rubbish, serve cocktails and cut sandwiches annually. Until 1975, no black man played at Augusta. Luckily, for the club's regular all-black team of caddies, conditions are improving. The loos in their accommodation now have doors.

In the third round, when a 20-mile-an-hour wind whistled through the pines and turned the putting surfaces into ice rinks, Tom Lehman took the lead with a 69. 'Who would have thought a kid from Minnesota would be leading the Masters?' Lehman said wryly. It wasn't so long ago since he had considered abandoning the Tour to coach golf at the University of Minnesota. 'I would have taken the job but I didn't want to have to rent out cross-country skis at the pro shop during the winter,' Lehman said.

A stroke behind the American came Olazabal, who had scored 67, 69 in the second and third rounds. Mize was in third place on 211. Norman had fallen away with a 75. For the third time in his career, Augusta, his nemesis, had whipped out its knives and (to quote Rick Reilly) carved him into sushi. He was still in with an outside chance, but it was Lehman whom Olazabal seemed most concerned about. 'I don't know much about him,' he said. 'You don't need to know much about a guy who can shoot seven under round here.'

José Maria Olazabal was two years old when he first picked up a golf club. The son of the greenkeeper at Real Golf Club de San Sebastian, he grew up in a stone farmhouse situated behind the ninth green, 35 feet from the putting green and 100 feet from the first tee. Golf was all he ever wanted to play. 'I didn't force him,' recalled Gaspar Olazabal, his father. 'He started himself. When he first began to walk, he picked up a club and began to hit and hit with it. He did it himself. He took to the sport.'

At 15, Olazabal was a small, light-boned boy with a delicate touch around the greens, who passed before John Jacobs's gaze as a member of Spain's national squad. At 25, he was the best young player in the world, his inspired performances at the World Series and with Ballesteros in the Ryder Cup indicating that a major victory was only months away. Then came the 1991 Masters. On the final day, Olazabal, within easy grasp of his first Green Jacket, chalked up a record quadruple-bogey seven at the 180-yard sixth, before bogeying the last to lose by a stroke to Ian Woosnam. It precipitated a two-year slump, during which Olazabal, who had always seemed impossibly composed and mature off the course, became obsessive to the point of madness on it. Perfection was what he wanted and the boundaries of that perfection, unobtainable in golf, seldom extended beyond ten feet from the hole. If an approach shot dared to run to 15 feet, he would slam his club down and, hands on hips, stand glowering at the green, steam issuing from his ears.

'He became very, very morose and bad-tempered,' Jacobs recalled. 'Funnily enough, we made an instruction video in May 1991, soon after he had taken five at the last and lost the Masters to Ian Woosnam, and I remember saying to him, 'Come on, stop looking so miserable. You didn't play well by your standards and you still got within a shot of the play-off.' What had upset him is he'd been such a winner as an amateur, and he had had all these victories as a professional, and that was probably the first time he had failed in the hot seat with a chance to win.'

Sergio Gomez, Olazabal's manager, watching with growing concern, began to feel that the game was destroying the man who is like a son to him, that Olazabal's reaction to less than ideal shots was so disproportionate it was as if he had lost a member of his family. 'I said to him, "If you behave like that when you hit a golf ball shot to 20 feet, what are you going to do when something really terrible happens? When your father dies, are you going to react the same way?"

A HEAVEN OF SORTS

The first thing that had to change was Olazabal's attitude. An astonishing outburst, prompted by Olazabal's appalling behaviour at the Tenerife Open in February, from Maite Gomez, Sergio's wife, for whom he has the utmost regard and who had hitherto shown him nothing but kindness, shook Olazabal profoundly. At the New Orleans Classic, where Olazabal finished runner-up to Ben Crenshaw, Gomez observed with something approaching awe: 'Yesterday he said to me, "Have you seen how beautiful this place is? How lovely the houses are?" Two years ago, he would never have noticed that.'

Next to undergo revision was Olazabal's swing. In March, Jacobs, in Spain on business, bumped into Gomez at the Andalucian Open. Sergio told him that the lesson he had given the young Spaniard at the Ryder Cup had helped, but he still wasn't happy. Jacobs went down to the practice ground to Olazabal. 'He asked me: "How do I draw the ball?"' Jacobs recalled. 'I put him in the right position and I said, "Hit it from here and you'll draw it."' Olazabal went home with second prize and won the Mediterranean Open the following week.

On the morning of the final round at Augusta, Olazabal found a note pinned to his locker. It was signed by Seve Ballesteros and it read: 'Be patient. You know what you have to do. You are the best player in the world.'

For the first time in several years, Olazabal believed it. Sergio compared his mood at breakfast to that of a matador about to enter the bullring. From the opening tee shot, he played to win and he rarely faltered. The pivotal hole was the 500-yard, par-five fifteenth. While Olazabal's approach only just cleared the pond, Lehman landed 15 feet from the pin. But Olazabal had been preparing for this moment all his life. Without hesitation, he stroked in a 30-foot putt from the fringe for an eagle. 'Great putt,' Lehman said. But he was fired up, not discouraged. 'I thought, "Okay, he made his, now I'm going to make mine right on top of it,"' he recalled. 'I hit a really good putt. It looked perfect all the way. A foot short of the hole, it was dead centre, but right at the very end it seemed to touch the front of the lip and take a 90-degree turn to the right.' Lehman fell to his knees and pounded the ground with his fists. 'It was like a stab in the heart,' he said later.

Back at San Sebastian, club members and friends of the Olazabal family had gathered to witness José Maria in his hour of glory. 'Here in the clubhouse,' Ramon Galdos, the club secretary, said, 'there was a crowd of us watching the whole four days. There were 25 of us and, of course, it was a very lively atmosphere. But when he reached the seventeenth, everyone got worried, very worried.' All except Gaspar, Olzabal's father. 'I was quite serene,' he remembered. 'I felt he was going to win. When he finished, we cracked open the champagne. We had it all ready. And we went on until three in the morning.'

Olazabal, who had just two bogeys in the final 56 holes, won by two strokes from Lehman, three from Mize and four from Kite, becoming the sixth European winner in seven years. His score of 69 gave him an aggregate of 279, nine under par. 'You will never know how happy I am,' he said.

Norman did not share his sentiments. His 77 had left him 13 strokes behind the Spaniard. He strode wearily into the clubhouse bar and leaned on the counter. 'Give me a beer for every bogey I've made,' he told the barman.

At San Sebastian, they were already planning the celebrations that would take place when the Masters Champion returned, including 'a dinner, a dance and all the honours that he merits'.

10

THE GREEN CARAVAN

'There are only two kinds of men in the world – those
who stay at home and those who do not.'

RUDYARD KIPLING

In the bar of the Hotel L'Etrier in Crans-sur-Sierre,
Switzerland, David Grice, the world-weary Fairway Travel
representative, was describing a typical week in the life of a
Touring professional.

'It's a circus,' he said, by way of introduction. 'What makes
my job difficult is that, when a player comes to a golf
tournament, everything is free. They get fetched and carried in
courtesy cars, and when they walk into the locker-room it's,
"Have some free balls, a free shirt, some free clubs." Travel is
the only thing they have to pay for, so they expect everything
to work perfectly and they get very upset when it doesn't.

'Then you get this false friendliness. But when they phone
up to make a booking each week it's very, very rare that they're
concerned about what their so-called friends are doing. You get
one or two little cliques – the biggest clique being the Scottish
– but, apart from that, they'll do exactly what suits them.

'When they get down to the airport on Monday or Tuesday,
there's a lot of camaraderie when they come together again.
Obviously, not everybody likes each other, but they will always
say, "Well done last week", or whatever.

'Then you see them on the plane. I sit in the last row, in
smoking, and look down the aisle and it's like someone's
thrown a pack of cards up and just let it fall. You'd expect the
ones who are friends to sit beside one another, but they don't.
You've got one sitting beside a fat old woman, another sitting

beside some kids. The moment we land, at the baggage belt, the whole mentality changes. They become a big family where they'll stick together and stick up for each other. It's like: "We're all in it together, fish out of water."

'Tuesday is when they let themselves relax. They practise, have a few beers, talk about football, have a laugh. On Wednesday, it goes quiet. They're thinking about the tournament; they're on a mission. Even best friends – if one's off early and the other's off late, the early one will stay in the hotel and have a bit of room service. Wednesday night, nobody's around the hotel after nine o'clock. On Thursday, it changes again. The ones that have shot 65 will be happy and intense and want to go to bed early. The ones that have shot 75 will be depressed, and they'll either go out on the piss or they'll sit in their room and phone their wife six times and want to slit their wrists.

'Friday's their big day. The players who have made the cut are overjoyed, they're thinking about the next two rounds. The guys who have missed it are miserable, demanding, cross. They're in a hurry to get home. The players who have qualified on the line are moping around. They're thinking: "What am I doing here?" I've seen players miss the cut and be happier than those who have just scraped through.

'On Saturday night, the professionalism comes in. They're thinking about the money. The guys in the top ten are looking to win, the ones lying twentieth or thirtieth are aiming for the top ten, and everyone else wants to finish in the top twenty or at least better than reserve money.

'On Sunday night, the atmosphere at the airport is the way it would be between four or five o'clock on Friday in a normal job. They're happy because their weekend's coming. They're all jovial and relaxed and they're having a few drinks. They've done the week's work and, whether they've won £2,000 or £20,000, they've accepted it. You get one or two that have a bad last round that just sit in the corner. They're obviously going to carry it all the way home with them. But the majority are happy with their lot. They just want to get home. It's, "Get me out of this fucking circus."'

THE GREEN CARAVAN

If it's Tuesday, it's not necessarily Rome. It might just as easily be Phuket or Puerto Rico, or Munich or Montego Bay, or even Berlin or the Czech Republic. Today, as it happens, it is Geneva. The sky is awash with a delicate blue, the ground is damp and aromatic, and the courtesy car is willing and able to take us on the two-and-a-half-hour drive to the skiing village of Crans-sur-Sierre, high in the Swiss Alps. Thank goodness for Swiss efficiency.

A curious mentality attaches to lifelong golf-circuit travel. Weeks are not divided into weekdays and weekends, but into laundry days, travel days, practice days, pro-am days and tournament days; and years are not years in the conventional sense, with Easter and Father's Day and Christmas – only seasons. Springtime begins with the Masters; summer exists at the Open; autumn is called to an abrupt halt by the arctic conditions synonymous with the Dunhill Cup; and winter signals the coming of the off-season and the departure of the top players, like snow geese, for exotic locations like Bali and Sun City, and the lesser players for Argentina and Nigeria.

It was September and we were on our way to Crans for the European Masters, the first qualifying tournament for the 1995 Ryder Cup, and thus the first of several million occasions over the next 14 months when we would be forced to write on that meritorious match. Also in the car was David Probyn, a blond-haired, blue-eyed, squeaky-clean tournament director, immaculately attired in the pin-striped shirt, navy blazer and red, green and blue tie that is the Boss-endorsed apparel of the European Tour. Probyn had been on the circuit five years. Previously, he had done contractual work for Sovereign Golf Holidays, but when an administrative position became vacant at Wentworth headquarters, he'd been taken on by the Tour.

Even Probyn conceded that, with one or two exceptions, Tour officials are peculiarly clone-like: short-back-and-sides, Boss uniform, bland, inoffensive and mildly arrogant in character. No doubt he is right when he says that the interviewers are looking for a particular type of person: one who will be able to deal with the lifestyle (which combines the existences of a millionaire, a bank clerk and a travelling salesman) as well as working with the same people week in and week out. 'It's almost a 24-hour-a-day commitment because you have to keep sponsors happy in the evening, which, if you've been out since five-thirty on the golf course, is not always what you want to do.'

Probyn's first real test of character came when he was dispatched to Darkest Africa to deal with the circuit there. The Safari Tour takes in Kenya, Zambia, Zimbabwe, Nigeria and the Ivory Coast (subject to local currency fluctuations, military coups, etc.), and has a long and scandalous past, which in its early days was oddly reminiscent of a Hollywood B-movie, in which the lions are moth-eaten, the dames are dizzy, and a group of camp white men dress up as gorillas. Tarzan lookalikes and caricaturish tribesmen with spears and leopard-skin loincloths. Probyn's experiences were fairly typical. In his capacity as tournament director, he was stationed in the middle of a Nigerian golf course beside one of only two available loos. In between rulings, he would watch people racing from all directions clutching toilet rolls. When a storm blew in, Probyn's job was to hop on to the back of a dilapidated motorbike and buzz along the fairways, tooting the horn to stop play. All went smoothly until he discovered that the self-appointed chief referee, a local government official, had taken it upon himself to tell players that anyone within two club lengths of the hole on the waterlogged greens could declare their putt a gimme.

There were the usual collection of travel nightmares. No Safari Tour event would be complete without them. In one instance, Probyn and his flock of fledgling pros set off on a flight from Lagos to Yamoussoukro, which was alleged to take an hour and a half but clocked in at 42. He and the players spent the night at the airport hotel where, upon finding excrement and insects on the sheets, they decided that their health would benefit immeasurably from a sleepless night spent playing cards in the lounge. The next morning they embarked on a three-hour bus ride through the jungle on uncharted roads. Returning, Probyn came within a whisker of being faced with telling 60 players that, due to over-booking, they would not be home for Christmas after all. It would have been more than his life was worth. Tour players might be adept at dealing with plugged lies or lateral water hazards, but let there be a hitch in their travel arrangements and they quickly become unhinged.

The mid-'70s and early '80s, the peak years of the Safari circuit, were a time of great unrest in Africa. Trigger-happy militia men, and government officials eager to stamp their authority on the crumbling monuments of colonialism, flexed their new muscle with glee. Private clubs were an obvious target. Not long after Zambia gained independence, a barbecue and disco were held at Luansha Golf Club for the Zambian Open players. The party was in full swing when the district governor took offence at something or other and left the club in a rage. Soon afterwards, a well-dressed official ordered the crowd to disperse. Neither the players nor the locals took any notice. Half an hour went by and the order was repeated, with the promise that force would be used if necessary. The party continued. All of a sudden, the doors flew open and 40 soldiers in battle fatigues rushed into the room. They cocked their machine-guns. Within seconds the party was over, the players and expatriates slipping and sliding in their frantic haste to reach the exit.

Anyone who knows Africa knows that such an incident is as likely to end peacefully, with smiles all round, as it is in a massacre. However, when tragedy did strike on the Safari Tour it came from an unexpected quarter. In 1974, the Zambian Open went to Mufulira, a small town on the Copperbelt. David Moore, a talented 18-year-old from Essex, and Gary Smith, also in his late teens, were put up by an elderly couple who lived near the course. Mr X was a miner by profession. A year or two earlier there had been a mining disaster, in which a shaft had collapsed and trapped hundreds of workers underground. Mr X played a key part in the rescue operation, crawling under the earth to survey the carnage and heroically hauling maimed and dying men to the surface. As a consequence of the horror he had seen, he had taken to drink.

One evening, Moore and Smith returned from the course to find Mr X under the influence. He began to shout at them, accusing them of flirting with his wife. He disappeared into his bedroom and returned with a shotgun. Everyone scattered.

Moore was slower than Smith and Mrs X, and Mr X shot him in the head. Smith dived into the bathroom, whereupon Mr X banged furiously at the door and threatened to kill him, too. Eventually, his wife managed to calm him down, and the three of them took the unconscious Moore to the local hospital. A senior British surgeon tried to save Moore, but it was hopeless. When Mr X heard the news of the young player's death, he went out into the hospital car-park and shot himself.

It was the unanimous decision of the players that Moore would have wanted the tournament to go on, and therefore it did and was won by Christy O'Connor, Jnr. A memorial service was held for Moore, the unfortunate victim of a terrible tragedy.

Back in the sanitised, eerily normal environs of Lake Geneva, Probyn was considering the small problems he faced in his role on the European Tour. 'The toughest thing about administering a golf tournament is making the right call in adverse weather conditions,' he said. Already his thoughts were turning to the Czech Open in the third week of October. Tour agronomists and green staff would be on site five weeks before the tournament to try to cure, or prevent the onset of, the grass diseases common at that time of the year, but they could not control the weather. Shorter days would mean that first tee-off would be around 7.00 a.m. and frost, not to mention rain, sleet and fog, would almost certainly be a factor. Groundsheets would be laid over the greens each night.

'It's very difficult because you've got such a wide range of guys,' Probyn said, not knowing then that the Czech Open would set a new benchmark in weather-related chaos. 'Some who are very easygoing and some [who] are not so easy. The toughest thing is, your relationship with them can change in an instant if you give a ruling that they dislike intensely. But by the same token, we're there to run golf tournaments by regulations set by the committee through elections. So you have to govern them at the same time as being employed by them, which can be a strange balance. But you also get quite a buzz from being associated with them. Some guys are good to have a beer with, but you can't get too close to them, because down the line someone's going to ask questions about how impartial you're going to be.'

THE GREEN CARAVAN

We turned off the highway and began the steep climb up to Crans-sur-Sierre. Wooden chalets and snow-capped peaks crowded the chocolate-box scenery. 'The Swiss are a neat and industrious people, none of whom is under 75 years of age,' Dorothy Parker reflected in *Constant Reader*. 'They make cheeses, milk chocolate and watches, all of which, when you come right down to it, are pretty fairly unnecessary. It is all true about yodelling and cowbells. It is, however, not true about St Bernard dogs rescuing those lost in the snow. Once there was something in the story; but . . . the present dogs are of such inclinations that it is no longer reasonable to send them out to work, since they took to eating the travellers . . . Skiing is extremely difficult, and none of my affair. The most frequent accident among ski-jumpers is the tearing off of an ear. The edelweiss is a peculiarly unpleasant-looking flower.'

Probyn stared unseeingly out at the vineyards and the mossy vertigo-inducing mountainside. He was thinking about the way in which the Tour tends to rob its followers of whole years; of how the speed of it steals away youth and the size of it swallows lives. 'Look at me,' Probyn said, his voice tinged with the resentment common even to golf's most ardent devotees when they consider how much the game has cost them. 'I joined the Tour at 24 and now all of a sudden I'm approaching 30. Okay, in terms of my career, I've moved on, but outside of golf my life hasn't benefited. You don't do anything at home. You just exist. You spend two days recovering and then you're gone again. You almost feel like an intruder. Is there life outside the Tour? I wonder about that sometimes.'

At Crans-sur-Sierre, I stayed at a small, family-run hotel called L'Etrier. There are three travel operators on Tour, Fairway, Traveleads and Randy Fox, and which of them one chooses to travel with generally has a lot more to do with the reps one is friendly with than the price. The average cost of a week on Tour is £450, including flights, accommodation and transfers. Players, who have the additional burden of their caddies' wages and, of course, meals, don't leave home for less than £1,000, which can easily become £1,500 or £2,000 if the tournament is in Dubai or Manila, or even, for that matter, in Madrid.

FAIRWAY DREAMS

Small wonder that players become disconsolate when the European Masters rolls around and they are suspended between 115th and 130th on the order of merit, with only two or three official events left in which to save themselves. On the European Tour, only the top 120 players keep their cards each season. Unless they are exempt through past victories, the rest of them have to return to the Qualifying School at Montpelier in the south of France in November, where they compete with 168 other would-be Faldos over six rounds (in invariably filthy weather) for 40 Tour cards. It is a grievously sad week and hard to stomach. Nowhere can one turn without seeing broken dreams and broken spirits and lives ruined for the love of an uncaring game. One mother sold her home so that she could pay for her son to realise a lifetime ambition at the school. He failed.

This was the subject under discussion when I joined Gary Evans, Richard Boxall, Derrick Cooper and the travel rep David Grice at the bar of the Hotel L'Etrier. They were talking about the nail-biting insecurity of their profession. Cooper, winner of the 1988 Madrid Open, was dangerously close to losing his card, and on edge. He listed the names of players who had come near enough to glory to smell it and then watched it ebb away: Denis Durnian, Nick Job, Phillip Parkin, Ove Sellberg, and so on ad infinitum. In Europe, at that very moment, a host of fine players were poised to return to the Qualifying School. There was Roger Chapman, who had won the Zimbabwean Open and notched up a string of second places in top-class European events; there was the promising Irishman Eoghan O'Connell, and there was De Wet Basson, the South African of whom great things were expected – to name just a few. Even if your card was secure, there were other humiliations. In America the previous week, Ian Baker-Finch, the 1991 Open Champion, had finished 14 over par at the World Series after shooting 82 in the second round. Too embarrassed to face the other players, he changed his shoes in the car-park each day. The general feeling seemed to be: there but for the grace of God go us all.

We moved into the dining-room, where ensued a lively discussion on the value of everyone's watches. Mine cost £20, so I wasn't eligible. Elsewhere, Ebels and Rolex were placed on the tables for inspection, with prices ranging from £2,000 to £7,000. On the men's Tour, these are the things that symbolise status: your wife, your car, your watch and your position on the money list – and not always in that order. They also represent the extremes. They show how chillingly easy it is to be a success story with a gold watch and cherry-red Porsche one year, and a wet, despairing face bound for Montpelier the next.

'This may sound harsh,' Gary Evans said, 'but if you can't make it through six rounds at the Qualifying School, you don't deserve to be out here.'

He spoke as one of the brightest prospects on the European Tour. Beside him, Cooper looked pale beneath his tan.

On Friday play was suspended for several hours as milky banks of cloud settled over the fairways. The topic of conversation in the press centre was not the weather but John Daly, who had withdrawn from the European Masters following an alleged assault upon a spectator at the World Series in Akron, Ohio.

According to Robinson, who witnessed this latest outrage, all week long Daly had been driving into other players. 'Are you in such a hurry to shoot 80?' Greg Norman's caddie Tony Navarro queried sarcastically, after Daly's ball had bounded through the Shark's group for the umpteenth time. Daly just ignored him. In the final round he hit several shots into the match of Jeff Roth, head professional at the Flint Golf Club, Michigan, on his way to a score of 83. Afterwards, Daly passed Roth's parents in the car-park. 'Where did you learn your etiquette?' Roth's 62-year-old father Bob asked contemptuously. Daly rounded on him. Words, as they say, were exchanged. At one point Daly is alleged to have called Bob's wife, Dolores Roth, an effing whore. Her husband seized Daly from behind and both men fell to the ground. They were separated by onlookers, and Daly strode away furiously. 'I hate this fucking Tour,' was his parting shot.

Now it seemed that an old back injury had been aggravated by the scuffle and Daly was voluntarily taking the rest of the season off to sort out his personal problems. Unsurprisingly, Reebok and Wilson, with whom Daly had signed a ten-year agreement worth an estimated $2 million a year in the summer, had taken the news badly. Jan Thomson, vice-president of Wilson Golf in the States, commented: 'We regret suspending John's contract and, while Wilson empathise with his personal and professional challenges, we believe that it is just as important to assure our customers and employees that the company expects the highest level of sportsmanship, decorum and professionalism from its professional advisory staff . . . Wilson and John will resume their relationship under a newly structured agreement when Wilson is satisfied that John has met specific behavioural and performance objectives.'

Zoeller thought the suspensions were unfair. 'I think John has taken a very bad rap for this latest episode,' he said. 'I'm not sure suspending him is the right way to go about it. He had a couple of hecklers, people in the gallery who got carried away. If they had security around John like they were supposed to have, it wouldn't have happened. What we didn't read was that John was the second guy to hit. That means the marshals in front had already waved those guys down. That's what bugs me. Nobody wrote that. He's playing with Neal Lancaster and Neal hits first. Then John hits.

'It's life in the fast lane. When you're on top, they're shooting at you. And they're shooting bullets. This one here was a direct hit.'

John Daly was not the only discontented player in the world. Like Wild Thing, Severiano Ballesteros's relations with the establishment were, to say the least, strained, and he had been unhappy with the general order of things for some time. Never one to let an opportunity go begging, he broached the subject in a roundabout way, informing us on pro-am day that he was considering playing more golf in America.

An air of bewilderment greeted this announcement. Ballesteros is not just an integral part of the European Tour, he is its lifeblood, its heart and soul.

'But why do you want to leave Europe?' queried one slightly anguished voice. 'What are you fed up with? The media?'

'No, no,' Ballesteros said. He smiled wanly. 'I wouldn't get fed up with you. Don't put everybody in one basket. I'm fed up with some things. In general, I'm not too happy.'

Gordon Richardson raised the matter of the BMW International Open. 'In Munich, when you were going to be fined for slow play, you said that you felt that you were being driven out of the Tour. Was that said in the heat of the moment?'

There was a pause. 'There are a lot of things I would like made better,' Ballesteros admitted. 'The players are a bit unhappy. I don't want to go too deep into the problem.' He studied his fingernails.

'What exactly do you mean?' Dai Davies asked.

'Well, when you say things to the committee, like, five, six or seven times, about why players are unhappy, and nothing happens . . .'

'What are you unhappy about?'

'You want to know too much,' Ballesteros said firmly and politely. It was clear the discussion was at an end. 'So,' he said with an attempt at brightness, 'the weather is very nice this week . . .'

Outside, mist and intermittent drizzle continued to disrupt the event. There were cold players, cross players and players throwing in the towel. Colin Montgomerie, who had been bidding for his third successive victory, missed the cut comfortably and afterwards exhibited his usual sense of diplomacy and decorum by referring to Crans-sur-Sierre as 'a dump'. One of the caddies – who, admittedly, has a tendency to embellish things – claimed that when a member of Montgomerie's match tried to cheer him up by urging him to think of all his millions, the Scot retorted: 'I haven't even spent last year's money yet.'

Meanwhile, the travel agents ran about like headless chickens. Due to the disruption in play, their bookings were now invalid, and they were desperately trying to accommodate the wishes of dozens of disheartened, I-want-to-go-home-and-I-want-to-go-this-very-minute pros.

'What do you do in a situation like this?' I asked Mark Watson, the Traveleads rep.

'Panic,' came the reply.

Later in the day, John McHendry came into the press tent to stare anxiously at the scoreboard. A former Walker Cup player once tipped as a future star of Irish golf, he was now contemplating the unappealing prospect of a fifth visit to the Qualifying School. 'It's demoralising more than hard,' McHenry said, without much conviction. He was 30 years old and had a new wife to support. 'I think if you go there with the right attitude, you'll get through. But it's hard to come off this Tour and go back to the School. The people who are there for the first time are up for it, because they view it as the opportunity of a lifetime. But if you've had a long, hard season on the European Tour, and you're a bit browned off with it all, it's very, very difficult to make it through.'

The Tour is relentless, forward-looking, shallow. It takes no account of friendships, relationships, marriages, children, pets or responsibilities. Whether you're fighting to make the cut, survive a deadline or earn a percentage, when you're ensconced in the warm bosom of your friends by the fireside of some cosy restaurant on a frosty night in Switzerland, home can seem as remote as the moon, and blood-ties as tenuous and ephemeral as silk thread. All that matters is the here and now – which is why some people are able to go conscienceless to red-light districts one week and bounce their babies on their knees and be perfect family men the next. It is an unnatural life and a highly artificial one. The Tour and home occupy parallel universes, and the former almost always has to take precedent. You know at least a year in advance that, barring an earthquake, you will be covering the Spanish Open on 5 May and the Open Championship on 16 July. But it is by no means guaranteed that you will ever find time to learn to play the piano, write to your grandmother, volunteer for a charity, walk the dog or celebrate your wedding anniversary. Not only are entire weeks wasted because you're always waiting for flights, waiting for play to resume, waiting for shuttle buses, trains and automobiles, but entire wars pass you by simply because technical idiocy doesn't allow you to find CNN on your hotel television. As the season grinds on, procrastination becomes a way of life. Everything not pertaining to the tournament currently taking place is put on hold. On returning to base, travellers without spouses are greeted with in-trays overflowing with unanswered mail, final demands and curt reprimands from forgotten aunts, while answering machines bleep with a dozen messages from concerned parents, hurt friends, angry bank managers and disillusioned publishers. Husbands and boyfriends are met at the door by growling dogs and blank-faced children. Daddy who?

'The problem is to be a good golfer you've got to be single-minded, and then when you go home, if you've got a family, you've got to not be single-minded,' D.J. Russell said. 'I think it's very hard to bridge the gap between a very individual sporting career and family life. You either have to have a very understanding wife, or your priorities have to change. The little white ball becomes less important.'

'It's big business now,' said Randy Fox. 'Players used to enjoy going to exotic restaurants. Now they can't afford to get sick, there's too much money. Look at Peter Smith [a talented Scottish player whose career never really recovered after he was rushed to hospital with a stomach haemorrhage caused by a chicken sandwich in Spain]. And five players had food poisoning in Germany. No, it's steak and chips or McDonald's, one drink, and then it's back to the room to watch satellite television. That's the No. 1 priority on Tour now when you're looking for hotels.

'It's changed a lot,' Fox said sadly, considering the unhealthy interest of the average Tour player in television, money and Nintendo games. 'It's how many millions now. They practise putting in their rooms every night. There's very little messing around – a lot of talk, but not much action. There's too much to lose. On Tuesday nights, there used to be 40 players in the discos. Now, there'll be three or four. It's really not the most exciting way of life. It's just an eight-to-ten-hour job. They're a homogeneous group of very serious businessmen. They could be next door to the Prado [Madrid's famous museum of art] and they'd never even know it was there. They hardly ever bring their families any more.'

But that is not to say there are no high jinks any more, just less. The top players like to tuck themselves up in bed at sundown and, with the exception of Ian Woosnam, let their hair down only occasionally with a spell of trout fishing or snooker. Of the rank and file, Malcolm McKenzie plays chess with sports psychologist John (Psycho John) Allsop, Gordon J. Brand paints, Ronan Rafferty adds to his wine collection, Ross McFarlane brushes up on his table-tennis skills (he was once ranked 20th in England), and Mark Roe, a former diving champion, plays practical jokes. These are not always popular. Some people like Roe's idea of fun and think it makes him one of the Tour's few remaining characters. Others think he is childish and wonder when he's going to grow up. His pranks have included: a record number of food-throwing fights in restaurants and on aeroplanes; cutting the toes out of Barry Lane's socks; removing the fuses from every single electrical appliance in Lane's room; sitting for 40 minutes in a hotel corridor until Lane opened his door, and then drenching him with a fire hose. The Ryder Cup player emptied Roe's mini-bar in retaliation.

Still, there are occasions when the Tour does need livening up. It used to be a standing joke that if 12 players walked into a restaurant on the US Tour, they would sit down at 12 tables, whereas in Europe they'd sit at one or two. Nowadays, even the Europeans take up six or even eight. They are also joined at the hip to their own countrymen. The Italian players eat together, as do the Irish, the Swedes, the Scots, the South Africans and the Australians.

'There's not a resentment,' Fox explained. 'There's just a nationalism.'

In the early days of European golf, few players had the luxury of the five-star service even caddies can enjoy today – i.e. courtesy cars, shuttle services to the golf course, gymnasiums, saunas and 42-channel televisions, and all the other essentials of stress-free travel. Indeed, most players used to take their cars to Continental events. Des Smyth drove the entire circuit one season with Warren Humphries. 'In hindsight, it was the worst thing I ever did,' Smyth said. 'It cost me money, in my opinion, because we were always sick and we were always tired, so we never won any money.'

'We played for nothing, so we won nothing,' D.J. Russell agreed.

Russell travelled with Ian Woosnam. The Welshman had a

campervan and Russell had a car and caravan, so they tended to go in the caravan. Later, they progressed to a car and B&Bs. In more stringent times still, Woosnam had travelled with Joe Higgins. Usually the penniless pair existed on a monotonous diet of chips and baked beans, but at one tournament they found themselves without even the means to afford these meagre rations. In the dead of night, they unloaded their practice ball bags, crept down to a nearby orchard and filled them with French apples. They gorged themselves without bothering to wash the fruit first, and spent the next few days being violently and copiously sick.

On another journey, this time from Scotland to Italy, their caravanette began to labour and wheeze. They prayed that the noise would stop. It grew louder and more persistent. At 12.30 p.m. they pulled over on a main street in Milan. They peered under the bonnet and fretted over the cost of a new engine and the very real chance they now had of being disqualified from the pre-qualifying event for late arrival. At 5.30 a.m. Woosnam rose and begged a ride to the nearest garage on the handlebars of a local's bicycle. A mechanic was persuaded to come and inspect the engine and it was fixed in a flash for the princely sum of £2. Higgins missed the cut at Monticello but Woosnam finished eighth.

'Did you think then that Woosnam would become as good as he did?' I asked Russell on the flight from Geneva to London.

'I suppose you both think you're going to be that good,' Russell said. 'But he was always convinced that he was going to be what he has been. Woosie's got a big front to him that makes him look as if he doesn't care. He tends to make light of things. But he works as hard at his game as anybody. He likes to make it appear that he doesn't really work that hard, but to win a major and become the world No. 1, you've got to be very determined. He's the most determined person I've ever met.'

Determined Woosnam may be, but at this point in time he had a very thin season. His – or, rather, IMG's – insatiable appetite for appearance money had left him cooling his heels in Jersey for most of the year. When he did appear at tournaments, he came in his private plane and stayed only long enough to enhance his Boozie Woosie image, cemented in the tabloid imagination by a fine, earlier in the year, for drunk driving. The public perception was that he had left his hometown in Wales for the Channel Isles tax-haven purely for mercenary reasons, but Russell said that in Oswestry his life had no longer been his own. Not that Woosnam seemed happy in Jersey. He complained of loneliness and said he had no friends to play squash or tennis or keep fit with. His golf suffered through a listless and negative attitude.

'I think the difference between Ian and Faldo is that if Faldo's playing badly, he says, "Oh, I'm concentrating on the majors," or, "Leadbetter and I are working on something in my swing,"' Russell said. 'Ian just says, "I'm playing crap." Faldo seems to make a positive thing out of playing badly, whereas Ian just tells the truth. It's also very difficult for someone like Ian to have gone from obscurity to world stardom. You can never be prepared for what that presents. He's a very private person and sometimes he'd just like to go somewhere and not be Ian Woosnam any more. It's nice being rich and famous, but at the same time he likes being one of the lads. Unfortunately, that privilege has been taken away from him. There's been a sort of getting used to it period for him. He's had to adapt to something that he finds very difficult.'

Russell thinks back to the uncomplicated days of their youth with a sigh. 'We often wish that we could go back to that time,' he said nostalgically. 'We often talk about it and wish that we could jump into a caravan and have £20 in our pockets for the month. I think the thing you miss from it is the sheer ambition and looking forward to every day.'

For his own part, he was looking forward to the day when his insurance policy came into effect. The US Tour have an excellent pension scheme which is based on the number of cuts made, but in Europe there's no security for journeymen. 'The hard thing when you're reaching my age is that the youngsters have got nothing else but golf in their life and they give it 110 per cent. All they dream about is golf – they live it and breathe it. Whereas, golf sort of gets in the way of everything else when you get to 40.'

He was biding his time until his own private pension plan

came into effect when he reached the magic age of 40 or, better still, until he reached 50 and could qualify for the most lucrative pension scheme ever invented for professional golfers not yet tired of delayed flights, lost luggage and airline food: the Seniors Tour.

11

FLEA CIRCUS

'The only place I can find him is on the sports pages.'
EDNA HAGEN, WALTER'S SECOND WIFE,
EXPLAINING HER DIVORCE ACTION

It all started in 1980, when a friend of Gordon J. Brand, the normally imperturbable Yorkshire man, asked him to post him some ganja seeds from the Jamaican Open.

'Ganja seeds?' repeated Brand. He thought they were something for the garden.

'No, no, no,' said his friend with some amusement. 'You don't plant them, you smoke them.'

Immediately, Brand was in a quandary. On the one hand, he relished the opportunity for intrigue – Dirk Pitt, the James Bond-type adventurer in Clive Cussler novels, was the hero he most identified with – but on the other, he broke out in hives at the mere thought of doing anything illegal. The vision of himself as Dirk Pitt won over. Despite being convinced that, ere the Jamaican Open ended, he would have descended without trace into a labyrinth of criminals and drug barons, he was determined to track the ganja seeds down. It was easier than expected. Every caddie that leaned drowsily up against the clubhouse wall was enveloped in a haze of marijuana smoke. There was no need to go looking for ganja in Jamaica, it came looking for you. Soon Brand was the proud, albeit terrified, owner of a handful of minute seeds. These his caddie demonstrated for his satisfaction, wrapped deftly in brown paper and tucked away in the golf bag.

That evening, Brand arrived at the hotel shuttle to find a policeman and a large Alsatian standing guard. His blood turned colder than a Saskatchewan winter. 'Oh, my God,' he thought in panic. 'The dog's going to jump all over me. It's going to smell the ganja seeds.'

'Never mind,' Brand adds now, 'that the dog was probably higher than the caddies.'

With a supreme effort, he prevented himself from turning himself in to the policeman and, circumnavigating the bus, leapt in the front door. Back in his hotel room, he removed the seeds from their hiding place in his golf bag and popped them into an envelope. Disaster! When he held them to the light, the seeds were clearly visible. For a moment, Brand despaired. Then he did what he always does in times of crisis and invoked his favourite action hero. 'What would Dirk Pitt do?' he asked himself. 'Scissors!' was the answer, and he rushed downstairs to obtain a pair. In the privacy of his room, he cut six pages out of a magazine, making holes for the seeds in the centre of three of them. This done, he sealed the envelope and printed the address in anonymous block capitals so that his handwriting couldn't be traced. He had the letter weighed at reception.

'Airmail to Africa,' he said to the woman behind the counter, thinking: 'She knows what I'm up to.'

In an effort to stave off the moment when the police came to read him his rights, Brand returned to his room for the sixth time and polished the envelope furiously in order to remove any fingerprints. Finally, he took the guilty package carefully by one corner and dispatched it in a hotel post-box.

In Africa, Brand's friend smoked the contents of the envelope and enjoyed them enormously. 'Well worth the effort,' he told Brand cheerfully. Recounting the story on the flight from London to Dubai, for the first big tournament of 1994, Brand shuddered. Dirk Pitt or not, he felt he really didn't have the nerve to make crime pay.

Like a cuckoo, Norman Dabell, the golf circuit's Inspector Clouseau, began the new season. 'We hadn't even seen him,' Mark Garrod of the Press Association said. 'He'd been playing in the pro-am. And the first thing we heard was: "Ahhhh!!!" Norman had burnt himself fixing coffee at the back of the press room.'

That had been at the weather-blighted Madeira Island

FLEA CIRCUS

Open, the first tournament of the year. Fog and inclement weather had disrupted every one of the three rounds and left the press and most of the field stranded in Madeira for three days when high winds prevented their flight from taking off. Norman had not reached Morocco, the next venue, until late in the week, and had left almost immediately, telling UPI, the Irish agency he freelances for, to 'take in agency', and making a break for the airport.

Norman is one of those men whom people unkindly describe as 'an accident waiting to happen'. Rarely does he wait very long. In Norman's hands, the most ordinary journey, the most innocuous hotel room, the most unadventurous evening out becomes fraught with peril. He has stepped out of a taxi cab in Nottingham, slipped on a cheese sandwich and broken his coccyx; he has rounded a corner at speed, collided with the chairman of the Caddies' Association, Martin Rowley, taken off over a fire hydrant and cracked several ribs; he has thrown his shoe at a mosquito circling a bulb and fused an entire hotel; he has screamed at a barman for refusing to serve him, only to realise that he was shouting at his own reflection; he has informed Kent Radio listeners that a player 'shit six soxes', instead of 'shot six sixes'; and he had leapt from the taxi in which he was attempting to catch a plane, in order to make a hysterical appeal to traffic exiting the golf club, jumped back into the wrong car and shouted 'Drive on!' imperiously to an astounded local.

Like Joseph Conrad, Norman began life as a seaman, although there the similarity ends. Conrad would not have crouched down over a sprinkler-head to examine his putt at the very moment that the greenkeeper switched on the irrigation. He would not have turned up at the Italian Open with no trousers. He definitely wouldn't have fallen off his chair during a live radio report and carried on discussing the leaders while lying on his back amid the wreckage. Once, during a round of golf in Sweden, Norman saw his partner's ball fly (as if directed by radar) into the muddy puddle which was all that remained of a dried-up pond. 'I can get that,' Norman declared, before setting out across the cracked expanse. Soon it became evident that a thin outer crust disguised a treacherous bed of quicksand.

Norman could not have cared less. His only concern was the golf ball. He floundered on, wrenching one foot from the mire and squelching in the next. Finally, he drew near to his ball. He reached for it. Then he took a step closer. He reached again. Then it happened. Like an old sea-dog robbed of his wooden leg, Norman toppled head first into the mud. 'Arghhh!!!' he wailed as he fell. Above him, two faces appeared on the bank. 'EXCUSE ME,' came a fruity cry, 'ARE YOU ENGLISH AND CAN WE PLAY THROUGH?'

Golf journalism has a long tradition of characters and eccentrics. Bernard Darwin, the father of golf writing, was, by all accounts, an upstanding citizen, but thereafter it has all been downhill. Take, for example, Jack Statter, the late *Sun* reporter. Statter had been stationed in North Africa during the war, and it had left a lasting impression on him. Upon meeting Bernhard Langer for the first time, he eyed the German quizzically and queried: 'Do you know that your dad bombed our fish and chip shop?' He wasn't to know that Langer's father had been locked away in a Russian prisoner-of-war camp in Czechoslovakia.

Being the *Sun* golf correspondent, he was seldom over-endowed with column inches. It was not unusual for him to be informed: 'Your space for tomorrow is 48 words – and that includes your byline.' This left him plenty of free time, which he employed to useful effect. He became Eddie Pollen's mentor when the former Ryder Cup player, not known for his IQ, started out on Tour, explaining to interested parties: 'I help him with his personal problems. For instance, when it's raining I tell him to put up his umbrella.' He spent hours assembling a DIY telescope in his bedroom so that he could see the time on the town clock-tower, only to discover that the clock had stopped ten years earlier. He puzzled for a period over the appearance of a different electrical appliance – now a toaster, now a kettle – on the back seat of his Beetle after late nights at *The Sun*, until he found that burglars had been using the vehicle to go on raids and were leaving him a tip. Mostly, however, he simply thought of Rommel, whom he idolised, and allowed his imagination to roam unchecked across the landscape of tournament golf.

Statter's most notorious exploit came at the Jersey Open in

the early 1980s. After an afternoon spent imbibing life-giving waters in the ambulance tent, he emerged blinking and befuddled and was struck by the sight of a squadron of army cadets, who had inadvertently wandered on to the course during a map-reading exercise, proceeding along the cliffs. Immediately, his imagination went to work. Rushing back to the press tent, he dashed off a few hundred words on the Channel Islands being reinvaded and golfers having to dive into bunkers to escape a hail of bullets. He then filed the story and retired for the day.

In due course, the *Sun* sports desk rang. 'We've had a rather good story from Jack,' they told Peter Dobereiner, the esteemed *Observer* correspondent, 'and we, er, wanted to check that it was true.' Dobereiner put them on to the tournament organiser who was even drunker than Statter. Asked to confirm the veracity of the report, he gushed, 'Absholutely. Every word.'

'The War Office went bananas,' recalled Dobereiner. 'They sent a colonel over to find out what was going on.' He and Renton Laidlaw were summoned to the tournament organiser's office, where they had to explain several times to an excited military man that the invaders in question had only been cadets and that they had not actually been carrying guns at all. 'He was shell-shocked, that was the trouble,' Dobereiner said of Statter. 'But he was a genius, no doubt about that. He was flawed.'

In the 'chalk and string' days of the European Tour, golf writing was a more precarious business than it is now. These days, whether one is in Birmingham or Berlin, the press centre operates at a sublime level of efficiency, mainly due to the efforts of the Sanderson family who run an up-to-the-minute scoring system. Dobereiner survived bus journeys through the tropics, Moroccan Opens where telephones were installed for decorative rather than functional reasons (nothing new there), and a coup in Nigeria where the President was killed on practice day. 'What was dangerous was that all the troops seemed to be on pot and they were sleepy and firing at random,' said Dobereiner, who took it all in his stride. Rather disturbingly, the military headquarters was sited alongside the eleventh hole and the golf club committee was composed almost entirely of senior officers from the army. Dobereiner spent the best part of five days playing cards with Harry Bannerman and pitch and putt with the neighbours, until eventually the rebels were arrested.

Dobereiner is unusual in that he is as wry and well spoken as his prose suggests; more often than not writers are the antithesis of how one imagines them to be. Pat Ward-Thomas, described by Alastair Cooke as resembling a Mexican farmer with five acres of beans that weren't doing well, used to dazzle his readers with lyrical and considered pieces in *The Guardian* each week, but in person was a walking keg of dynamite. In *Golf À La Carte*, Dobereiner recalls how 'Pat's famous temper could be detonated by the slightest incident, such as the frustration of American hotel breakfasts which required him to unwrap butter pats, pierce milk cartons and open plastic marmalade pots. He was never at his best in the early morning . . . and his electrifying roar of "Damn these bloody parcels" caused waitresses to drop trays and strong men to slop their coffee . . . Once embarked on a tirade, Pat would warm to his theme, laying about him with increasingly extravagant language until what began as a small mishap with a sugar sachet developed into a wish that the entire blank country should blow itself into oblivion with its own blank bombs.'

According to Dobereiner, Ward-Thomas had spent the war in a prison camp and this had 'soured him to a degree and drastically shortened his temper'. He remembered standing behind the eighteenth green at the Masters with his colleague, watching the leader take an interminable age to putt out. Ward-Thomas, who was on deadline, bristled with impatience. Finally, he was unable to contain himself any longer. In a stage whisper that could be heard three fairways away, he burst out: 'DOESN'T THIS MAN REALISE MY LIFE IS EBBING AWAY?'

Apart from the time when he ripped off his blazer and challenged the Reuters correspondent to a duel at the World Match Play, Norman has rarely been known to become violent. He did almost throttle Frank Clough with a telephone cord, but that was purely accidental. Indeed, even when the incident on the Costa Brava degenerated into complete mayhem,

Flea Circus

Norman managed to refrain from lashing out. Of course, that evening had begun like all the rest: with a deceptive calm. Shortly before midnight, Norman, enjoying the balmy air, had stepped out on to his hotel balcony with a glass of red wine, unaware that the modesty rail concealed his boxer shorts and made him appear naked. When he eventually retired, he was kept awake by the cistern, hissing and gurgling incessantly. When he could stand it no longer, Norman flew out of bed and began plucking aggressively at sundry fittings behind the toilet. One came off in his hand. Even as he was pondering this development, the bathroom flooded to a depth of two feet. 'No!' cried Norman and plunged his arm into the hole in a desperate attempt to stop the flow.

But already the water had slipped under the bedroom door and set off down the marble passage. Downstairs, the night porter was buried in his newspaper when the switchboard began to chirrup furiously. 'Agun gone loco, Agun gone loco!' screamed Norman down the line. All hell broke loose. After an initial crisis period – during which the night porter, misunderstanding Norman's frantic cries for aid, had raced to his door with a tray and two bottles of Perrier only to discover Norman crouching, like the boy and the dyke, over the toilet bowl – the maintenance man had to be uncovered, which was no easy task at 3 a.m. When he eventually returned to his post, the night porter was shaken and dishevelled, a shadow of his former self. It had been a long and extremely trying evening. Earlier on, he had had to deal with the arrival of the police. A woman in the block of flats opposite had seen a naked man parading up and down on the hotel balcony. She wanted him arrested for indecent exposure.

Every circuit has its own unique ambience. The Australasian Tour is like an extended package holiday, all beaches and barbecues, oddballs and children, and an easy-like-a-Sunday-morning atmosphere prevails at all times. The US PGA Tour is rather more clinical. Players, officials, caddies and journalists don't just stay in different hotels and receive vastly differing privileges, they move in different time zones altogether. The European Tour is like a family – everyone looks out for everyone else. We stay in the same hotels, eat in the same restaurants and, after all these years and with all the added millions, our tournament venues are still suspended somewhere between gypsy encampments and sophisticated travelling circuses.

Each Tour stop has its accompanying rituals and we cling to them tenaciously, serial nomads in search of stability in a fluid and unreliable world. In Dubai, there is the market with its fake designer T-shirts, cassettes and watches, there's the Gold Souk, and there's breakfast overlooking the Emirates putting green in the cool marble splendour of the clubhouse.

One morning, while we were tucking into croissants, scrambled eggs and pineapple, Ian Wood of *The Scotsman* announced, somewhat melodramatically, that he might be tempted to do something drastic if another Faldo press conference contained the words, 'fine-tuning with Lead'.

'Why don't you pre-empt him?' *The Guardian*'s Dai Davies suggested. 'Say to him: "Nick, have you been doing any fine-tuning with David Leadbetter recently?"'

'Fine-tuning with Lead, perchance?' experimented Wood.

We moved on to a discussion of press conference banalities, of which there are many. 'The most famous must be, "I'm just going to take it one day at a time,"' Davies said. 'How the hell else can you take it?' The same applies to one game at a time, one step at a time, one decade at a time . . .

In post-round press conferences, Phil Mickelson, the gifted American, addresses every reporter as 'sir' or 'ma'am', and his interviews are filled with sycophantic references to his parents, his caddie, his manager, his great-aunt Bertha and his playing partners, Mr Watson, Mr Crenshaw, etc., all of whom were a pleasure to play with and an inspiration to him as a toddler. Fred Couples's interviews are frank and rambling. Ballesteros's are witty and self-deprecating. David Gifford's are spoken almost entirely in a whisper, and every second sentence Greg Norman utters is followed by the words, 'No question about it'.

'Don't you think that there's such a thing as too much?' I asked the assembled group, still thinking about the Shark, who was playing in the Desert Classic and the Asian Classic the following week. 'I mean, Norman has an Aerospace Gulfstream

FLEA CIRCUS

III jet worth £10 million, a Rolls-Royce, a Range Rover, seven Ferraris, a couple of ordinary cars, an 85-foot custom-made fishing boat and a mansion in Palm Beach.'

'Ah,' said Woody, 'but does he have a Swiss penknife?'

When Dale Hayes, the South African, won the Order of Merit in 1975, there were 17 events with a total prize fund of £427,917. Eighteen years on, Colin Montgomerie earned over £700,000 when he became the European No. 1 after playing 24 events. In 1994, the prize fund for the season was £24.5 million, and there were 37 events taking place in 18 countries.

Nowadays, nothing is left to chance. Endorsements, win bonuses, and prizes for everything from low round of the week and golfer of the month, to most improved player and winner of the egg and spoon race, are so abundant in tournament golf that all aids, assistants and advisers are considered grist to the mill. Each January there is something called the Apollo Week, at San Roque in Spain, which is effectively a marketing opportunity for manufacturers and a survival guide for aspiring professionals. There, mock press conferences are staged and golfers are introduced to the gurus, clubmakers, psychologists and fitness experts that are indispensable to the modern player. As a consequence, the gauche rookie, with his empty bank account, ill-fitting clothes and little-boy-lost air is a rare sight on Tour now. Instead, these new kids on the block sport the latest haircuts and strut about cockily in their Titleist visors, Ashworth shirts and Dockers khakis – their caddies scurrying after them bearing king-size Mizumo golf bags – secure in the belief that anyone talented enough to survive the hell that is the Qualifying School is owed a living by everyone else. More often than not, you'll see them six months later, limping along like pricked balloons, but at the start of the season their heads are in the clouds and nothing and nobody can keep them down.

Jonathan Lomas was the first of these young guns to stroll into the Desert Classic press room. Nicknamed Johnny Cash because of his alleged reluctance to part with money, he had more reason than most to feel confident, having had nine top-10 finishes and two victories on the Challenge Tour (the European satellite circuit) the previous season. He had shot a first-round 66. A fresh-faced 25-year-old, he rattled off his birdies and bogeys like a veteran.

On the whole, golfers are ten times more articulate than, say, footballers or British Rail platform announcers, but that doesn't make them all politicians. For every David Feherty there are 20 players who think that sparkling repartee is an inexpensive brand of champagne, and Dobereiner's imaginary interview with David Graham is not too wide of the mark.

Dobereiner: 'What went wrong?'

Graham: 'Tripled five.'

Dobereiner: 'I can now go straight to the typewriter and begin: "David Graham's challenge faltered with a third round 76. An otherwise solid performance was marred by a torrid seven at the innocuous 370-yard fifth hole, where the players enjoyed a light following breeze. Graham reeled from the course ashen faced and groaned: *I played that hole like an arthritic granny . . .*"'

Lomas's press conference did not require any embellishment. With little prompting, he reeled off a breezy commentary on his week so far. He was staying at the house of a former Miss Trinidad and Tobago, his caddie was a South African woman, and he was concentrating on blocking out the pressure. There was no trace of shyness or hesitancy in his speech, and no false modesty whatsoever. His whole demeanour conveyed an unmistakable message. It was: 'I'm here to stay; get used to it.'

It is perhaps because this 'What do you mean, you haven't heard of me?' attitude has become the norm among young players, that Ernie Els stands apart from the crowd. He is 24 years old, his achievements are enormous, and yet there is not an arrogant bone in his body. He does not go in for macho posturing or philosophising, and there is nothing affected about his manner. There is just a sleepy calm, a half-smile that lights up clear, dreamy eyes, and a breathtakingly beautiful golf swing – long, smooth and rhythmical. The fire burns very deeply in Els but no less brightly for all that.

At the Emirates course in Dubai, the young South African shot a record-breaking 61, nine under par, to take a five-stroke lead in the first round. Afterwards, he waved away compliments good-naturedly. Born and raised in Johannesburg, he has a typically Southern African reticence and dislike of self-promotion, and a habit of talking down his accomplishments. He had telephoned his dad, who, he said, thought he was joking. When he was asked the next day how he had celebrated, Els replied: 'I had dinner and one beer. I guess that was my celebration.'

The only time Els betrayed the slightest irritation was when he was compared to Gary Player, whose consecutive victories in the SA Open, Masters and PGA championships he matched at the age of 22. 'Like Gary says, "Can we compare wallets?"' was his sardonic response. 'No, it's nice in a way but we're totally different, we've got totally different golf games. Gary always had to work his way around and fight it out. I try and enjoy the game, at least. It's hard to do sometimes, but I try. It's nice when people say that but I don't care about it, believe me.'

Even more impressive than his wins in South Africa or Japan was Els's ability to deal with his success equivocally and with the minimum of fuss. 'That's his personality,' said Sam Feldman, his manager, proudly. 'You're never going to change him.'

Wherever Els was, Feldman could be seen running around like an Afrikaner uncle, benevolent and excitable. 'Ernie's very laid-back in a lot of things and he lets a lot of things go,' Feldman said. 'He doesn't like confrontation. But he's very strong willed. If he doesn't want to play somewhere he'll say so and that, quite honestly, is the end of the story. He's not as easy to do business with as he is with everything else. He's quite adamant about what he wants. He's stubborn. I'm not saying that's bad, but there is a different side to him. I've stopped nagging him because he says, "You're like my father now. Don't nag me." But I got to a point where I understood what I was dealing with. Some people are highly motivated by training 14 hours a week and eating the correct foods. Ernie's not like that. Maybe if he was, he'd go backwards.'

As a boy, Els won the World Junior in the United States at the age of 13, became a scratch golfer the following year, was Eastern Transvaal's senior tennis champion and a first-class cricketer and rugby player.

'I also did athletics,' Els added rather more quietly.

Feldman burst out laughing. His charge is not known for being overly energetic off the course. 'The only place he runs to now is the bathroom,' he teased.

Nevertheless, he admitted that Els had not been wholly unaffected by fame. 'The notoriety did get to him. One moment he was just somebody playing golf in South Africa, and the next everybody knew him. I think that put pressure on him because all of a sudden he realised that every week he's got to perform. For whom? In our discussions, I've always said to him, "You must do what you want to do. The people that care about you will always be there for you whether you shoot 86 or 66." There's always next week. It's a 30-year career. It's not going to be done in a week.'

On Thursday, we were invited to an event billed as an 'Arabian evening', although the two Irish musicians rather clouded the issue. Seemingly intent on massacring the most beloved of Irish folk music, they stood on the stage where we had expected to see Arabian Nights unfold and wailed to an unappreciative audience. To begin with, there were no belly-dancers in sight. Indeed, at the outset there had not even been a bus. We had waited on the steps of our hotel, a hungry posse of journalists, while eight o'clock came and went and a chill desert wind blew ice into our veins. Tempers quickly frayed.

'Do you think we might need another coat?' I asked vaguely, when headlights finally shone and a bus came roaring up the drive.

Gordon Richards lost his temper. 'How can you say, you think we need another coach? I mean, really. You'll just have to make do with this one.' And ignoring my spluttered protests, he climbed on board.

Norman was the last of our company to arrive, wearing a silk jacket with multi-coloured triangles that would have been the clothing of choice for jugglers in the last century. We were relieved to see that he had come without his razor. The previous year, travelling in a similar bus, he had turned up late, flustered and unshaven. Midway to our destination he had produced a battery-operated razor, switched it on and proceeded to saw away at his jaw. The driver cocked an ear in alarm. 'A slow puncture,' he decided and, slamming on brakes so hard that we all almost flew through the window, he leapt from the vehicle with his spanners and began hammering at the tyres and poking irritably at the undercarriage. Norman kept quiet. Slowly and surreptitiously, he put away his shaving kit and sat looking about him in wide-eyed innocence.

Tonight, fortunately, all was peaceful. We sped through the night on the wide, smooth roads of Dubai, passing the broad, dark humps of camels and shaggy silver-topped palms. A large yellow moon climbed ponderously up the sky. At last, we turned off the main highway and onto a desert road designed to forcibly extract every tooth from one's head. We travelled like this for some time until blazing lights indicated that we had arrived at the beach home of our host, Mohammed Al Abbar, Director General of Dubai's Economic Department.

Everybody who was anybody appeared to be there. They were drinking champagne amid the silk carpets, Arabic coffee pots and lace-covered four-poster beds, or gazing into roaring fires on the beachfront – oil sheikhs, men of Bedouin extraction, scores of expatriates and professional golfers. Greg Norman sat gingerly in a chair, with a plate of tandoori prawns, attempting to combat a severe bout of hay fever. Darren Clarke and Eoghan O'Connell, the Irish players, were alternately tossing back cans of Heineken, gnawing at giant drumsticks and sucking on a hubbly-bubbly. Norman "Officer Dibell" Dabell, who works for Irish regional papers like the *Cork Examiner* and is fiercely protective of his subjects, informed us that Clarke was on a diet. This news was greeted with derision. Based on the evidence before us, we decided that Clarke was of the eating-Kellogg's-bran flakes-while-wearing-trainers school of fitness. Later in the season he was to prove us wrong.

We departed for the culinary village, where a feast fit for kings lay smoking on the dunes, and piled our plates high with snowy rice, barbecued lobster, sweet and sour prawns and stuffed peppers. All were delicious. Expatriates and pro golfers, having eaten their fill early on, lolled about on cushions with hookahs. The Irish musicians lent a surreal element to the proceedings.

The seasonal passage of a golf writer is, it has to be said, accompanied by the not infrequent dispensation of what is collectively known as 'bung' – i.e. logoed shirts, dinners and golf games. For no other reason than the fact I write about golf, I have shaken hands with the royal family in Monaco, watched Shirley Bassey sing beneath the stars in Dubai, been to Disneyworld in Florida and received enough sweat-shirts to clothe a small football team. Most free gifts are sent the way of charity, but Golf World's Gary van Sickle does a humorous impression of a greedy journalist: 'Thank you very much for my complimentary gift. Please may I have two more.'

Not all journalists are greedy and not all expense accounts are generous, as Ron Wills might have testified. Eating with several of his fellow golf writers one evening, Wills was overcome with dizziness and stepped outside for a breath of fresh air. Minutes later he passed out. In the meanwhile, a large bill arrived at the table. Since there was not enough money to cover it, Mark Wilson went in search of Wills, finding him prone in the gutter. Wills recovered consciousness to find the man from the *Daily Express* emptying his pockets without the slightest concern for his well-being.

The highlight of this particular evening was the appearance of the belly-dancer who, it transpired, was Canadian. She was practised at her art none the less, and a great believer in audience participation. On several occasions she gyrated her way into the crowd and urged men to dance. Many expatriates seemed to be old hands at belly-dancing and cheerfully obliged. Mike Britten, a diminutive British freelance, turned her down. I think he was afraid that Norman, who has not spoken to him since threatening to drive him into the ground in the summer of 1993, would make cruel jibes at his expense.

Somewhere near midnight we decided to call it a day. Mike led the way across the desert to the car-park.

'Lawrence of Arabia,' someone said.

'Lawrencette of Arabia,' Gordon joked.

We piled into the bus, cold and tired, our breath making cartoon bubbles on the window. We steeled ourselves for the bone-shaking ride across the desert. The engine started – one bump, two bumps, three . . . clatter! A knife bounced out of a coat pocket and fell guiltily to the floor. Ten pairs of eyes stared accusingly at the offender. Jock McVicar blushed scarlet to the roots of his hair.

'Well, well, well,' cried Mark, in the tone of a policeman apprehending a criminal. 'What's all this, then? Stealing the sheikh's silver?'

'No, I was just . . .'

'Go on, spit it out.'

'Well, it was just that I had my glass in one hand and my plate in the other and I had nowhere to put my knife and fork . . .'

'A fork, too! What else have you taken? The crystal wine glasses? The salt and pepper?'

And for the remainder of that one-hour journey poor Jock had to endure our taunts, and explain over and over exactly how he had ended up with the silverware of his host in the top pocket of his tweed coat.

In every respect, it resembled a badly acted scene from *Carry On Cleopatra; Arabian Nights* it was not.

On the final day of the Desert Classic, I went out with Norman Dabell to watch Norman, the golfer, play. With his taut, sinewy frame, capped teeth and shock of yellow hair, the Shark resembled nothing so much as Ken, Barbie's companion. 'He doesn't look real, does he?' I remarked to Dabell.

'He probably isn't,' Norman said. 'It's probably a stand-in.'

Greg Norman's usual war-cry had been rather muted after the third day of play. 'It just seems that Ernie blitzed us in the first round,' he admitted, looking with awe at Els's eight-stroke lead. 'If I shot 62 tomorrow, maybe . . .' His voice trailed off. 'I'd like to see it blow really hard tomorrow,' he began again, knowing full well that we knew that he knew he was just whistling in the wind.

But experience is a powerful asset. Els was nervous, he was unsure of himself. He didn't know whether to target the pins or play conservatively. Norman watched him hawk-eyed. 'He hooked off the tee on five,' he told us later, 'and I said to myself, "If you can get a two-shot swing early on, it might make all the difference." Because I could see he wasn't in sync.'

On the front nine, Els drove out of bounds, he three-putted, he took an unplayable from a bush. He opened the door wide enough to drive a bus through and none of his pursuers took advantage of it. 'I felt edgy,' he said after signing for a 71 and his first European Tour victory. 'I've never felt that way before. I was scared of making big numbers instead of just going out there to attack the golf course like I did the first three days. It was funny.'

Norman was impressed. He had been astounded to hear that Els had never won in Europe before. 'He's a lot calmer than I was fourteen years ago,' the Shark admitted. 'He's got more of an even keel about him . . . I just hope he keeps his long, flowing swing. If Ernie tried to shorten his swing, it would hurt him a lot.'

'Is he capable of winning a major championship?' a reporter asked.

Norman pursed his lips. 'Anybody can be a major winner if you've got it in your heart,' he said. 'But a lot of outside agencies come into effect when you get to that level. I've seen a lot of guys get to that level and then back-pedal. But he's good enough to do it, no question about it.'

REPORTAGE

12

GOLF IN THE GHETTO

The road to Soweto Country Club is lined with shanties belonging to the three million inhabitants of the infamous township. Litter drifts across the scarred brown fairways, which are open to those who can afford the £10 membership or £1.75 green fee – although even that is beyond the reach of many who would like to enjoy the bare-roomed clubhouse and the ragged greens.

This is the heart of black golf in South Africa. This is where Mawonga Nomwa exchanged one dream for another: when the bloodshed scuppered his plans to be an electrical engineer, he turned to golf. Here, at least, hard work might bring reward.

It was not easy. At 24, Nomwa might be the future of black golf, but his mailbox is not exactly flooded with offers of support. Even the endorsements it does yield are double-edged. When the Development Trust paid R1,000 (£190) to put him through the Tour School, Nomwa justified the outlay by winning the thirteenth card. Thereafter, he was on his own, and three tournaments went by before a local bank stepped in and he could afford to play again. 'I couldn't sleep at night worrying about where I could get the money,' he said.

Nevertheless, Nomwa, who finished 29th at the Wild Coast and equal 27th in the South African Open, knows he is luckier than most. Like the friends he caddied with as a teenager in Soweto, he grew up in relative poverty in a small brown house a few hundred yards from the course. They played football together among the fruitsellers and garbage tips of Pinville. But Nomwa's father, a clerk, wanted his son to have a chance, and bought him as set of second-hand clubs. The boy's first set of cards at a respectable course gave him a six handicap.

Meanwhile, John Mashego, the country's best black player

since Vincent Tshabalala, winner of the 1976 French Open, was struggling to survive. He has spent five of the past eight years without a sponsor. Since turning pro at 31, a year after taking up the game – 'When I gave up football, I thought, "What can I do that will take me away from the township, away from the violence?"' – his has been a lonely trail, ridden with hardship and opposition: "I've been called names. People say, 'Hey, caddie, come here."'

Passion is all that kept Theo Manyana going during his 28 years as a pro. The eldest son of a labourer, he learned the game as a caddie, hauling the bag in baking sunshine for a loaf of bread and the odd coin a round. On the long road home he would stop to play golf on a handmade course carved from wasteland: 'There were no fairways and no rough, just jungle and sand greens. We took our picks and shovels and we made it.'

But the condition of makeshift courses was the least of Manyana's worries. More upsetting was the refusal of the South African PGA to allow black members until 1981 – and then only ten – and of the clubs to allow black players to practise at tournament venues. When Tshabalala, a member of the South African team, boycotted the 1977 World Cup in protest, he was banned by the SA PGA for two years, which ruined his career.

'It was like a nightmare. It made us lose all confidence in ourselves,' Manyana recalled. 'And every time we were not allowed to play we were told, it's the government, it's the government, but later we found out that it wasn't the government, it was the clubs.'

That was certainly true for caddies. Paul Malathane, a five handicapper, is a former political activist whose flight into exile in 1977 was partly the result of an incident where he was not allowed to accompany a British player into the clubhouse. He returned in 1993, and now juggles his career as a medical practitioner in the military with carrying Gavin Levenson's bag on the SA circuit, but he claims there are still events where only white caddies are allowed into the clubhouse.

Manyana is now a tournament director on the SA Tour. At times, his position has been more contentious than he can bear but he has vowed to hold on, knowing that the success of Nomwa and 150 other black professionals depends on his support. It also depends on a change in attitude among élitist white clubs and both black and white sponsors.

'When you go to black businessmen and ask them to help you play golf, they ask, "What is that?"' Mashego said, 'They are not really educated about golf.' Manyana agreed: 'You talk sponsorship to such a person and his reply will be, "I work hard for my money. You go out and do the same."'

As yet, golfers have little choice. Even supposing they could afford the green fees at the better courses, they would still find it impossible to buy quality equipment. This year, the Development Trust has begun running a few two-day tournaments to help under-privileged players, but no benefactor has been found to help pay the registration fees, entry fees and subscription, amounting to some £120.

That doesn't stop them from crowding on to the rough-and-ready Soweto Country Club, the only black club in the country, to try. 'If you went there over a weekend, you'd be shocked at how many people are there,' said Manyana, who estimates that there are 1,000 black players in the township alone. 'It is okay for beginners, but for professionals like myself it can only damage your game. The greens are like fairways. You need a hammer for a putter.'

A barefooted ten-year-old hits a grey, scuffed ball with an ancient club. He comes here every day after school. Like Nomwa, he dreams of something better. Unlike Nomwa, who hopes his eight-hour practice regimen will eventually bring him glory at Augusta, he has yet to focus on specifics.

'To win the Masters, you might have to practise for six hours a day,' a fellow Sowetan told the young professional. 'I'll do ten,' Nomwa said, determinedly.

13

A Final Round in Purgatory

April 1996. Merv Norman never wanted his son to be a professional golfer. When the 17-year-old Greg decided he would rather play on the Tour than fly fighter planes, Merv told him that he would never make it and cast him adrift emotionally. Greg rose to the top of the game and won two major championships, but Merv never hugged him, never told him he was proud of him. When a television interviewer asked him: 'So, what do you think of your son's brilliant career?' Merv's only response was: 'Well, it'll do till something better comes along.'

Last Sunday, Greg Norman's dream turned to dust. In the cruellest manifestation of sporting injustice in memory, the world No. 1, so long denied in the US Masters, suffered the worst collapse in major championship history – turning a six-shot lead into a five-stroke deficit – amid scenes so harrowing that when it was over, the gallery was muted in its acknowledgement of Faldo's victory.

The sense of horror, of numb disbelief, was overwhelming. What should have been Faldo's shining hour – the day he shot 67 to win his third green jacket and join that rare group with six or more majors – became tainted. Yet it is hard to imagine a player showing more compassion in victory, or conducting himself with more grace or humility in such awkward circumstances. 'I don't know what to say,' he said to Norman. 'I just want to give you a hug.' And Norman cried because Faldo, whom he had respected but never liked, could, at a time like that, embrace him and say he was proud of him when his own father never would.

It will be a long time before the scars of that final round are erased. It will be longer still before the gallery who streamed so hopefully through the gates on that clear, blue morning, clutching picnic baskets and periscopes, can rid themselves of the images of golf as a prolonged car crash – of Norman taking a bogey at the first from a greenside bunker, bogeying the fourth and sailing over the green, pulling his approach into the trees at the eighth, watching a near-perfect shot run off the green at the ninth.

At the tenth, Frank Williams, Norman's manager, was fretting about Norman's wife Laura. 'She's a wreck,' he said. He wasn't doing too well himself. He put his hand over his eyes as the Australian hit a poor chip to ten feet and then missed the putt. Faldo made a solid four. At the next, Norman's 14-foot birdie putt rimmed the hole and his missed the return from three feet. Faldo made his par and they were level. Laura had disappeared. Williams held his head in his hands. An American sportswriter sidled up to him. 'How do you feel around now?' he queried breezily. 'Great,' said Williams. 'I have every confidence.' Crestfallen, the man hurried away. 'Christ,' said Williams, 'how does he think I feel?'

He stared down at the twelfth tee, sweating. Norman hit his ball into the water. He took a double-bogey to Faldo's par. Wordlessly, Williams wrapped his arms round Laura. A horrible silence settled over the gallery. 'I feel sick to my stomach,' a spectator said.

Beside the thirteenth, an eerily perky David Leadbetter, Faldo's coach, watched as Norman fidgeted on the fairway. 'His routine has changed by six or seven seconds,' he commented. 'He's gripping the club and regripping it. He can't get comfortable.' His own player was the very model of cool, collected control. There was a moment of tension when Faldo took a five wood out of his bag, but he replaced it, hit a peerless two iron into the green and matched Norman's birdie. 'We talked about this last night,' Leadbetter said. 'I told him, nobody's shot a low number to win the Masters since you came from five behind to beat Raymond Floyd in 1990.'

At the fifteenth, Norman's chip for an eagle shaved the hole. Both men made their birdies. In a confused attempt to pull off a last-minute miracle, Norman hooked his tee shot into the water at the sixteenth and Faldo led by four strokes. As the ripples gave notice of Faldo's imminent victory, Norman stood on the tee like the battered hero in a Jean-Jacques Rousseau work: 'Plunged into an incomprehensible chaos where I can make nothing out, and the more I think about my present situation, the less I can understand what has become of me.'

After the agony came the analysis. Had it been anyone else, it is just conceivable that a 77 would have been put down to a terrible day on the most precise of courses, but Norman is the golfer who shot 76 to lose the 1986 US PGA to a holed bunker shot from Bob Tway, who blocked his final approach to miss out on a Masters play-off the same year, who lost play-offs to Fuzzy Zoeller in the 1984 US Open, Larry Mize at Augusta in 1987, Mark Calcavecchia in the 1989 Open and Paul Azinger in the 1993 US PGA, when he three-putted the second extra hole.

That being the case, his ignominious crash was attributed to 'choking' – something that is difficult to accept. Choking is a word that denotes, in the ugliest possible way, loss of nerve, lack of bottle and a degree of yellow-bellied cowardice that is utterly inconsistent with every aspect of Norman's life and personality. This is a man who has looked death in the eye more times than an undertaker and never flinched. He has saved two lives, hugged the wall at 180 m.p.h. in IndyCar, run out of oxygen at 88 feet under the sea and risen to the surface no faster than his own bubbles with only a mild case of the bends, and patted bull sharks in ocean caves.

Once, Norman was in an F-14 jet when the pilot told him there was a small problem. The wing flaps wouldn't go down. That meant that the plane couldn't slow down enough to land on the tiny aircraft carrier bobbing far below them. For five long minutes the pilot wrestled with the controls and a crash landing on terra firma began to seem inevitable. Then the wing flaps resumed service. Afterwards, Norman was asked if he had been afraid. 'Oh, no,' he said. 'It just meant we got to look at the sunset longer.'

Herein lies the clue to Norman's long history of blow-outs. He is not only fearless; he has no idea how to be afraid. He doesn't have a safe shot, he has a death wish. He makes the worst decisions under pressure of any great sportsman in living memory, and he makes them because he has a tendency towards self-destruction and he believes he is invincible.

'I put all the blame on myself,' said Norman, whose 52nd second-place press conference was an affair of such dignity and class that even Bobby Jones would have been hard pressed to live up to it. 'Even if I had played halfway decent, it would have been a good tussle with Nick. I let it slip. I made a lot of mistakes. Call it what you want to call it, but I hit a couple of poor iron shots and paid the price.' Yet, he added: 'Not everything can be perfect your whole life. Maybe these hiccups that I have inflicted on myself are meant for a reason. I think there's something waiting down the line for me that's going to be really good.'

Regardless of how history remembers the 60th Masters, nobody can take away Faldo's achievement. For the first time in his career, he looks truly happy, contented to the depths of his soul. He has survived a divorce, a season in hell and the worst dustbin-digging excesses of the tabloids, and he has emerged a warmer human being. His natural sense of humour, hidden for so long, bubbles to the surface constantly, even on the course, and he is measurably less intense. As he walked to the tee in the third round, Brenna Cepelak, his American girlfriend, called his name. He came over to her. 'I love you,' she said. 'Me you too,' he said in Faldo speak.

After the final round, Faldo said that he had set out to shoot 65 or 66 and just chip away at Norman: 'I shot 67, which was still the best round of the day, and things turned around. By the time we went through the twelfth, I had a two-shot lead. Then it was mine to lose. I wasn't counting my chickens until I hit the last shot out of the bunker on to the green at the eighteenth. Greg could have holed that putt on seventeen, I could have hit a tree. I could have taken six and he could have had three. I wasn't putting my head down until that ball went to the green. Greg's a great player, a great competitor. The man's got the drive and the commitment, and he'll be back again.'

In a strange way, it was harder for the people around Norman to accept Norman's loss than for the man himself. Norman might have been haemorrhaging inside but he was philosophical. 'I don't know how I could ever convince you that I know I screwed up today, but it's not the end of the world,' he said, retaining, through his pain, the ability to recognise that, when all is said and done, golf is only a game – a great game, a game of breathtaking cruelty and unparalleled joy – but a game none the less.

He glanced up at the television on which Ben Crenshaw was helping Faldo into his new emerald coat. 'God, I'd love to be putting the green jacket on,' he said with feeling, 'but life's going to continue. I'm sad about it. I'm going to regret it. I've let this one slip away and I've let others slip away, but it's not the end of my life. I'll continue to win golf tournaments. I'm not going to fall off the face of the earth because of what happened here.'

14

OR ELS

Michael Jones, the son of senior golfer David, knew very well he shouldn't be in the locker room at Royal Lytham, but he just had to see Ernie Els play the final hole of the 1996 Open Championship. An aspiring golfer himself, he had crept through the clubhouse in muddy boots and over-long shorts, and now he watched with a friend as the young South African putted out for a five to finish second behind Tom Lehman.

Minutes later, the locker-room door burst open and a frustrated and desperately disappointed Els burst in. 'He didn't see them at first and he was effing and blinding and banging doors,' recalled David Jones with a laugh. 'Then he looked up and said: "What are you boys doing here?" When they explained that they weren't really supposed to be there, he said, "Just hold on a minute," and he went away and returned with three beers. He is now their total hero. And that sums Ernie up. He's a terrifically pleasant guy. He's the sort of guy you couldn't help but wish mega-success for.'

People have been wishing Ernie Els mega-success ever since he turned up at the World Junior, aged 14, with a thatch of blond hair and a slightly less refined version of the elegantly beautiful swing that has made him great, and dispatched America's little darling Phil Mickelson. Last year, when he won his second US Open at Congressional, the most striking thing about him was not the blazing intensity with which he steamrollered down his opponents over the final holes, it was that he has experienced fame, fortune and disaster and emerged largely unscathed. Apart from a house in Orlando and a farm in gorgeous George on South Africa's east coast, he is still the same easy-going, raw-boned kid who lasted the longest in the survival of the fittest that was Oakmont in the 1994 US Open.

'That week was no different to any other,' recalls Els, the world No. 1. 'I was out there, I was playing well, I knew I was playing well and I just believed that I had the game and I was going to win. I was young and I made a lot of mistakes, but mentally I was as tough as anybody that week.'

It is inevitable that Els should draw frequent comparison with that other prodigy and world No. 1 contender, Tiger Woods, whom he overcame in a playoff for the Johnnie Walker Classic in January, but time after time Els's tortoise approach to the game (calm manner, effortless swing) wins support over Tiger's hare (fiery intensity and back-breaking swing) when it comes to longevity. 'Never mind Tiger, Ernie is the man for the future because of the way he handles all this,' Jones said. 'There are no violent mood swings. He seems very centred in himself. He treats it like a game, not like the end of the world. There is no whiff of prima donna about Ernie Els.'

'In my view, he's the man, not Tiger, long term,' agreed Southern African businessman John Bredenkamp, owner of the management company Masters International. Bredenkamp, who has known Els since he was a teenager and handled his finances for a period early in his career, remembers that Els always stood out. 'You could just see the natural raw talent was there. The mechanics were so smooth.'

After a round of golf with Els and Woods, one of the greatest tennis players ever to take a court told Els's coach Robert Baker than he thought Els would win more majors because he was more intensely focused in the crucial closing stages of the tournament, whereas 'Tiger always had a cold or an injury or an excuse. You have no idea what it's like to be there in the last set,' he continued. 'Mentally, Ernie has the edge over Tiger.'

When Els won his second US Open last year at Congressional – which, along with Oakmont, the scene of his first US Open victory, has the most brutal rough in American championship golf – Frank Nobilo remarked that Tiger might be long but Ernie was strong. Tiger, he said, hit the ball huge distances, but Els, with his 6ft 4in, 15-stone frame and rugby-forward shoulders, could take a five iron out of the rough, actually connected with the back of the ball and move the ball forward, which is a significant advantage on any USGA layout. Interestingly, Els also hit more greens than any other player at both US Open victories. But it was the intense focus that the tennis player spoke of which separated him from his rivals, most notably Colin Montgomerie, on the final holes in 1997. While Montgomerie elected to play for the wide part of the green at the seventeenth rather than flirt with the lake, then proceeded to take three to get down, Els executed a shot that was breathtaking in its audacity – a towering 212-yard five iron that arced towards the water and landed 12 feet from the pin. It won him the title.

'Standing there on the fairway, I was quite intense, to be honest,' recalls Els. 'I was really feeling the pressure. But I'd hit a five iron into four or five feet in the [rain-delayed] morning round and that gave me confidence and a little bit of bravery in my heart. I'd hit my three wood shorter than Colin's tee shot and I knew that if I could hit my second in there on the left, it would put pressure on him. My swing was good and I wasn't really feeling any negative thoughts. I was very positive.'

It is moments like these that show that Els's smiling, unruffled demeanour hides a competitive fire that burns as bright as Arnold Palmer's ever did. Els just keeps his emotions under control. 'He's definitely not as laid back and cool as everybody thinks,' says Johann Rupert, chairman of Rothmans, who took Els under his wing shortly before he exploded into world golf with victories in the 1992 South African Open, Masters and PGA, and arranged the sponsors invitations that gave him his start in Europe. They have been close friends ever since. Rupert remembers Els cursing for an hour after the first round of the US Open, then putting for an hour and sorting out the problem. Els recalls his emotions after bogeying the seventeenth and eighteenth holes for a first-round 71. 'I was really angry at myself, really angry. I didn't even hit balls afterwards. I was working so hard on that first 18, getting up and down, and then to finish in that style made me feel like I was going back to where I was at Kemper [previous week] when I missed the cut. It was a big tournament for me because I was sliding a bit. I hadn't won a big tournament for a long time. I went back to the house and my mum was there and she always has a calming effect on me. She said that I shouldn't be so hard on myself because it is only a game. It was something I had to work out for myself, but maybe without them I wouldn't have won.'

As a boy, it was temperament that separated Ernie from his older brother Dirk, who seemed to be the better of the two. When things went badly, Dirk's blood would boil and he would immediately start to play worse. Ernie, by contrast, slowed down and tried to think more clearly. Little by little, he would get his game back on track.

'Ernie Els takes after his mother,' Rupert says. 'If Ernie had taken after his father, Monty would have been a very tame comparison. Dirk is a superb golfer. He still hits the ball 40 yards past Ernie. But Dirk wears his emotions on his sleeve.'

Els's ability to keep his passions under tight rein led to several misapprehensions about him, most commonly that he doesn't exert himself on the range or in the weight room and that he isn't particularly bright. 'People don't know how hard Ernie works,' Rupert says. Certainly, he isn't known to be overly active away from the course although, ironically, he hurt his shoulder last year playing 'Tarzan' in the gym with his father and brother. 'The only place Ernie runs is to the toilet,' Sam Feldman, his ex-manager, once joked, and Bredenkemp paints a picture of Els as a Fred Couples-type figure, relaxed and homely. 'Ernie's exercise is jumping in and out of the pool,' he says with a laugh. 'He likes being at home and watching TV. He's not a complicated person, and that's one of his assets.'

In golf, where over-analysis leads to paralysis, there is no greater asset. Watching Els work with Robert Baker, a former Leadbetter assistant, is an education in how to take a golf lesson: a swing, a glance, a comment, end of instruction. Enlightened, Baker's pupil works contentedly on his own.

The idea that Els might not be intelligent is extraordinary to Rupert, one of the wealthiest and most successful businessmen in Africa. 'I've watched him in his inter-personal skills and he's got good judgement of people and their characters,' he says. 'Certainly anyone who thinks he's not intelligent is making a mistake. He's not about to open up to just anyone, and the fact that he's reticent leads people to think he's not intelligent. I think he's highly intelligent and analytical.'

He believes that Els will become a good businessman, although for now he leaves it all to Nic Frangos of Legend Inc. 'Quite frankly, at 28 he shouldn't be worrying about business. He needs to concentrate on winning,' he emphasises.

There is no doubt that Els has more than his share of personal and professional attributes, but it has not been plain sailing. On the course, Els has seen major opportunities evaporate painfully at the 1995 Open at St Andrews, after he three-putted 14 times in four rounds, at the US PGA at Riviera where he was leading by three strokes going into the final round and shot 72 on a perfect day, and the 1996 Open at Lytham, where he drove into the bunker at the seventieth hole, took five up the last and lost by two strokes to Tom Lehman.

'After the fifteenth, I was one or two behind at Lytham,' Els recalled, 'and I thought, here we go. But I tried to fade the ball at 16 and came over the top of the ball, and at the eighteenth I was in-between clubs. I was disappointed when I walked off 18. I felt like I'd had a chance. At Riviera, I had two different emotions. One was that it was a bit of a blow-out on my part, and the other was that it was like running the 100 metres and pulling a hamstring halfway. But I feel like it's history, it's gone.'

This year, like several others, he was also poised for success at Augusta, a course made for his game. Paired with Jack Nicklaus on the last day, he saw his chances slip away. 'I don't think I've found a formula for playing that course yet,' Els adds.

He is proud to have won two majors before his 30th birthday, but his heroes are the people who have achieved longevity and success at the highest level (Gary Player, Jack Nicklaus, Pete Sampras) and he expects more from himself. 'You look at some of the great players and they won a major a year for about ten years,' Els says, 'and you think: I'd better start working a bit harder.'

Through it all, Els has stayed unspoiled and relatively untouched. He has won two majors, four World Match Play titles and some 18 events world wide, earned several million and appeared in America's celebrity bible, *People* magazine, smiling in a jacuzzi with his girlfriend Liezl, and has remained much the same as he was at 20.

'It was hard at first,' Els admits. 'Success came pretty quickly – I'd almost say easy – and it came at a bit of an unexpected time. I expected to win two majors from about 26 on, not at 24, because I only started playing international golf, really, that year. You're out there by yourself, not knowing too much about yourself or even the game of golf, and it is hard. Now I just try to live my life and keep it as simple as I can.'

'He's not changed a lot,' Rupert says. 'The problem is not that one changes, it's that people around one change. I think he's noticed that there are a lot more hangers-on these days. But he still goes to the cricket and the rugby with his old friends and he's still prudent with money. And he never speaks ill of others.'

'He's a nice fellow,' said Peter Thomson, five-time winner of the Open, 'and I think that nice fellows do well in the end.'

Long after he ceased to have any business involvement with Els, Bredenkamp's lasting impression is of Els's decency. 'I can't speak more highly of the guy,' he says. 'He's phenomenally talented and he's got no airs and graces. It's very difficult for people not to be affected by success in this business and he isn't. He hasn't changed, he hasn't forgotten his friends. His parents are wonderful. They're a very close family.'

'When you get to know him, every now and then you wonder, is this for real?' says Rupert of Els's enormous gifts and apparently irrepressible goodness. 'It's almost too good to be true, that a nice guy should also be able to do everything it takes to be one of the top three players in the world. But it is true. He's a very loyal friend.'

To Els himself, if he has changed at all, it is for the better. 'Hopefully I've matured and my values have changed a little bit. I don't take everything for granted any more. I've got a really great lifestyle, to say the least. To be 28, to have a farm in South Africa and a really nice home in Orlando and do just about what I want to do is really something special. Sometimes I lie in bed and try to appreciate it a little. I call my parents a lot more, which you don't really do when you're young, call my grandfather and try to see my friends down here. Golf is still my most important thing, but the whole situation has cooled down a bit. My desire will never cool off, but now I'm thinking of other things, like settling down. It's so beautiful here. Other things have come into it.'

15

SOUTHBOUND EXPRESS

July 1995. Outside the Royal and Ancient clubhouse John Daly was communing with the crowd. Having practised what he preaches by driving the eighteenth green, he now moved at a pace somewhat slower than a dawdle, tucking the fan mail gratefully under his arm, swapping smiles with a woman with a poodle and reaching out a meaty paw for *The Killer Swing: John Daly's Guide to Long-hitting* and autographing it with a careful red scrawl.

'About the only thing in college I ever learned how to do was sign my name,' observed Daly, a contender in the Open Championship. 'All I ever did was sign the test and leave.'

To the purists, both Daly and his game are too brash for links golf. 'He can't just overpower the Old Course,' one said after Daly had claimed that six of St Andrews's par fours were within reach of his driver before hitting two and narrowly missing two more. 'It takes time to understand its subtleties,' added the purist. Greg Rita, Daly's caddie, disagreed. 'For a power player, his short game is very underestimated. He has a really good touch around the green and he's pretty imaginative. And when things are going well for him, he's very, very competitive.'

It was a telling remark. Lionhearted when things are going well, Daly has in the past been the first to quit when they were going badly. Take, for example, the 1994 Open at Turnberry. On the second day, he went out in 32 and was tearing up the field when he came to the tenth. There, he drove on to the beach. A concerted search by the gallery failed to reveal his ball and Daly proceeded to the eleventh with a thunderous face. When he reached the green he four-putted for a seven, knocking in the last with a careless backhand and notching up a 40 on the inward half.

'I'm going home to tear the knife out of my heart,' he said melodramatically before finishing last in the Open for the second time.

Nevertheless, ever since Daly first crashed into our consciousness he has had two redeeming features. The first is his obvious talent. Daly's game is golf without frontiers. Only Seve Ballesteros has played the sport with such all-or-nothing abandon, with such freedom of movement and independence of thought.

The second is his loyalty to the public. Had any other player uttered the words 'I just play for the fans' as often as he has, it would have sounded like a marketing ploy. With Daly, though, it was a mantra, the only constant – apart from his 'grip it and rip it' motto – in the chaotic swathe he cut from his rags-to-riches victory in the 1991 US PGA championship to alcohol rehabilitation centres and beyond.

A cynic might say that Daly is best viewed from a distance; it is hard to be entirely convinced by him up close. If a man's eyes really are the windows of his soul, then Daly's house is empty or, at best, haunted. 'He's very extreme,' his wife Paulette conceded.

In Holywood, Daly's alcoholism, chocolate binges, broken marriages and stormy outbursts might have passed without comment; in the mineral-water world of professional golf he was an outlaw from the outset. He was suspended twice by the US Tour for, among other things, walking out of a tournament and endangering the lives of the public by driving a ball over their heads, before visiting an alcoholic rehabilitation centre at the instigation of the Tour's commissioner in those days, Deane Beman.

'I'm just basically going to say that there was no 1993,' he said and, after a brief period of exemplary behaviour, took the rest of 1994 off after a car-park scuffle with a spectator last September.

'How dare he say any of us are on drugs,' Greg Norman retorted when Daly, tired of being the Tour scapegoat, declared at last year's Scottish Open that he wasn't the only one with problems and that it was possible there were players on cocaine.

'I'm not the one who beat up my wife. I'm not the one who

is an alcoholic. I'm not the one who tears up rooms. If I had done the things he's done I'd have been ostracised by everyone.'

But is he good for the game? 'I wish you hadn't asked me that,' said Larry Mize, a former Masters champion and a born-again Christian. 'I've played with him twice, and both times he handled himself very well. On those occasions he was good for the game, put it that way.'

Recently, a more sinister hobby has been added to Daly's list of obsessions. The day after he shot 71, 77 to miss the cut at the Colonial in May, a congratulatory picture of him appeared in an advertisement in a Memphis paper. He had, it seemed, won $100,000 playing a $100 slot machine at a showboat casino in Tunica, Mississippi. The following month, when he pulled out of a tournament at his home course of Southwind, Memphis, complaining of a migraine, there were reports that he subsequently visited the casino twice.

'It's not out of control,' Daly insisted when he was interrogated about his gambling. 'It's not what people are saying. Yes, I gamble. I gamble for fun and pleasure. I do it because I can and it's relaxing. It's the most relaxing thing I do besides playing guitars.' Then he said: 'I love it so much that I spend 12 to 24 hours at a time at the casino. I'm not going to quit gambling.'

There has been much speculation that his latest pastime and its associated debts may have contributed to Daly's decision to halt his move to Rogers, Arkansas, which is near to his home town of Dardanelle. Daly denies that is the case. 'They say it's a buyer's market right now,' he said after explaining that he had taken his $895,000 home off the market. 'We've kind of decided to stay here.'

If anything symbolises Daly's feckless, rootless existence, it is his home-owning history. In his early years on Tour, after the break up of his first marriage, he travelled the circuit in a trailer, going from place to place in splendid isolation.

Later, when his drinking began to get out of hand, he moved to Castle Pines in Colorado to escape the influences of the city. When he had 'killed', as he put it, that house in a drunken frenzy in December 1992, he and Bettye tried to start afresh in the exclusive suburb of Isleworth, Orlando. Their divorce settlement presented Bettye with the Isleworth home and Daly built a new one in Memphis.

Theoretically, the worst of Daly's troubles are behind him. He met Paulette, his third wife, at the Bob Hope Chrysler Classic two years ago and they appear to be happy. 'We've had our hard times,' Paulette said, 'but then everybody does.' The downside is Daly's headaches. After a hangover-free drinking career, he now finds himself tortured by terrible migraines lasting days at a stretch.

Doctors have advised him to cut down on caffeine, but it his sugar intake that arouses more concern, carrying as it does the risk of diabetes. At one stage he was consuming up to 16 Diet Cokes, five packs of Marlboros, several bags of M&Ms and a pint of chocolate yoghurt daily. 'It's actually getting easier not drinking,' said Daly, who sends a urine sample every month to the Tour, not because he has to but because he wants to. He has been sober for three years. 'It's coping with the headaches and sugar rushes and all this other crap I have to deal with that's the hard part.'

In the press centre at St Andrews, Daly, who has not challenged a major since the Masters in 1993, was reminded of his red-faced departure from Turnberry.

'I was hot,' he confessed ruefully, referring to his mood rather than his temperature. 'Everything just went south.' When pressed on the likelihood of a repeat performance, he replied: 'I hope I don't do that again,' in a voice of someone who suspects that he probably will in the not too distant future.

On and off the golf course, Daly faces a race against time. Will he mature, calm down or win the fight against himself before his obsessions and addictions destroy him? One can only hope so. Without his free-flowing swing, his colour, his talent and his wildness, golf, not to say the Open Championship, will be the poorer.

FAIRWAY DREAMS

16

How to Play Golf and Stay Happy

Mission Hills, Rancho Mirage, March 2000. The Nabisco Championship (known to the players as the Dinah Shore and lesbians worldwide as an excuse for the largest gathering of gay women on the planet) is the major championship Laura Davies most wants to win, so she has prepared for it the best way she knows how: with a little gambling, a little shopping and a lot of phone calls home to her mother. With Karrie Webb in the field, there has, of course, been quite a bit of practice, but that hasn't stopped Laura from living life to the full amid the cinematic beauty of Rancho Mirage, with its palms, mansions and hazy circle of snow-capped mountains. She has no patience at all with ungrateful Tour players.

'I think if people stand back and realise what they're doing and how much money they're earning and how much fun we have travelling round the world, then they'd think, what am I doing complaining?' says Laura, taking a leisurely swipe at a ball on the Mission Hills range and watching it explode like a scud missile into the blue. 'People save up two years' wages just to come on holiday for a week where I am now and I'm trying to win a major championship. That's not hard work, that's fun.'

She puts down her club and contemplates the culture of preciousness that now exists on the men's Tours (the US Seniors' Tour, which Robinson describes as being full of 'evil, bitter old men,' being the worst). 'I can understand No.152 on the money list moaning because he's not having any fun,' Laura says. 'He's not earning any money and it's a hard life. You're away from home 34 weeks a year. But when the top players start moaning I think, "Hang on."' She leans on her bag and grins disarmingly.

Laura Davies may be the greatest player women's golf has

ever seen, but she is also the most irreverent. In golf, the majors are sacred. The best players are not only supposed to win them, using a near-scientific combination of diet, discipline and hard work, they're supposed to accord them due reverence. There is not even the faintest possibility that Tiger Woods would make a side trip to a casino on his way to winning the Open Championship, or that Nick Faldo would forgo his pre-Masters warm up in order to fit in a game of ping-pong or blow a few hundred in the Gap; for them, the majors are a matter of deadly earnest. Fortunately, Laura has never been all that good at doing deadly earnest. That serious, superior superstar thing has never sat well with her. She has Seve Ballesteros's artistry on the course, but none of his intensity. She has Colin Montgomerie's vast natural talent and lack of regard for practice and coaches (she's never had a lesson in her entire life), but none of his spoilt sulkiness. She has Greg Norman's exuberance and passion for Ferarris, spending sprees and living life at 100 m.p.h., but none of his hardness, arrogance or obsession with money.

'I'm not interested in worrying about tomorrow's round until tomorrow,' Laura says.

Laura Davies has been the best thing to happen to women's golf since Nancy Lopez, ever since she turned up at the Curtis Cup at Muirfield in 1984 with tousled hair, ill-fitting trousers and a pout, and hit the ball further than any woman anywhere on her way to demolishing two experienced Americans. So shy that she once compared her fear of public speaking to that of 'a trapeze artist with vertigo', she threw off her inhibitions only in the heat of competition. 'She'd rather lose a tournament than win and make a speech,' her father Dave recalls. 'But that's all changed now . . . She's a lot more self-confident. In fact, too self-confident. When I think of when she was younger, she was a shrinking violet.'

It was sport that brought Laura out of her shell. Dave had always been very competitive, running and swimming and playing football, hockey and cricket, and Laura caught the sports bug young. At seven, she loved to play soccer with the boys. The local YMCA only had a girls' team for Over-12s but Laura, tall and strong for her age, wanted to play so badly that

Dave pleaded with them to allow her to be a defender. At first, they refused point blank. Finally, they gave her a grudging trial. 'So she played her first game, stood there, didn't move, with her hands on her hips,' Dave says, remembering his daughter's resentment that they didn't take her talent on faith. 'Finally the ball came to her, she dribbled the ball all the way up the field and scored a goal. Then she just turned around and said, "There you are."'

At 14, she discovered golf, tagging along with her older brother Tony. Soon, she wanted to try it for herself. 'Tony and I were always competitive with each other,' she told Liz Kahn in *The LPGA: The Unauthorized Version*. 'We had bets on everything we did. I wouldn't have a putt without a bet on it. Even at Trivial Pursuit we'd play for a fiver or there was no point.' As a family, the Davies were an unstoppable 10-pin bowling team, and Laura had the lowest handicap and highest average (158) of the women in their league. She also ran cross country and played hockey, netball and rounders.

At 16, she decided that golf should be her life and quit school to work on her handicap, reducing it from 26 to scratch in just two and a half years. To support herself, she took odd jobs in a supermarket, bookmaker and garage near her home in Coventry. Victories in the English Intermediate and Welsh Strokeplay earned her Curtis Cup selection at 20 years of age, and at 22 she turned pro, borrowing £1,000 from her parents to see her through the 1985 season. Tony agreed to caddie for her.

In the second round of her first Tour event, the Ford Classic, Laura shot an 85 and missed the cut. She elected to dig into her £1,000 for some cheap accommodation. Tony spent a freezing night in the car. A week later, she took a six-shot lead over Jan Stephenson in the first round of the Hennessy Cup in Paris. She finished runner-up to the American superstar and came into the press centre in tears. With cruel timing, Colin Snape, the Tour's executive director, had decided that Laura, cash-strapped and chubby, was wearing 'scruffy trousers'. He fined her £50 for bringing the Tour into disrepute. This announcement was greeted with outrage. Jan Stephenson fumed that Laura had so much talent it should have been irrelevant if she played in her bra and pants. 'You should encourage players of her ability,' she told the press. 'She could be the Seve Ballesteros of the women's Tour.'

To Laura, who was and is painfully self-conscious about her weight, the experience was devastating. Her talent was so enormous that she went on to win the Belgian Open with an eagle, birdie, birdie finish and top the money list that season, but her size was never far from her mind. For years she wore tank tops or sweaters even when it was baking hot because she felt she looked 'less big' if she was covered up, and once she confessed that while other professionals watched highlights of their rounds on television and noticed the angle of the clubhead on their backswing, she worried about the size of her shoulders. The result was a tendency towards feast or famine. When Gary Player took her to task about drinking 15 Cokes a day, she decided that she needed to diet. A Slim-Fast advert seemed like the answer and, in about a two-year period leading up to June 1993, she lost three and a half stone. Years later, she told Kahn that it was 'one of the greatest achievements of my life'.

The effect that Laura's weight had on her sense of self worth was unfortunate, to say the least, particularly given that she was actually very pretty, just not in the narrow definition dictated by fashion magazines. But what made it doubly difficult is that her detractors put it together with her whimsical approach to practice and decided she was squandering her talent. In the early days, her appearance constantly led people to underestimate her. In 1987, when Laura shot a 66 in the first round of the Dinah Shore, the *Los Angeles Times* writer John Cherwa, who hadn't seen her hit a shot, wrote: 'The leader is Laura Davies, a 23-year-old lass from England who, despite her six under par 66, is not expected to be leading after Sunday's final round. Leading a golf tournament after the first round is akin to leading the 10,000 metre walk after the first lap. Who really cares? Davies won slightly more than £37,000 in 1987, which equates to about $50,000 here in the colonies. The winner of the Dinah Shore gets $80,000. Better tell Maggie Thatcher there's no need to hang by the phone.'

Laura finished 33rd, tied with Nancy Lopez, and sent Dave to ask Nancy for her autograph because she was too shy to ask her hero for it herself. Four months later, she beat Ayako Okamota and JoAnne Carner, one of the most feared competitors in women's golf, to become the first non-LPGA member to win the US Open. 'When Laura hit the ball, the earth shook,' said an awed Carner.

From 1986 onwards, there was no stopping Laura. She won four tournaments, including the British Open, in her second season, and held both the British and US Open titles by the end of the next. When she joined the LPGA Tour in 1988, she missed three successive cuts and then finished birdie, eagle, birdie to beat Lopez in the Jaimie Farr Toledo Classic. 'We don't think of Laura as a rookie. We're just petrified when she makes the cut,' was Carner's droll comment.

Far from failing to fulfil her potential, she managed to live life and have fun in a way that 99 per cent of professional athletes could only dream about while clocking up more air miles than any golfer since Gary Player. In 1994, she won the Thailand Open, the Standard Register Ping, the Sara Lee Classic, the LPGA Championship – her second US major and ninth victory in US – the Itoki Classic (in Japan), the Australian Masters, the Ireland Open and Scottish Open, becoming the first golfer ever to win on five Tours in a single year. She dominated the world rankings and became the first British player ever to win LPGA money list. She also came within a whisker of winning a third US major when she arrived at the 18th in the Dinah Shore leading by a shot. A wayward eight-iron and a three-putt cost her victory.

'That's the major that I should really have won,' says Davies. 'I took it hard. If I never win the Dinah Shore, that particular loss will be the loss that's more annoying than anything else.'

She picks up her club and launches another few balls towards the purple mountains. Five weeks earlier she had had laser eye surgery the day before the LA Open, teed up in the tournament and led from start to finish. 'I should have had it done in the off season but I would never have done it,' grins Laura. It was, "Oh, I've got you an appointment for 8 a.m. tomorrow." That's the way it had to be.'

Now, she was planning to do her best to stop Webb, who had won four of the last five events.

'I think I've practised more in the last three weeks than my caddie's ever seen me practise,' Laura grins. 'I'm trying a bit harder. I'm not going into gyms but I am hitting a few more shots because I want my irons to be more consistent, I want my drives to be consistent, I want to hole more putts. And that's purely because of Karrie Webb. Because she is, I think, the best player there's ever been. She's definitely testing Nancy Lopez's record.' As if aware that Karrie is, ultimately, a rival, she adds: 'I think Karrie's incredibly good but I think I can be as good as she is. I'm not that good yet but I think I can be. I want to be. I think I can raise my game.'

Dave Davies is, as people are fond of pointing out, a slender man. They tend to refer to him as 'thin' or 'skinny', as if to exaggerate the contrast between him and his famous daughter. In actuality, the difference is most marked in their faces – in Dave's shuttered cynicism and Laura's frank blue eyes. Where Laura is warm and expansive, Dave is abrupt. Where Laura is spontaneous, Dave plays his cards close to his chest. Even his body language is suspicious as he hunches over his plate of cold meats and beetroot in the sponsor's pavillion at Mission Hills and casts his mind back to Laura as an accident-prone child.

'When she was about 18 months old she tripped over and hit her face – her teeth – on the fireplace,' he remembers. 'She chipped a piece off the fireplace but her teeth were fine. She used to intimidate other kids when they were crawling round. She'd get 'em in a corner.'

In 1967, when Laura was three, the Davies moved to Marietta, Georgia, where Dave worked as an aircraft design engineer for Lockhead. Dave remembers the next four years as a difficult time. 'Laura's mother didn't like it over here. Hated it in America. They went back and I stayed here.'

At that age, Laura was still too young to understand anything except a vague sense of hurt. Years later, she told her biographer, Lewine Mair, that she felt more of a benificiary of circumstance than a victim because she had been left with family on both sides of the Atlantic, but she only started to see Dave regularly when she joined the LPGA Tour. He travels to eight or ten events a year.

Dave had greeted the news that Laura was turning professional with some scepticism. 'I didn't think she could make a living at it. I said, "Make sure you think about it." But she hasn't looked back.'

They had in common a passion for gambling. While Laura's mother is a restraining influence, Dave had stopped in Vegas on his way to Mission Hills. 'Laura's basically shy until she's around people that she knows and she's doing something she enjoys and then there's no shyness. We were in Vegas in November and everybody knows her. They know me because of her. We always stay at the Desert Inn. As soon as people see me there, the pit bosses go, "Where's Laura?" She does bet rather a lot.'

Laura, who learned gambling at her grandmother's knee, betting on the horses on a Saturday afternoon, says her motto is never to gamble more than she's prepared to lose, but she did tell Mair that she had once lost £4,000 when the limit she'd set herself was £3,000. 'I was cross. I knew I had gone too far. It was obscene to have lost that amount of money in a world where so many are struggling.' Another time, she put down £20 and won £27,691.34. She admitted to Kahn that it was part of her personality to gamble. 'I enjoy the adrenalin pumping so hard that it's like being up there with a chance of winning a tournament. Sometimes I stop when I'm ahead and I've walked out of a casino in London and run to the car because I've won so much money I was afraid of being mugged.

'Lots of people gamble to try to win money. I gamble for fun, and I know I will lose. Gambling and golf go hand in hand. Nine out of ten golfers gamble, even if it's only a $10 Nassau. I'm sure some people think I'm mad, but I think they're mad, some of the stuff they go for, like drink, drugs or smoking.'

Periodically Dave and Laura run into PGA Tour bad boy John Daly, an acknowledged gambling addict, who is said to have gambled away $51m of his $48m earnings in the course of his career.

'Yeah, well, he's a bad gambler,' Dave says unsympathetically. 'I was talking to his friend. He tells me that John plays the $1,000 slot machines and doubles up on the twelve playing blackjack. Stupid crap like that. No wonder he loses.'

Laura's motto is never to bet more than she can afford to lose, which is still a considerable sum. In 1993, when she won the Australian Ladies' Masters, she prepared for the tournament every morning in the hotel casino or on the tennis court. Once, playing in a tournament in Santiago, she spontaneously decided to fly to Vegas, spent the night there and return before her tee-off time the following morning. Then she couldn't get out of Vegas because of fog.

'Right in the middle of the damn tournament,' Dave says with something akin to approval.

'Where does she get that from?' I ask. 'Is that from you?'

He grins. 'Probably.'

'Does that mean you wouldn't advise her to do anything different?'

'She wouldn't listen anyway,' Dave says.

Asked what they did together apart from gamble, he says abruptly: 'Well, she gets on my nerves a bit and I get on hers. Her latest thing is for me to return to England and for her to buy me a house over there and for me to sell up over here and move back. I told her I'll have to decide. Because I've been over here for 33 years. The way of life, I know everything. As a friend of mind said, I've spend more than half my adult life over in this country. All my friends are here. Laura says, "Well, you've got friends – me and Tony." I said, "Two people? I've got hordes of them where I live."'

To Dave, Laura is overly generous. He would rather she saved her money for a rainy day. He'd rather she drove something sedate like a Volvo as well.

'When I'm driving, she wants me to speed up always. When she's driving, I want her to slow down.'

Success, he said, hadn't changed her one iota. 'Well, she's so natural. She doesn't have any pretences. But when she's playing there's only one thing she wants to do and that's be No.1. She doesn't enjoy watching Karrie get all the limelight.'

'You must be very proud,' I say. 'She'll go down in history as one of the game's greatest players.'

'Sometimes I am,' Dave murmurs.

I stare at him. 'What do you mean?'

He looks away. 'No, I suppose that's wrong,' he says at last.

'I am very proud of her.' There is an awkward silence. 'She's going to the palace in November to receive her CBE,' he says hastily. 'So I'm flying over. It's my turn to go to the palace. My son and myself.'

He still finds it extraordinary that she's come so far. 'Never a thought came into my head that it would be her second time at the palace and she'd be invited to tea parties with the Queen,' Dave marvels.

The fairways at Mission Hills are as vivid as astroturf, the crowd colours like jewels. Between palms, willows and eucalyptus trees rush golf carts shaped like miniature Rolls Royces and Mercedes Benzes. A convertible sails by with a windswept dog in the front seat – a St Bernard-type creature, only twice the size. In the players' cafe, Alison Nicholas, Laura's pint-sized former Solheim Cup partner, was wrestling with a frozen sherbet lemon and remembering her first encounter with a shy, awkward Laura at the 1981 British Amateur. 'I knew she was going to be a great player,' says Alison, who was beaten two and one. 'At that point, she'd just try to hit it as hard as she could. Obviously, it meant she was a bit wayward but over the years she managed to tone it down.' She considers her friend's progress. 'She's just an incredible talent. She hits the ball phenomenal distances but also she's got a fantastic short game. I don't think you'll see another player like her. You've got to rate her as one of the greats.'

In 1990, Alison and Laura, who share a love of football (Laura, Liverpool and Alison, Sheffield Wednesday) and Tepinyaki Japanese food, often roomed together when they first started playing in America, were paired together in the first Solheim Cup at Lake Nona. In the first foursomes match on the first morning of the event, they beat the seemingly invincible pairing of Pat Bradley and Nancy Lopez two and one. They were brought down to earth with a crash the next day when they were beaten four and three by Beth Daniel and Betsy King. Even psychological warfare didn't help. 'I think I've got to them,' Laura told Nicklaus after she annoyed Daniel and King by making them putt a short putt. Alison laughs at the memory. 'Five holes later, we were shaking hands. I said to

Laura, "I don't think we got to them."' The US ultimately scored an embarrassing 11½–4½ victory over Europe but that early foursomes match was no less memorable. Two years later, the Nicholas/Davies combination helped Europe to even the score, but not even Alison would deny that it was the sheer force of Laura's personality that willed the underdogs to an emotional 11½–6½ win over the US. Not since Ballesteros boarded Concorde for the 1987 Ryder Cup has any one player had such an inspirational effect on a team.

Laura and Alison beat King and Daniel by a hole in the foursomes and Patty Sheehan and Juli Inkster by a hole in the fourballs. Of the second match, Alison says: 'She was incredible. She holed putt after putt after putt that day. She was so bad. She was putting so well that she'd wink at me when the ball got halfway to the hole to say, "That's going in." It was just extraordinary. She would go, "How's that?" and it hadn't even got to the hole yet. Majestic.'

'She has the most natural ability of any woman I've ever seen,' says Tour player Trish Johnson, a close friend of Laura's. 'She loves sport and she loves playing sport and it shows in everything she does. She loves life. I'd pay to see her play and I wouldn't pay to see any other player play.'

Both Trish and Laura are football mad and Trish's favourite memory is the time they went with four friends to see England play Tunisia at the World Cup in Marseilles. 'Our idea of bliss, really,' Trish says. Laura's idea of a perfect day is to be at home and go shopping with her mother Rita in the morning and watch sport on television all afternoon, with a little gambling thrown in for excitement.

On the course, Laura's aim is to raise her game to the level Karrie Webb is currently operating at, although some would argue she has nothing to prove. In 14 seasons, she has won 59 events and $4m. In her worst year, she still won twice. If she'd been a man, she would be lauded as one of Britain's greatest sportsmen. Instead, relatively few people care.

'Monty's had a lot of wins but he hasn't had 59,' says Laura. 'David Beckham would probably be the only one who was more high profile. I don't mind that. It doesn't bother me.'

Ask her if she thinks it might be a blessing to be spared

some of the pressures of players at that level of fame and she finds it difficult to imagine they would bother her at all. 'It wouldn't worry me. People coming up and talking to you, I think it's quite entertaining. The word fame is irrelevant to me because I don't think I'm famous. I'm just someone lucky who's having good craic and if someone wants to come up and enjoy having a conversation with me, that just doesn't worry me.'

After 15 years at the top, Laura is still Laura, gleeful, spontaneous and relaxed about life. She is, however, trading in her Ferarri for a BMW.

'Getting sensible in me old age,' she grins.

17

THE REINVENTION OF NICK FALDO

Nick Faldo is a precise man and he knows to the second when he experienced the most painful moment of his career. It was December 1999 and he was a guest on the BBC's Sports Personality Awards, watching a film review of the century's greatest British sportsmen. When it came to golf, Faldo, Britain's greatest golfer, was stunned to find he was not even acknowledged by commentator Peter Alliss.

'They had a stupid excuse,' says Faldo, still hurt by what he sees as a deliberate snub. 'He did a three-hour interview and it got cut out. Baloney! All he talked about was [Colin Montgomerie's] incredible achievement winning seven Order of Merits. Never mentioned my name, let alone what I had done. The two seconds they had was me lifting my arms up when I holed the putt at Augusta in 1996. The BBC filmed the British Open, for crying out loud. Afterwards, I said to Dad: "I don't want to retire and I'm forgotten. I want to be remembered for more than the two seconds the BBC gave me."'

For much of his 20-year career, Faldo has been notorious for being one of the coldest men in British sport, at times better known for being aloof, arrogant and self-obsessed than for winning six major championships. 'He's a hero,' Alliss once said, 'but he doesn't fully understand that he's a hero.' But the rollercoaster of the last six years has left him profoundly changed.

Along the way he has seen the death of his 15-year marriage to Gill, the demise of his relationship with American student Brenna Cepelak, his engagement to Swiss PR executive Valerie Bercher exposed to the dustbin-digging excesses of the tabloids, split with his coach, lost his caddie, and fallen to 119th in the world, any one of which could have left him a broken man. Instead, they have left him softened and chastened. More willing to live for the moment. More careful to cherish the things that are precious.

Valerie, for instance. She sits cross-legged on the floor of their rented Surrey house, blonde hair framing intelligent brown eyes and a perfect smile, and intervenes whenever she feels it necessary. Faldo towers over her in his armchair. His soft green shirt is stretched across his athlete's chest and pale thick arms. He is laughing as he recounts the catalogue of disasters that have come their way recently.

'What was so difficult about last year is that we knew that everything would be resolved – there was a light at the end of the tunnel – but we didn't know what speed we were heading towards it,' says Faldo.

'We would sit and solve one problem,' agrees Valerie, 'and then there'd be two new ones.'

Faldo grins, recalling them wading through failed business ventures, divorce papers and property crises. 'We'd go through five or six problems and then go, "Oh, by the way, I'm playing crap as well.""'

For a man so famously private, so long regarded as an emotional iceberg, there is a sense of shock in the admission. It's a sign both of how far he has fallen and how far he has come. Sitting in the calm, cream living room, with its bright vases of Berberers and family snapshots, there is a vulnerability about him that is unimaginable when he is striding unseeingly across the golf course or narrow-eyed and defensive at a press conference. Yet there have been times when he has been seriously depressed. When he separated from Gill in 1995 and missed the cut at last year's Open, the lows were so bad that if it wasn't for Valerie and his friend and business adviser Danny Desmond, chairman of the Bride Hall Group (his first ever sponsors), he would, he says, have been finished.

'It's very hard when you've got three kids and you don't want to hurt them,' says Faldo, eyes seeking Valerie's for support. 'You don't want to hurt any more people than necessary and, obviously, the kids, God! The to-ing and fro-ing with your emotions and what are you doing and is it the right time. That was heavy. It went on for a long time. I didn't come up for six years.'

THE REINVENTION OF NICK FALDO

When he did surface, it was to find that his career had been reduced to mere statistics. For a long time, Faldo had been content to let his clubs do the talking. The BBC's omission had brought it home to him that if nobody cared about him, nobody would care enough to remember him.

George and Joyce Faldo named their only son Nicholas Alexander because they wanted him to be a star. He was a former military policeman who worked in the financial planning department of ICI plastics. She was a cutter and pattern maker for Cresta Silks. They lived in a two-bedroomed Welwyn Garden City council house and dreamed of a future in which their son would win the Tchaikovsky piano prize, rival Laurence Olivier on the stage or model at Harrods fashion shows. Eventually, they realised he was only interested in sport. One of Faldo's earliest memories is attempting to chop logs in the back yard with a hickory stick given to him by his maternal grandfather, but not knowing about golf he gravitated towards other sports first. He tried swimming but the training bored him. He tried tennis but they told him he was too tall. He tried team games but they wound him up.

'I guess I was an individualist. I used to come back and throw my bike against the wall. I'd just ride up and let it go. Crunch! I'd come in and go, "So and so didn't do the right thing."'

Then he tried canoeing. 'My father and I got the kit – the classic – built a canoe in the upstairs bedroom and then thought: "How do we get it out the house." We had to take out the window. And then I took it down to the river and got attacked by a swan. That was the end of my canoeing.'

His critics have always considered these childhood anecdotes as evidence that he was over-indulged by pushy stage parents, but Faldo laughs out loud at the notion that he was spoiled.

'Was I spoilt! I was traumatised. I went to a new dentist a couple of years ago and she says: "Did you have a dreadful illness as a child, or was it malnutrition?" I said: 'It was my mother's cooking. There's a joke about my mum and her mince – 101 ways to cook mince – and we used to eat salads three times a week, even when it was snowing.'

Once, when Joyce went to fetch him at school, she found him in the midst of a scuffle with another boy. To teach him a lesson, she turned the car around and left him there.

'They said, "Nick's having a fight in the corner,"' grins Faldo. 'So she went home.'

When Faldo turned on the television in the spring of 1971 and saw Jack Nicklaus win the Masters, their worries were over. They took him down to Welwyn Garden City golf club, booked a course of six lessons and Faldo was hooked. He spent three months hitting balls into a long jump pit at a nearby school before being taken out on to the course. His first score was 78 (minus three lost balls).

In 1973, aged 16, he left school to focus on golf. He vividly remembers the sense of separation he felt on his last day in class, the awareness that his friends were turning left and he was turning right.

'I guess that's when I got labelled a loner. But I was very happy being out there on my own, working on my game. I didn't have a social life at all. I played golf from dawn to dusk. Came home, food was on the broiler, ate, went to bed. And I literally did that rain or snow. So I didn't have girlfriends or anything.'

Over the next two seasons, he went on to become one of Britain's best amateurs, winning 10 titles at junior, county and amateur level in 1975. In the process, he suffered the fate common to a lot of successful sportsmen whereby, having been denied an adolescence, he lacked social skills. Years later, Alliss outraged him by describing him as 'the classic only child', but now, in hindsight, Faldo wishes he had spent less time alone as a young player. Now he wishes he had been able to switch off.

'I've been talking about this with Valerie,' Faldo says. 'You know, I never had a gang of mates where you bomb down to the pub and you have a social crowd, might be six guys, six girls. Never had that. There might be the odd mate, the odd girl, or what have you, but there was never a group of buddies.'

There's a story Faldo likes to tell about Jack Nicklaus, the greatest golfer of all time, who at his peak would respond to questions about other player's victories with a tart: 'I don't know and I don't care.'

THE REINVENTION OF NICK FALDO

Champions, Faldo insists, are by necessity focused on themselves. They do what they need to do and leave. 'I mean, you're in a professional sport, for crying out loud, and you're out there to win,' he says impatiently. 'You're not just out there to waft it around and hope something happens. You've got to show the other guys you've got a little mettle because that's how you beat them. But then they automatically assume that this carries on into your private life.'

From the start of his career, Faldo did everything his own way; some might argue the hard way. Headhunted by Houston University, he lasted ten weeks before the torture of academia and a disagreement with the golf coach over practice time, or lack thereof, had him demanding a ticket home. Back in Britain, he turned professional in April 1976. He finished 58th on the money list that year, and topped up his tiny earnings with a $2,000 cash windfall at a tournament in Nigeria. He remembers sitting in his hotel room, pushing it around on a table.

'I'd never seen so much money,' he says.

Two years later, he was on his way to becoming one of the best young players in Europe, appearing in the Ryder Cup team and winning the second of four PGA Championships. He was also married.

'You wish somebody would have slowed you down,' says Faldo, who wed pretty Melanie Rockall at 20, 'but I guess like all youngsters you know what you're doing. It must be very difficult for parents. Yeah, that was the classic – too young and all a mad whirlwind . . . I'd certainly advise my lot to do it differently.'

By 1984, the marriage was over and Faldo was preparing to marry Gill, a former IMG employee with whom he had had a headline-grabbing affair, and embark on the riskiest, most controversial decision of his career. Months after winning his first US Tour event, he approached David Leadbetter and asked him to throw the book at him. It didn't matter to him that he had finished No.1 in Europe with five victories the year before. Faldo's eyes were on golf's biggest prizes, the British Open, US Masters, US Open and US PGA Championship. To get them, he needed to start from scratch.

The journey to greatness took three long years, during which Faldo beat balls till his hands bled. It culminated in victory in the stormswept 1987 Open at Muirfield. Along with the glory, he found himself being criticised for winning golf's greatest championship, in driving wind and rain, in a conservative, predictable manner. Eighteen pars, people raged. Couldn't he have made a birdie?

At the golf course, his focus was on playing; off it, his awkward sense of humour (the kind that produced lines like 'an oeuf is an oeuf' and made him sing 'My Way' at prize giving) and apparent inability to make friends with other pros made him the butt of constant jokes. *Sports Illustrated* came up with a line about Faldo's idea of an evening out being 'dinner for one' on the hotel balcony, and as recently as last month's US Open, players were taking bets on how many words he would speak to his amateur partner in the practice round. Six, said one. Eight, said another. His partner counted 14.

'The reason why I've found it difficult to be with other golfers is I don't like talking golf off the golf course,' Faldo explains. 'I never wanted to sit down with the pros in the evening and go, "What about the 14th today?" I think that's why I've never made a conscious effort to make friends on Tour.'

In the meanwhile, his career moved relentlessly forward. In the space of four years, he won two Masters and two Opens and yet far from serving to dispel the image of him as a mechanical player and socially inept man, they only seemed to increase it. In 1992, for example, when he had won support by bursting into tears after a brave and hard-won victory at Muirfield, he lost it with what many considered the worst speech in memory, thanking the media 'from the heart of my bottom'.

Faldo chuckles unrepentantly. 'Some guys still think that was the best line ever delivered.'

At the time, however, the constant battering stung. In 1995, Faldo decided to relocate to the US Tour, partly to escape the press, partly because the courses and practice facilities were far superior to Europe and partly to explore new horizons. He went, he thought, with the blessing of his family.

'That was one of the twists,' Faldo says sardonically. 'Gill pushed me on it, said, "Yeah, you should do it."' Then she changed her mind. She said, "No, the children are in school here and they're going to stay here."' And that became a major difficulty, a major burden. I'm over there, the kids are back here and that was obviously another factor to the relationship not working. I needed some support. Because it's hard work. To play on Tour on your own is horrible.'

He wasn't alone for long. When his marriage hit the wall, he began a liason with 20-year-old Cepelak. On the course, his decision to move to America paid off more richly than he could have hoped, and in 1996 he won his third Masters after an emotional encounter with Greg Norman. It was during that final round, when the Australian suffered one of the greatest collapses in sporting history and turned a six-shot lead into a five-shot deficit, that Faldo first showed the grace and compassion that lurked behind his arrogant facade. 'I don't know what to say,' Faldo told him, 'so I'm just going to give you a hug.'

Faldo was not to know then that that might be the apex of his career. That from that moment on, the gradual disintegration of his ordered world would take its toll on his game even as he appeared smiling in the papers with Brenna.

Ironically, the man who is viewed as a loner and enjoys spending time alone, working out in the gym or dreaming up business projects, has never been out of a relationship since the day he turned 18.

'On the course, I'm happy to be on my own; off the course it's totally different,' concedes Faldo. 'I've always had the company. I've never had a period in the last 20 years or so when I haven't had a partner. I've never had a period where I've said, right, be on your own, sort yourself out. I've found that difficult. I think you need a buddy to help you on that. Men, at home, need to be organised. You need someone to do your ironing, washing, whatever. There's nothing worse than waking up and looking after yourself.'

In a sense, Faldo suffered four divorces in as many years: first Gill, then Brenna, then his coach, then his caddie. As Gill's lawyers and the tabloid hounds unleashed their full fury upon him, the second most important relationship in his life hit the rocks. Faldo says of his 13-year bond with Leadbetter: 'You could argue who's helped who and who's been good for who. We were good for each other, put it that way.' Leadbetter maintains that Faldo sent him a fax to fire him. Faldo's version is somewhat different. There was a letter but it was a letter that came out of hurt, anger and more than a little bewilderment.

In golf, it is the ephemerality of the game that both thrills and terrifies. In 1997, Faldo won the LA Open with a sterling performance, effortlessly seeing off a barrage of top talent. The next week, nothing felt the same. According to Faldo, Leadbetter's response was to do a 180 degree about-face on method and announce that from now on they were going to try something called the 'Dynamic Golf Swing'.

'Had me out there doing all sorts of funny drills,' says Faldo, who stood in the sun trying to hit bunker shots with his stomach and putt with a two-inch backswing. 'This is what led to the bust up. We pursued this, totally alien to what I'd ever done before, and the thing that didn't twig was he said that the guy who had the most dynamic golf swing on Tour was Ernie Els, because it's smooth and there's no energy loss. And that didn't ring a blimming bell. It's like, why not go watch Ernie for an hour. It would probably have done me more good than trying to get different parts of the body moving at different speeds.'

Faldo's game began to go south at an alarming speed. No .4 in the world after his Masters victory in 1996, he plummeted out of the top 50 in 1998, out of the top 100 in April 1999 and finally sank to a dismal 187th in the world in August last year. For a man who had once been the most dominant player on the planet, with a game so mechanical and finely tuned as to be flawless, it was a stunning fall from grace. His confidence drained, Faldo clung with grim faith to his teacher's new philosophy, even when he injured his arm. Then Leadbetter called Faldo's manager John Simpson and told him he couldn't fit the 1998 US PGA Championship, one of the four events where Faldo most needed him, into his schedule.

'Obviously, his father had died back in June and he was using that,' Faldo recalls, 'saying he was sorting the estate out.

In fact, he was finishing a golf book. I thought, well, after 13 years, that's a great show of support, but okay. It's almost like he was saying, "You're down. I can't help you."'

There is a sense he felt that people were deserting him like rats fleeing a sinking ship.

'If the guy can't even call you in the week and go, "I can't make it but how's it going? What are you doing?" you feel that maybe he thinks you're a lost cause. It's not going to happen.'

After that, the blows came thick and fast. His turbulent two and a half year relationship with Cepelak ended. It righted itself shakily after she took a nine-iron to his prized Porsche, causing thousands of pounds worth of damage, but was never the same once he met Valerie in September 1998. Bercher and he were engaged just over a year later and planned to marry in the summer of 2000.

But in the end it was the loss of the other woman in his life, his caddie of ten years, Fanny Sunesson, that hurt the most, not least because it was so unexpected. Last November, on the day he presented her with a Jeep Wrangler to celebrate their first decade together, she told him she thought they needed a break from each other. The collapse of his game had been hard on both of them. Devastated, Faldo pleaded with her to finish the last couple of events of the season with him.

'But typical Fanny, she's spinning in her head all the time,' says Faldo, who is still friends with Sunesson, 'so as soon as we get to the Johnnie Walker in Taipei, the first two minutes I'm with her, she said: "I still think we should part." So that put a real negative on it because you've got somebody working for you who doesn't want to be there. I said, "Fine. I'll get a caddie down in Australia." So that's it. There's no ill feelings. It was just bad timing and a little bit the way it was done. But it's all done and dusted now.'

Faldo hired a new caddie and prepared to start the millennium with a clean slate, but there was one more crisis to come. In June, after years of unrelenting criticism, he found himself in the unlikely position of being defended by the British press when Mark James, the former Ryder Cup captain, published a sensational account on his reign. It included a vicious personal attack on Faldo and led to a banner headline in the *Daily Mail*: 'I tore up Nick Faldo's good luck letter.'

'That was a bolt from the blue,' says Faldo. Such was the strength of feeling against James's actions that he had little choice but to resign on 1 August, but not, Faldo claims, before he discovered that James had 'fabricated the story to make it look as if I'm unloved, not wanted as a future captain.'

As far as he could tell it was a grudge match, dating back to 1995 when he constructively criticized the poor practice facilities and courses in Europe, and James responded by calling the top players 'Fat Cats' who took appearance fees. 'That's always bemused me,' says Faldo. 'He became the Tour spokesman on my comments. So I've never seen eye to eye with him on that. But why he's been storing all this up to have a dig at me, I don't know.'

Nick Faldo is in his sanctuary. He stands up to his thighs in sun-dappled water, fly-rod in the crook of one arm, and holds up a brown trout it has taken him less than ten minutes to catch. The smile he wears is as wide as the Wiltshire river. He is hemmed in by greenery and regarded by two curious swans. He lowers the speckled fish gently into the water. 'Go on,' he says, 'have a breather.'

In the darkest moments of the last half dozen years, this peaceful river where kings once fished became Faldo's retreat, a hiding place from one bitter blow after another. Now it's a source of happiness. On his weeks off, he and Valerie take 'the babes' and enjoy picnics by the river with his parents. Joyce makes him laugh by cooking fry-ups on a calour gas stove she's had for 35 years, and his father, kept on a rigid diet by his mother, sneaks cream donuts whenever her back is turned.

Anyone who knows Faldo will tell you that the biggest change in him – a new warmth, a new openness – has come over the last year or so, and it's not a coincidence that it's happened in the time he's been with Valerie. They met at a tournament in Crans-sur-Sierre, Switzerland, where Valerie, whose only previous contact with golf was a vague notion that Tiger Woods played the game, thought he was a 'nice looking, smiling guy'. Faldo was still seeing Cepelak; Valerie was engaged to designer Olivier Delaloye.

'We were both in the same boat,' says Faldo, 'both trying to end relationships.'

'Unhappy relationships,' Valerie adds.

At the outset, Valerie doubted they had anything in common and suspected that, at 40, Faldo's taste in music was confined to Dire Straits, but she was amazed to find out how alike they were. So was Faldo.

'The first movie we went to see was *The Full Monty*,' he says. 'I mean, it's a very English movie, isn't it? And she got it all. She's laughing at everything. And I thought: This is great.'

'Selection criteria,' teases Valerie. 'Does she like *The Full Monty* or not?'

Theirs is a relationship based on mutual trust and affection. He calls her 'V', she calls him 'Dude'. The tabloids have made great play of the 16-year difference in their ages, but if anything it is Valerie who seems the stronger of the two. 'Being a golf wife is a terribly secondary existence,' Melanie once said, adding: 'You exist only as a satellite,' but it is hard to imagine Valerie being anyone's satellite. She speaks three languages, has a degree in social sciences and politics, and has that rare quality, intelligent compassion. A confirmed non-golfer, she has looked into the rarefied bubble occupied by other golf wives and decided that she has no interest in becoming a career shopper. Instead, she is encouraging Faldo to engage in real life and real charity. To brave claustrophobia in the stale darknesss of Giza's pyramids. To sail down the Nile and see the poverty beyond the palm trees. To go to China and actually venture out to climb the Great Wall. To take benevolence beyond the safe confines of junior golf.

In some ways, they are complete opposites. Valerie likes to sleep in, Faldo likes to powerwalk at 5.30 a.m. Valerie is gregarious and loves to be with her friends. Faldo is happy with his own company.

'He's been like that all his life,' Valerie says a little sadly. 'He's learned to be like that.'

Ask Faldo who his support system was in his early days on Tour and he is briefly at a loss for words.

'Just me,' he says at last. 'I've been my own everything.'

'Which is maybe not a good thing,' says Valerie. 'He's learnt to keep an awful lot of things to himself, inside. Emotions, problems.'

They consider the media's version of events. 'That's another thing,' Valerie says. "Nick Faldo, multi-billionaire." We see numbers in the papers we can't believe. Either Daddy's hiding the money or . . .'

'We went through the divorce, all the financial problems with that, the paperwork with that,' says Faldo. 'You're talking about a year's worth of paperwork.'

But after years of emotional stress and financial wranging with divorce lawyers and Gill, Faldo is finally able to see a future in which he can just enjoy being with Valerie. His biggest concern remains his children, Natalie, Matthew and Georgia. Before he proposed to Valerie, he asked their permission, and it is a great comfort to him that they love her as much as she loves them. He is well aware of the scars his escapades have left on them. Both Valerie and he encourage them to communicate and ask questions, particularly 13-year-old Natalie, the oldest, who hears things about her father from her friends and comes home wondering if they're true.

'The relationship he has with his children is amazing,' Valerie insists. 'My parents are not divorced. I had my dad every day from six o'clock till the time I was going to bed but I wasn't this close to my father. All the time that he spends with his kids is quality time.'

Later, when Faldo goes out of the room, Valerie says: 'He's very soft and very sensitive. Almost everything hurts him. He doesn't show it, of course, but even some things that he reads in the press that he knows are bullshit, he still thinks of it during the night. Can't sleep.'

Asked what she thought might suprise people about him, she says: 'He's a very warm person. He likes to touch.'

His ability to shut out the world amuses her. 'He focuses on something and anything can happen. I can be talking to him, next to him, and he's not listening.'

'That's intentional,' Faldo says when he comes back, giving her a sly sideways glance.

'We laugh a lot,' says Valerie. 'Nobody knows that he has a great sense of humour.'

THE REINVENTION OF NICK FALDO

Once a workaholic and an obssessive, Faldo's trials have shifted his focus to Valerie, who plans to have children 'once Nick is around to enjoy them'. The test of their relationship will come when Faldo finds his game again, as he started to do at Loch Lomond and the Open last month, and rediscovers the seductiveness of competition. After a lifetime of putting golf first, he may, one suspects, revert to type.

When they pose for photographs, they pretend not to be speaking and sit at opposite ends of the sofa, arms folded like sulky children. 'The cold one,' Faldo jokes, referring to his icy image. He slides over and puts his arm around Valerie. 'Come closer,' he tells her. 'You're too far away.'

Nick Faldo is thinking about the things that scare him in life. He decides that nothing does.

'Horse riding,' says Valerie.

'Horse riding,' concedes Nick.

'Skiing,' Valerie reminds him.

'Skiing,' admits Nick.

Ignoring his protests, she tells the story of their first, and possibly last, skiing trip together, where she attempted to help Faldo and Georgia, now seven, negotiate the baby slope – a slope which even Faldo admitted had less break than a green. Three-year-olds were racing down it fearlessly. Valerie told him to wait at the top while she skied with little Georgia, then she would come back for him. Halfway up the ski-lift, she spotted him. He had removed his boots and was walking down.

'Honestly,' scolds Valerie now.

'I'm just scared,' confesses Faldo. 'If something goes twang – a knee – I'd be so annoyed.'

Apart from skiing, not much scares Faldo these days, not even the thought of losing the game he has dedicated his life to pursuing. For anyone who has ever viewed Faldo as a sporting robot, with nothing of real value in his life apart from beating balls, the equanimity with which he has accepted the fact that his best might be behind him might come as a surprise. But Faldo is a man who has stared into the abyss and realised that there are so many worse things in life than not being No.1. And so much that's better.

'In modern sport, you've got your spell and hopefully you can stretch it out as long as possible,' says Faldo, 'whether it's two years, five years, ten years. And that's been a difficult thing to accept – maybe that was my era and it is now gone. How do I get all of that back?'

He stretches his long legs out in front of him and contemplates life after golf. He has a million dreams and plans. There is his course-design business, his junior golf programmes, his interests in the internet golf company 18 Global, his charity work, the sports centre with facilities for the underprivileged and the disabled that he has had ambitions of building since he was a boy.

'If I'm going to be remembered,' Faldo says, 'I want to be remembered for what I did on the golf course and what I did off it. I took from the golf course but I gave it back. Not to look good. I've had these visions since I was a kid. But I'd love to think I'd created something that could last forever.'

But not even Valerie believes that he could live without the physical thrill of hitting golf balls. Or even without winning. Over the last year, as Faldo has come closer to unscrambling his game technically and stripped away layers of negative thought with sports psychologist Kjell Enghagen, he has come to realise that the secret of his success was inner confidence. That, in days gone by, his cold focus had people beaten before he stepped on the tee. And deep down, some part of him recognises that there might be a trade off. In finding himself, Faldo might have lost the very ingredient that made him a champion.

18

MAJOR EXPECTATIONS

Forest of Arden, June 2000. Colin Montgomerie comes striding into the English Open press centre with a long, loose stride and a flushed face but – a moment of consternation from the press officer with his clipboard here – he doesn't go into the interview room. Instead, he marches towards the rogues' gallery of reporters, causing us to eye each other in sudden panic to see which of us has upset him, but, no, his face is wreathed in smiles and he beckons us all forward like a storyteller with a juicy tale or a mother hen rounding up her brood, balances easily on the edge of a makeshift table and scans the leaderboard on which his name appears just below Michael Campbell's, who has, after all, had a record round.

'Stay where you are, stay where you are,' Montgomerie says with an airy wave. Without preamble he tells us: 'I hit the ball very well but I think the putt I missed at 18 threw me.' We scramble for our notebooks and hurry to his side as he rattles through his round. 'Great short putt. I just missed it. Not to worry, not to worry, but to be out in 31 would have been very good.'

At the end of any tournament no place but first does for Montgomerie, but in the opening rounds he is confident enough to see victory from any place on the leaderboard. He checks Campbell's progress, which is somewhat slower and more defensive than the previous day's 63, the round of his life.

'Should he expect to win from that position?' asks one reporter.

Montgomerie gives him a beatific grin. 'I would if it was me,' he says.

Ever since the start of the season, Colin Montgomerie has been relaxed. Serene almost. On the course, the bluster and sulkinessness that often mars his face or his actions and makes him appear petulant and bad-tempered to the galleries, has been largely absent; off it, he has been a dream.

'I'm mellowing,' Monty told me at the B&H International Open at the Belfry, grinning to reveal tiny white teeth. 'I haven't mellowed but I'm mellowing.'

It was a cold, rainy afternoon in the grim north and Montgomerie had just completed a five-hour round with a pro-am team at the Belfry and endured a lengthy grilling by the press on his new Callaway ERC driver – outlawed by the USGA but not the R&A because it's 'trampoline' effect sends the ball some fifteen yards further – and yet he was the picture of contentment. He's not handsome in the Hollywood sense of the word, nor does he have the taut athleticism of players like Tiger Woods, Nick Faldo and Greg Norman, but his robust health and tanned strength lend him plenty of appeal and he has in common with those champions an aura of unshakeable, indomitable confidence.

In the dozen or years that Montgomerie has been on the circuit three conflicting images of him have emerged. The first is the Monty that the public often see, the one the tabloids love to poke fun at. That Monty is the bad-day-at-the-office Monty, red-faced and scowling, prone to chewing the ears off camera-clicking members of the gallery, hecklers, marshalls, scorers and small children. The second is the self-important Monty, the one who poses like a lord in the pages of *Hello* magazine in a mansion in which gilt is the chief accessory, and makes fatal declarations like, 'If we can't beat Paraguay, we might as well go home,' at tournaments like the Dunhill Cup at St Andrews, before being soundly trounced by Paraguayan Raul Fretes for his trouble. The third is the Monty away from the golf course, the one adored by his friends, family, most reporters and Prince Andrew. That Monty is bright, articulate, eager to please and almost impossible not to like. And, fortunately, it was that Monty sitting before me now, explaining in a small voice that the confidence he exudes is an illusion. That he has a lot of self doubt.

'I show confidence,' Monty says, 'and I have done since I started. But at the same time, you'd be surprised. It doesn't always feel that way.'

Major Expectations

Apart from being phobic about flying, he is, he says, insecure about golf. 'I'm in a position now where everybody wants to beat me. I'm the sort of target, if you like, and sometimes it's not as easy to achieve the wins as it might seem. I'm expected to do well and it's always the most difficult thing when you're expected to do well to actually go and achieve it.'

Colin Montgomerie may be the most unique player in golf. Golf is a game defined by its quirks and intangibles, its lack of respect for talent, for greatness, for industry, and not even Faldo, with his scientific dissection of the swing, proved immune to the slumps which strike them all. But in Europe, at least, Monty has been invincible. To him it's because he believes in life after golf. When he takes a break, be it three days or three months, he puts the clubs in the cupboard and doesn't take them out until the day before his next event. At tournaments, he does the bare minimum of practice. If he is working on something particular, he might spend an hour or two on the range. Sometimes, he just hits a few wedges. Other times he doesn't bother hitting anything at all. His approach to coaching is similarly lax. He can take it or leave it. Mostly, coaches like Bill Ferguson just confirm what he already knows.

None of this would be extraordinary if Montgomerie wasn't the No.4 player in the world, behind Tiger Woods, David Duval and Ernie Els. Since arriving on Tour in 1988 and finishing 52nd on the money list, he has never, ever gone backwards. He won the Portuguese Open and finished 25th on the Order of Merit the following year, was 14th the next and fourth and third after that. In 1993, he won the Order of Merit for the first time, since when he has ruled the European Tour all but unchallenged for seven successive years. Unfortunately, he's 37 years old and has yet to win a major championship.

'I'd rather have had my career, the one I've had, the consistency of it over the last nine years, than win one week and go into oblivion,' Montgomerie says positively. 'I won't mention any names . . .'

In 1992 Montgomerie sank a five-foot putt on the last hole at Pebble Beach and felt that, with the sea winds blowing like fury on the Monterey Peninsula, he had a good chance of becoming US Open champion at his first attempt. Jack Nicklaus agreed. In an astonishing lapse of judgement, he congratulated Montgomerie on winning the title, despite the fact that the leaders were still out on the course. Moments later, Tom Kite began his back nine charge and Montgomerie was relegated to a humble third place. He was devastated. 'This will help your career – not winning,' a friend told him. Now, Monty knows he was right. The following year, he won the Order of Merit for the first time and the year after that he tied for the US Open after 72 holes, only surrendering when the flaming temperatures and brutal rough of Oakmont turned the playoff into an endurance test won by Ernie Els. Then came the ultimate disappointment. With his name on the leaderboard and his game at its peak, he came out to play the final six holes of the rain, delayed second round at the US Open in 1997, was heckled unmercifully by the wet, intoxicated crowds and dropped six shots.

'I regret the second round at Congressional because I should have won that week,' admits Montgomerie, beaten again by Els. 'I played brilliantly that week. Three rounds of 65, 67, 69, which was fantastic golf. I regret the second round because I shot 76 and that lost me the tournament. There were outside circumstances there. I'd just won the previous week at Slaley Hall and coming over there tired I made a huge error. Instead of flying from Newcastle to London, I drove, and the next day I flew out to Washington tired, arrived on Monday afternoon and played on Tuesday and Wednesday. I shot 65 the first day. I was playing the best golf I've ever played in my life – much better than I am now – I should have won that event. I regret the second round.'

And so Montgomerie was saddled with the game's cruellest label – the best player in the world not to have won a major – with all of the deficiencies it implies. The pressure mounted. The better he played in regular events, the more questions were asked about his performances in majors. When he missed three cuts in four years at the Open, he was treated as a national joke. In US majors, when his heart-on-a-sleeve face showed he had allowed it to get to him, he was pilloried by the galleries. At the Open, he was crucified by the tabloids.

'What you don't do is read the press that week,' Montgomerie says ruefully. 'I've learnt that in a hurry and so has my wife. Because the first thing that's said about me at a major is that I haven't won one and it's a failure. Colin Montgomerie is a good player but he hasn't won a major. There's always a "but" after my name. And I would like that to get off my back as soon as humanly possible.'

In golf, as in life, winning is not enough. It's essential to win in the right way (if you're tax-man lookalike Mark Brooks and you beat uncharismatic Kenny Perry in a dull US PGA Championship playoff, it doesn't count), with the right amount of charisma (if you're dour Paul Lawrie, fat Craig Stadler or your name is Andy North, then being the Open, Masters or US Open Champion doesn't count) and the right attitude (if you're Vijay Singh and you shout 'Kiss my ass' to Augusta, hours after winning the Masters, it's frowned upon). Greg Norman, who has more than 80 titles to his name, will never be considered a greater player than Nick Faldo, who has won less than half of that but has six majors to Norman's two. And Monty was keenly aware that history would leave him out in the cold if he never won a major at all.

Perhaps that's why the aura of bliss he had cultivated so carefully earlier in the season transformed into a mushroom cloud of misery when he finished so far behind Tiger Woods in the US Open at Pebble Beach that his position in the field was actually irrelevant. For most players that wouldn't have been the end of the world, but the US Open was the major Monty felt he had the best chance of winning. When it all went horribly wrong again he was temporarily crushed, but he recovered both his game and his sense of humour at Loch Lomond and could well have won the title again had it not been for his old nemesis Ernie Els. Then it was on to St Andrews for the Millennium Open Championship, where his failure to win a major was once again thrown into sharp relief.

'This is not now or never,' Montgomerie snapped on the eve of the tournament when he was asked if he thought he had a finite amount of time to win a major. 'If I don't win this Open that doesn't mean I can't win one. Mark O'Meara came in here when he was 40 and wasn't saying that. I believe I've got, say, five years at this level left, right? Let's say I'm in the top 10 for the next five years. I have been for seven years in a row now. I'm very proud of that fact. I think I can remain in the top 10 in the world for the next five years. If I achieve that I have 20 opportunities to win a major, right? This is just one of 20.'

For the most part, Monty was in a fairly good mood but some of the questions he was asked would have tried the patience of a saint. Like Jack Nicklaus, he was fed up with being grilled about Tiger Woods. Even a simple generalisation about the course set up and how 67 was a good score around St Andrews, was greeted with the response: 'You talk about less experienced players perhaps getting into trouble. Are you trying to say Tiger is not quite the favourite everyone might think?'

'I never said he wasn't experienced, for God's sake,' Monty snapped. 'First American question, first American question, about Tiger Woods. All I said was, we're all hitting it an awful long way now becase of the conditions of the course. A lot of people can drive the last right now. I did it yesterday. I've never done that before. Now that's his length nullified on that one particular hole for a start.'

Undaunted, a second reporter piped up: 'I know you're getting fed up with people talking about Tiger Woods . . .'

'Yes, I am,' Monty said shortly. 'Next question.'

Then the tournament began. In his heart of hearts, Montgomerie does not believe he can win the Open, so his attitude is always soured from the start. The differences between him and Tiger Woods, who takes every course on its merits and concerns himself with his own game and no one else's, were spectacularly highlighed in the first round of the tournament. Tiger reached the turn at one under par and wore an expression of total contentment. He was relaxed and patient, confident that things would go his way. Monty was also one under par at the turn. He, on the other hand, was on the verge of a seizure. He looked like a man enduring the worst day of his entire life. And he behaved like a man enduring the worst week of his life right up until he had signed his scorecard on the last day and melodramatically blamed his putting.

'It's 20 years too late for him to be behaving like a spoilt baby,' one observer said. Earlier in the week, the *Telegraph*'s Martin Johnson had remarked that there was so much steam coming out of his ears after his round that the locker room resembled a Chinese laundry.

Certainly, it's true that not one day of the Open went by without Montgomerie delivering some self-pitying diatribe on the disaster that was his round. None of his rounds were in fact disasters. He shot 71, 70, 72, 70 to finish five under par for the week, which, though not good enough for him to finish in the top 10, was by no means a catastrophe. And yet asked for his reflections on the four days, he ranted: 'I've just finished my round, you know. It's very difficult to ask someone for their reflections on a week like this after he's just finished his round. I think that's quite an unfair question to ask at this stage, you know. Give me a week or a month and I'll come back to you on it, but right now it's very difficult to reflect when you've just finished your round.'

On the European Tour, tales of Monty's outbursts of petulance and pomposity are collector's items. Nothing is funnier than Monty when he is puffed up with self-importance or Monty attempting to deal with the many cruel tricks life plays on him (Mr Bean had an easier time trying to stuff his Christmas turkey), and it's difficult not to have a soft spot for him if only because he provides such good copy. Take, for example, the time he was contending in the Irish Open and came into the press centre limping.

The journalists looked at each other. 'Did something happen?' asked one.

'Did something happen?!' cried Montgomerie. 'DID SOMETHING HAPPEN? I sprained my ankle signing autographs, that's what happened.'

'Can I make a suggestion?' came a voice from the back. Monty was thunderstruck. Too taken aback to object, his blue eyes swept the room until they alighted on the innocent face of *Mirror* reporter Tony Stenson. 'What suggestion?' demanded Monty.

'Don't sign autographs while you're walking along,' Stenson said brightly.

A muscle worked in Montgomerie's jaw. 'If I didn't sign autographs while I was walking along,' he said icily, 'I would never make my tee-off time.'

On another occasion, he was asked if he had heard about the death of Gene Sarazen.

'Very sad, very sad,' said Monty. 'He was a wonderful player and a good friend till the end.'

This announcement was met with some bemusement since no one had been aware that the two men even knew each other. 'Were you close?' he was asked.

'Oh, yes,' Monty said nostalgically. 'Me and Gene . . . You know I was right there when he made his hole-in-one at the Postage Stamp at Troon. I saw it all, I had a front-row seat.'

'That's very interesting,' said one of the journalists. 'You know, we should get hold of the BBC footage on that. You'd be easy to spot – a blond curly-headed boy, right there in the front row.'

'I didn't say I was in the front row,' Monty snapped. 'Actually, I was quite far back.'

They go on. My own personal favourite is the time BBC radio reporter Tony Adamson tried to get an interview with him at the 1994 Dunhill Masters at Woburn. There is no player more obliging than Montgomerie when it comes to setting up interviews but few more evasive when it comes to actually pinning him down to do them. Adamson spent most of the week arranging times to speak to Monty only to have him wriggle out of it at the last minute. Finally, he managed to get him to promise faithfully to do a live interview with Radio 4 after the third round of the tournament. With his producers and listeners standing by, he went to find Montgomerie.

'Can't do it now; I'm sorry,' Monty told him.

Half furious, half panic-stricken, Adamson reminded him of his promise.

Montgomerie sighed pitiously. 'Can't,' he said sadly. 'Bereavement in the family.'

Adamson was immediately sympathetic. 'Gosh, I'm so sorry,' he said. 'Why didn't you tell me?'

'It's alright,' said Monty in martyred tones. 'You weren't to know.'

Later, Adamson relayed this story to a Scottish colleague. 'Bereavement in the family?' queried the man. 'What bereavement? Oh, you mean the death of the Montgomeries' Filipino au pair's mother?'

There were literally hundreds of these anecdotes. Once, Monty leapt into his courtesy car at the Dunhill Cup after being beaten by yet another obscure golfing nation (Paraguay, India or China, I forget which) and slammed the door theatrically, leaving his wife Eimear standing outside. Another time, he was making his annual attempt to be an amiable person at the 1994 Open at Turnberry when the gods conspired against him in the first round. Throughout the day, he had managed to stay calm while enduring the flagrantly evil machinations of incompetent scorers, photographers and mobile phone users. He had looked on enviously as his playing partner, the flagrantly evil Gordon Brand Jnr, destroyed a whin bush after hitting his ball into the rough, but he restricted himself to a small, 'Hopeless,' when he shanked his own six-iron shot into the Wee Burn at the sixteenth. Left to his own devices, he might have gone back to his hotel room and screamed silently into his pillow, but when he came off the eighteenth green the media were waiting to pounce.

First up to bat was *Mirror* writer Ken Lawrence. 'Well, Colin,' he said. 'You've shot a 72. Is there a way back?'

Montgomerie tensed. He looked heavenwards for support. He went beserk.

'IS THERE A WAY BACK?' he screamed. 'WHAT DO YOU MEAN, "A WAY BACK"?' Only four people have ever broken par on this course. I shot 72, not 82.' And with that he was off, leaving the *Daily Record* to gleefully inform readers that: 'The reformed Monty lasted only 293 minutes.'

Away from the Open and the unrelenting pressure to win majors, Montgomerie was once again tranquil and in control. In Europe, he was as powerful a presence as Woods is everywhere he goes and it was clear that he enjoyed being both fêted and feared. Nick Faldo once accused him of operating in a comfort-zone in Europe because he refused to relocate to the US Tour, but there were much bigger impediments to Montgomerie's desire to win majors than a perfectly natural desire to stay in the country where he was happiest. For a start, there was his attitude. As amusing as many Monty stories were, it was hard to believe that his temperament – sunny with a 90 per cent chance of thunderstorms – didn't affect his performance. He was too easily distracted. Woods gives the impression that nuclear war could break out on the perimeter of the fairway and he wouldn't even look up. Montgomerie, as someone once said, can hear a man thinking about opening a packet of crisps at a hundred paces. In the 1997 US Open at Congressional, his biggest regret was dropping six shots in six holes in the second round. But the main reason he dropped those shots is that the wet, alcohol-fortified crowd heckled him. Woods would have blocked out the noise. Monty allowed it to get to him.

In some ways, what it boiled down to was a lack of discipline. Europe's big three – out-of-shape Montgomerie, tubby Lee Westwood and scarlet-faced, cigar-smoking Darren Clarke – all pride themselves on their casual approach to practice, their refusal to darken the door of any gym and their unfettered enjoyment of rich food and wine, but it's no coincidence that the men who have been world No.1 over the last decade or so, Woods, Faldo, Ballesteros, Norman and Langer, are all fine athletes who, at the time of their reign, had spent thousands of hours in the gym and on the range and could have happily competed in any sport you could mention. That's not to say that if Monty, Clarke and Westwood suddenly adopted Pete Sampras's training schedule they would coast to victory in every major, but rather that their lack of interest in going the extra mile to be the best in the era of Woods, the hardest working man in golf, raises question marks about their commitment to winning golf's biggest titles.

There was no doubting Monty's ambition but perhaps, deep down, the only son of James Montgomerie, former chairman of a Leeds biscuit factory and now Secretary of Troon, cares most about winning and not necessarily about winning majors. Winning for its own sake obsesses him.

'It's the fear of losing,' Monty admits. 'I hate losing at anything. It's not the money and it's not fame, because I don't really like either of them, to be honest with you. Fame is getting in the way now in the way it didn't before, and money . . . I'm not playing in this event for money. I'm playing to win.'

The other factor is that there is so much more to Monty's life than just golf. As tempestuous as his marriage was in the early days, Eimear and his three daughters still come first, before golf, before majors. 'I'm very, very lucky,' Monty says. 'I married the right person. At 21 years old, as I was, and she was 21, you think you know everything. You don't. You know nothing at all. But I married the right person and that's what's kept my home life as settled as it is. She's absolutely brilliant. She's intelligent. She's my best social asset. She's just excellent in every way. She's brought up three lovely children. I've been away. I've been putting a roof over their head as opposed to bringing them up, so she's been the stability, if you like, throughout, and that's what keeps me going when I'm away from this.

'My life with her is great and we have a stronger marriage now than when we married ten years ago and we're more in love with each other. I'm actually having a good time away from here, and that's what keeps me going to succeed. She's as ambitious as I am. If she wasn't as ambitious as I was, we'd have grown apart. She had to come along with that, and she was able to do that, which is fantastic.'

But as loathe as Monty was to admit it, time is running out for him on the course. With the majors of 2000 gone, he had, by his own calculation, just 18 more chances to win one. Take into consideration his record at the Open and the fact that his game doesn't suit Augusta and you might say he has just nine chances left. Nine opportunities with Woods in the field is not many. If he never won a major would he regret it? Would he rue the chances missed, the times when the red mist has descended?

'No, never regret it,' says Monty blithely. 'I'd take the career I've had and run right now. Right now.' He laughs and it reaches his eyes and lights up his whole face. 'If I don't win another tournament, I'll be happy with the [PGA Championship] being the last one. I've won 29 events now and been fortunate to do so and to have that consistency and the Order of Merits that I have in my trophy cabinet. I pass them every night and I always look at them and think, "Well, that's okay. That's very good." No one else has got that. Even the Seves and the Langers and the Faldos, brilliant players, didn't achieve that. They've all won majors and good luck to them but they haven't won seven Order of Merits.'

He grins. 'And not just that,' he says proudly, 'seven in a row.'

19

TALKING TO TIGER

Tiger Woods was proceeding up the eighth fairway at St Andrews with the burden of history, expectation and several hundred million dollars of endorsement and betting shop money on his slim, athletic shoulders and yet he looked as relaxed as a honeymooner on a beach in Barbados. A succession of poor approach shots had lent a ferocious intensity to his drives but the explosion of energy was limited to 30 seconds or less and never removed the look of focused contentment on his mobile young face. He turned his head to follow the bright flicker of seagulls across the sky. He laughed at a comment from his caddie Steve Williams. The removal of his golf glove was an unhurried affair.

In athletes, stress manifests itself in a hundred small ways. Even a man as po-faced and robotically controlled as Nick Faldo was before he gained a set of emotions showed his anger with ticks in technique, cruel jibes at his caddie, slammed clubs and sarcastic asides to hapless marshalls or members of the gallery. But on and off the course, Woods exhibited a zen-like calm. Above him, the scoreboard showed the Native American Notah Begay (Tiger's old college roommate) at six under par, six strokes ahead of Woods. Woods holed out for his eighth straight par. He strolled off the green with his hands in his pockets. When you're 24-years old and have won 26 of the 102 tournaments you have entered – your most recent victory being a belief-beggaring 15-stroke victory in the US Open at Pebble Beach, you tend to have more faith things will go your way than most 24-year-olds do.

It was the 129th Open Championship and Woods was embarking on an epic quest: to become the youngest player since Jack Nicklaus and only the fifth man in history, after

Nicklaus, Hogan, Sarazen and Player, to win the Grand Slam. He had come well prepared. Instead of chasing dollars at a tournament or beating balls back home in Isleworth, Florida, he had taken a leaf out of Tom Watson's book and chosen the easy rhythm of rural Ireland. Hours after stepping off a plane from the States, he had shot 64 to win a charity pro-am at Limerick. He then spent the rest of the week fly-fishing with Mark O'Meara, now more famous for being Tiger's friend than for winning the 1998 Masters and Open.

They made an intriguing pair. O'Meara, the chief architect of the 'Ryder Cup players should be paid' controversy, is colourful and frequently charming and can always be relied on for a provocative quote, but he is also as hard as nails and universally regarded as a phoney. As one American writer observed, the interesting thing about O'Meara's phoneyness is that it goes all the way through. He's not superficially phoney, for the benefit of the press, say, with a mean side underneath. With O'Meara what you see is what you get. Which makes you wonder about Tiger. Other members of his entourage include Earl Woods, the original Green Beret, who trained his Tiger by jiggling change on his backswing and employing other military psychology to ensure he was bullet-proof and generally invincible when he fulfilled his destiny as the best player on the planet, Tida Woods, who looks more like Imelda Marcus with each passing day, his coach Butch Harmon, a tough cookie in the O'Meara mould with a particularly poor line in interview excuses (once, at a Spanish tournament, he told me he couldn't do a pre-arranged interview because he felt uncomfortable doing an interview in a country where he didn't speak the language – the fact that I spoke English and wrote for an English paper was neither here nor there), his girlfriend Joanna Jagoda, a pleasant, independently-minded University of California at Santa Barbara graduate, his caddie Steve Williams, a tough but likeable Australian whose lips are sealed tighter than the Vatican vaults, assorted people from his management company IMG (his original agent Hughes Norton, a.k.a. the anti-Christ, was replaced after procuring Tiger's multi-million dollar Nike and Titleist deals by the tough but upstanding Mark Steinberg) and, of course, friends like Michael Jordan. Toughness was what all of these people had in common and Woods himself had it in spades.

None of it altered the fact that he had a startling ability to make the right choices, on and off the golf course. Those choices had led to a 12-stroke victory in the 1997 Masters and a seemingly unnecessary two-year swing change which subsequently rewarded him with eight wins on the PGA Tour, including the US PGA Championship, in 1999. He earned $6,6m in the US, almost $3m more than his nearest rival, David Duval, and a total of $7.6m. His adjusted scoring average, 68.43, was the lowest ever. Towards the end of the season, he embarked on the longest streak of victories since Byron Nelson's famous 11 in 1945, winning four times in succession that season and twice at the start of the next. On arrival at St Andrews, he had already won five times worldwide in 2000 and made $5m. His career total was almost $20m. He managed all of this while conducting clinics for inner-city kids across America, leading a relatively normal home life and satisfying the demands of sponsors like Nike and American Express who would help him earn an estimated $1b by the time he was 30.

If all of that was a recipe for the kind of stress only known to other multi-million dollar entertainment people like Michael Jordan and Madonna, you would never have known it from Tiger's demeanour.

'Have you dreamt about this week at all?' he was asked in his pre-tournament press conference.

'Dreamt about it?' said Tiger, amused. 'No. Have you?'

Even being grilled by 700-odd media people, his serenity was palpable. You wouldn't exactly describe him as a quote machine – since he had been asked every question in the universe a thousand times at least, there is a sense that he was mentally going, 'That's question No. 23,' and answering by rote – but he was polite, he was sincere and he very rarely let on that he thought a question facile or unoriginal.

Asked if he felt that it was to his advantage that so many people thought he would win the Open (the bookmakers had him at 15–8), he said simply: 'Whether the odds are 15–8 or

100–1, as long as I can go out there and give a wonderful effort, give it everything I have, then I look back on it, whether I win or lose, and say that I gave it everything.'

He spoke of the strength of his desire to play and to improve and said that he had never thought he could love the game more than he did as a boy but somehow that love had grown with maturity and understanding. He talked about his security detail, and how they were there not just to help him but to help the spectators. 'A lot of the kids are here and the adults don't care about the kids, they run right over them. I was playing in Ireland and one of the kids just got trampled over by an adult. He was knocked down and his arm was bleeding.' He denied that he feared for his personal safety.

'Do you still get those hate letters, or has all of that eased off now?' someone asked.

'Nothing has changed,' Tiger said quietly.

'Nothing has changed?'

'No,' said Tiger.

The moment passed. Inevitably, he was asked about the Grand Slam. Astonishingly, he said that right then, at that point in his career, winning the Grand Slam would not necessarily be the greatest accomplishment of his life. 'People might think I'm crazy, but to win three consecutive US juniors, I think that's probably the hardest because of the age limit. You can't keep playing. At 17, you're out. And as anyone knows, there's a dramatic difference between 14, 15 and 17-year-olds, whether with a person who's twenty-four or thirty, there's not as great a difference. To win at that level three consecutive times, 18 matches in a row, that's not bad.'

'But at the end of your career, no one is going to remember that, probably,' a reporter pointed out.

'No,' Tiger agreed. 'But I will.'

And then he went out to try to win the Open Championship.

Tiger Woods was not always so sanguine. There's a story he tells about a Sam Snead exhibition match he and Earl attended at Calabasas Country Club when he was just six. Every two holes, a new group of people had an opportunity to play against the great man and Tiger's chance came when Snead reached the par three seventeenth. Not having the strength to carrry the creek in front of the green, Tiger somewhat ambitiously tried to land his ball on a nearby cart path and bounce it onto the putting surface. It didn't work. The ball missed the path and landed in the creek.

'I got in automatically,' remembers Tiger, 'I'm going to play it. The ball was sitting up. From behind me, Sam yells out: "What are you doing?" I turn around; I'm dumbfounded. I'm just going to hit the shot. And he says, "You can't play that. Just pick it up and drop it. Let's go." Well, I didn't really like that very much. I remember turning around, looking at my ball and I said, "I gotta hit it. I don't want to drop it, it's a penalty." So I hit a seven-iron right out of there on to the green, all wet, two-putted, got my bogey and bogeyed the last. I made bogey, bogey and Sam beat me by two, par, par.'

At six, Tiger was already a veteran. Born on 30 December 1975 to Earl, a lieutenant colonel in the Green Beret in Vietnam and Kultida, a Thai native, he grew up in Cypress, California, near Los Angeles. He was still in the cradle when he began imitating Earl's swing, ten months when he picked up a club and knocked a ball left-handed into Earl's practice net in the garage, and barely two when he appeared on the Mike Douglas Show and won a putting competition against Bob Hope. At three, he shot 48 over nine holes. His first teacher, Rudy Duran, recalls him having skill and imagination at five. Television footage of him at that age shows Tiger's swing to be a remarkable miniature version of what it is today.

Between the ages of eight and fifteen, he won the International Junior tournament six times. He won also three US Junior Amateurs (no other player has managed more than one) and a record three US Amateurs to become one of the most successful amateurs in history. His professional debut on the US Tour was the best since Horton Smith in 1931.

But it is easy to get bogged down with records and lose sight of Tiger as a person. In many ways, Earl was the archetypal stage parent but the destructive possibilities of that were offset by two crucial factors. In the first instance, nothing that Earl wanted for Tiger (for him to be the world's greatest golfer) could come close to what Tiger wanted for himself (to be the world's greatest golfer). Plus, Earl insists he always told his son: 'I don't care if you play golf. You can be a plumber. Whatever you choose, I just want you to try to be the best.' Second, Earl loved Tiger unreservedly. Nowadays, he gives motivational speeches to the inner-city kids who attend his son's clinics and it's not difficult to believe that the words he uses are the same he has been telling Tiger since he was born: in essence, love yourself, tell the truth and be your own person. 'Tiger cares about you,' he says. 'For too long you have been told and conditioned that you ain't gonna be nothing.' There is some emotional rhetoric about conditioning and prejudice in the US of A and then he orders the children to 'stand up. We love you. Say this: "I believe I am somebody."' He speaks so passionately that even pressmen cry.

As a boy, Woods was focused beyond his years and, for the most part, as schooled in the game's etiquette as his father had groomed him to be. Ken Adler, a member of the USGA's junior championship committee, told the *Detroit News* that he remembered him as 'a very delightful young man. He was fun, laughed, was pleasant to be around. Not a difficult kid at all.' But a local broadcaster who had tried to conduct a live interview with him at a junior tournament in 1991 had a different view. 'He was already a huge national story. We had him on SportsWrap after he had a rough day. He was a brat. Totally unresponsive. I told him he sounded like he didn't want to talk on the radio and he said, "That's right."' Nine years later, the broadcaster ran into Tiger at the Masters, reminded him of the interview and told him how impressed he was that he had matured into his role as the world's best player.

'He looked a little stunned when I first mentioned what a jerk he had been but he flashed that big grin when I complimented him.'

When Tiger turned pro in 1996, preceded by more hype and hyperbole than even Hollywood could conjure up, he showed every sign of being the jerk he had threatened to become on bad days as a young boy. In press conferences, he was eerily controlled – programmed almost. His gift was undeniable but his temper bubbled constantly beneath the surface and he seemed perpetually to be suffering from coughs and colds, aches and pains. In between winning assorted Tour events and the Masters by 12 shots, he attracted a stream of bad publicity for spurning an invitation from the President, failing to attend a Jackie Robinson memorial, failing to turn up to a dinner held in his honour, etc. There were disapproving grumbles from Nicklaus and Palmer and, when he allowed Fuzzy Zoeller to be guzzled by the wolves that set upon him after the stupid remark about Tiger serving fried chicken at Augusta's Champions' dinner, it did not augur well for the future.

It's hard to say why Tiger changed or even when Tiger changed. Possibly it was because he was taken under the wing of Michael Johnson. Possibly it wasn't. Suffice to say that when he arrived at the Open Championship in July 1999, he had become a man. As the fittest, most hard-working golfer on the PGA Tour, he had filled out noticeably, but he had also acquired a sort of star sheen. There was an aura about him. However, the most noticeable difference in him was in his attitude. He was still a 23-year-old, with a 23-year-old's penchant for cursing and adolescent humour, but somewhere along the line he had opted for grace. He was courteous, confident rather than arrogant, and he had perfected the art of the well-crafted, non-controversial quote. His incredible smile was seldom far away. But he was still controlled. Too controlled in some ways.

'Tiger's very cold,' said a close friend of Eldrick's as we clambered through the gorse at St Andrews in a vain bid to watch him retain the lead with an effortless 66 in the second round. 'He's a very well brought up individual as far as his purpose in life goes, but as a person he's very cold. He doesn't let anyone interfere with his goals.'

SATURDAY, 21 JULY 2000

When you're a genius, there's a danger that everything you do will be reduced to statistics – some of them fairly bogus. The fact that Tiger played 63 holes of major golf without a bogey, for instance. Had the Open followed the US Open, that would have been one thing, but it discounted the Western Open, where Tiger hadn't performed particularly well, in between. That said, there was nothing bogus about the sheer ease with which he went about conquering St Andrews. It was all put into perspective on the first day when Woods drove into deep rough, knee high and tangled, at the Road Hole 17th. Half an hour earlier, Begay had made triple bogey from the same position, visiting the Swilken Burn en route. For reasons known only to himself and Steve Williams, Tiger stood in the grass laughing and laughing. After a few experimental chops, he swung at the ball with all his strength, removed a bale's worth of hay, and left the ball just short of the green. As commentator Peter Alliss said, 'People don't realise the strength of the man. The average [Tour] player could not play that shot.'

Left with a treacherous putt on to the green, Woods stroked the ball to about three feet, thus turning an almost certain bogey into a clever par. 'That's why Tiger's No. 1,' someone said.

'I figured anything in red would be good,' Tiger commented when he came in with a 67 to lie a shot behind Ernie Els, 'and I've accomplished that.'

Poor Els, one of the most gifted players of his generation, was rewarded for his efforts with yet more questions about Woods. 'Guys, that's unfair,' he said wearily. 'Let's talk about my round or get on the phone and call Tiger.'

By Saturday, Tiger was the only player anyone was interested in.

'Calling David, Fred, Sergio, Ernie, Tom and Steve, we request that you boys get your butts into gear and put up a fight against Tiger at the weekend,' ordered a blackboard outside the famous old Dunvegan Hotel at the start of the day. 'Anything less is not acceptable.'

Els and Duval et al tried their best to comply but the psychological strain of battling a force of nature proved debilitating. Els birdied the third, fifth, sixth, eighth and tenth but drove into a gorse bush at the twelfth and never recovered.

TALKING TO TIGER

Steve Flesch climbed to 10 under and David Duval was a shot of Tiger standing on the fourteenth, but whenever anyone drew near to him he simply shifted gears and cruised away. Duval showed the most spirit, taking advantage of an outrageous stroke of good fortune at the last to turn a possible six into a three. His aim, he said, had been to get into the last group with Tiger.

'Why? Because you get to look him in the eye. If I can swing the golf club and putt like I have the last two days, I can show him that I've got a golf game going too. And to play in the last group in the oldest championship in the world with the player who is undoubtedly the best in the world right now is an experience you definitely want to have.'

Out on the course, a marshal asked Prince Andrew to step outside the ropes because he didn't have the appropriate armband.

'That's the Duke of York,' a reporter informed him in a hushed tone.

'I don't care if he's the Duke of Hazzard,' growled the marshall. 'He's not coming on the fairway without a proper armband.'

In years to come, when Tiger's performance at St Andrews is analysed, it won't in terms of fireworks. There were few of those. Rather, we will remember the relentlessness of Tiger's march. His dominance of the event was so total, his mastery of the course, the field, the elements and his emotions so complete, that there was never any point when it seemed he might be overtaken. Even players who drew within two or three shots of him seemed to fall on their own swords as Woods swept calmly along, unruffled and unpressurised, never at any point appearing to extend himself. When a 67 left him six strokes ahead of the field going into the final round it was all but inevitable that he would win the Open on Sunday and complete the final leg of his career Grand Slam.

Tiger gave one of his trademark fist pumps after sinking a six foot birdie putt on 18, and kissed Joanna on his way to the recorder's hut. 'Are you going to hit balls?' she asked him.

He looked up at the clock on the R&A clubhouse. 'Seven o'clock,' he said. 'Yes, I am. But the range closes at seven.'

'Get them to open it again,' Butch Harmon told him.

'We tried that last year,' Tiger said. 'It didn't work.'

When he had gone, she told a new acquaintance: 'I've got no golf in my background. When I met him two years ago, I didn't even know what the Masters was.'

In the press room, Woods was asked whether, with a six shot lead and the Grand Slam in sight, he found it hard to stay in the present.

'No,' he replied, 'because I understand what it takes to play in the final round of any tournament. You can't let yourself look ahead to the final outcome because if you don't take care of the present, the final outcome may not be what you want.'

'It's all in his hands,' said Irishman Padraig Harrington. 'It always was.'

SUNDAY, 22 JULY 2000

In his heyday, Nick Faldo used to tell people that his dream was to impact galleries to such an extent that they would look back in decades to come and say: 'I saw Nick Faldo play.' Doubtless some will, but I know I'll be saying: 'I saw Tiger Woods play.'

On Sunday, I walked the Old Course with Tiger Woods and watched him pass into legend and it was, from start to finish, unforgettable. Some 50,000 people crowded ten deep among the low dunes and inhospitable gorse bushes, craning over the ropes and balancing precariously on milk crates, desperate to catch a glimpse of sporting genius. Mostly, they were frustrated. Apart from the fact that the Old Course is probably the worst viewing course on the planet (if it was a new course being presented to Tour directors today as a possible venue, they would fall off their chairs laughing), there were so many people on the fairway that at times it resembled the Macey's Parade.

There were batallions of photographers and film cameramen, men with rakes, referees, marshalls who had finished with earlier matches and were using their marshall status to get an unobstructed view, men with giant fluffy booms, squadrons of bald men with radios performing no obvious function, cheeky spectators, radio reporters, policemen, Woods' security detail and, of course, journalists.

The weather reflected David Duval's fortunes. At first, it

was sunny and optimistic, with seagulls wheeling in a clear blue sky and the icecream vans doing a good trade. When he was making a birdie charge to draw within a few shots of Woods, it was positively summery (a rare thing in St Andrews). Then, at the tenth, he made his first three-putt. By the time, he reached the eleventh green, the sky was completely overcast. At the twelfth, where he handed the title to Woods, an icy wind had begun to blow.

It is true to say that there were stretches of the round that lacked in atmosphere. There was no dramatic tension, no electricity in the air and none of the tears and sense of theatre that went with Jean Van de Velde's riveting 18th hole finish at Carnoustie, Costantino Rocca's 60-foot putt through the Valley of Sin at St Andrews in 1995, Greg Norman's 1993 victory and all three of Seve Ballesteros's triumphs. What is not true is that it was boring. It was, in fact, mesmerizing. This was a 24-year-old who had survived all the disadvantages of minority and yet risen, through love, strength of will and fanatical dedication, to demolish records that have existed for centuries and become the youngest player by two entire years to win the modern Slam, and those who find that boring need to go to their doctor to get their pulse checked. Either that, or take up Xtreme sports. Golf is not for you.

There was the occasional heart-stopping moment. Usually they came after one of Woods's tee shots, which came off the club with the whining swoosh of rockets. 'My God,' breathed one man after watching Tiger's drive on five. A few gasps accompanied Duval's near-misses and there was a sickened silence when he found the Road Bunker on 17 and dug himself a quadruple bogey eight.

From Tiger's point of view, the only part of the event that was not choreographed to perfection was the seventy-second hole of the tournament and that was only because it was beyond his control. The huge crowd, frustrated by four days of poor viewing on the Old Course, swarmed across the fairway after Tiger and Duval had driven and tried to get across the Swilken Burn. Heavy-handed marshalls shoved a few into the water and Tiger had to force his way through the crowd and across the Swilken Bridge. It was not until after he had hit his approach to the green that he was able to relax and enjoy the applause and even then it was cut short by the antics of a voluptuous streaker, the fifth that week.

But nothing could detract from the magnificence of Tiger's achievement. His final round 69 gave him victory by eight strokes, the largest winning margin since 1982, and the modern Grand Slam. He also became the first player since Tom Watson to hold the US and British Opens simultaneously.

'It really is hard to put it into words,' said Woods with tears in his eyes. 'The emotions . . . To have a chance and opportunity to complete the Slam at St Andrews, the home of golf, is something very special.'

Asked how he felt about joining the four legends who had achieved the modern Slam, he said: 'Those are true champions. They've won countless tournaments, they've been the cream of the crop, they've been the most élite players, not only of their time, but ever, and to be spoken of in the same breath as those players is very, very special.'

But even in that moment of glory Tiger managed to cling on to the grounding Earl gave him, still such a powerful influence in his life that he makes his bed every morning, whether at home or in a luxury hotel, and irons clothes that have been freshly dry-cleaned. Musing over what suprised him most about his own achievements, he decided that it was: 'The fact that I've only missed one cut as a pro.' He had, he said, expected to be at this point in his career sooner. 'But, you know, the swing change took time.' It was a simple statement of fact, said with confidence but without a trace of conceit.

'I think it was a spectacular performance, to say the least,' Duval said of Tiger's achievement, which included being the only player in the field not to visit one of St Andrews 112 bunkers during the course of the week. 'He simply didn't make any mistakes and he captitalised on what he needed to capitalise on. He played very efficiently. That's the best way I can put it.'

Tom Watson felt that Tiger had raised the bar to a level where only he could jump over it. He described Tiger's 15-shot victory at the US Open as 'the greatest achievement in the history of the game', and said that Woods played golf supernaturally. 'He's swinging the golf club better than I ever swung the golf club and he has more power than I ever did. He might be putting like I did but that's the only thing I can see that might be equal.'

'He's obviously got a great inner confidence,' said Faldo, whose scoring record Tiger had beaten. 'He's got the mental power to say to himself: "Hey, I'm on my way to winning another major or I'm on my way to winning six tournaments in a row or 11 out of 20." Most guys, just the success would automatically make them throttle back and say, "Well, this can't go on." He's basically said: "Well, this can go on." The old thing where you can't win every week, he's basically said: "To hell with that. I can win every week." And that's his goal. He's taken all the bits that everybody said you couldn't do with golf and said: "I can do them. Why can't we do them?" It's just a different level.'

But not everyone was overjoyed at Tiger's success. Many seemed to feel that he was so dominant and his victories so predictable that the game's chief attraction, its capriciousness, was taken out of it. Robbed of its mystery and fun, golf, people said, would die. Leaving aside the sheer ridiculousness of this argument, even the most prejudiced observer should have been able to see that Tiger Woods was not just good for the game, he was the best thing to happen to golf for half a century. The largest crowds ever to attend an Open watched him win at St Andrews and a third more Americans watched it than had the previous year. Television deals and prize money had gone through the stratosphere. People who would never have been caught dead on a golf course prior to his arrival were taking up the game in their millions. Racial barriers were being broken down every day. Golf was finally becoming cool.

The question was, who would step up and challenge him? Ernie Els, who one would have thought might be able to, said after finishing second that he did not think that even if he had played his best he would have been able to get to 20 under par and beat Woods. It was a breathtakingly defeatist statement. Woods's score was only one stroke better than

Faldo's a decade ago, and yet nobody went around saying that Faldo was supernatural and playing a different Tour and that his score was unattainable. For the most part, they simply said that conditions favoured low scoring that week and that Faldo was on his game. One wondered what the effect of having no rivals would have on Tiger in the long term. Great players actually thrive on competition. They never shy away from the battle. There was a wistful note in Woods's voice when he talked about how much he enjoyed it when Els and Duval briefly made a run at him. He wanted more of it. Failing that, he simply went on alone, to compete against history. In the end, history might be the only opponent capable of matching him.

29 August 2000 WGC – NEC Invitational, Firestone Country Club

Tiger Woods was little more than a silhouette against the falling Ohio night when he put on a dry golf glove with the number 21 written on it and aimed an eight-iron at the pin on the 18th hole. Twenty-one is Steve Williams's favourite number and that's where he wanted his boss to finish below par. Woods was, as ever, in his zone, relaxed and comfortable. He was remembering the nights when, as a young boy, he and Earl had crept on to the Navy course in southern California and played in the darkness, calling the shots to each other and listening for the ball to fall. He could still recall the feel of the club in his hands, the simple joy he had taken in the game. His club flashed. The ball landed stiff. A birdie gave him victory by nine shots.

How is greatness defined? Is it by statistics? Tiger had won five of his last seven events, three of which had been major championships – making him the first man since Hogan in 1953 to win three majors in one year. He had also won 15 of his last 26 events and four of the last five majors. He had won so often, so effortlessly and so convincingly that measuring his achievements against the accepted benchmark of the world's greatest golfer – Nicklaus's 18 majors – began to seem slightly quaint. Even at his peak, Nicklaus didn't routinely win majors by 12 or 15 shots – the equivalent of Secretariat winning by 30 lengths every time he left the stable. He was, of course, competing against Player (nine majors), Watson (eight) and Palmer (seven), as compared to Duval (none), Mickelson (none), Love (one) and Singh and Els (two), but he never gave the impression that he had oceans of talent held in reserve. He never made the most gifted of his peers seem embarrassingly inadequate by comparison.

Is greatness also a state of grace? Nicklaus and Bobby Jones were the only golfers Tiger could be compared to at all, but Tiger transcends his sport in a way that only people of the calibre of Muhammad Ali, Michael Jordan and Wayne Gretsky have done. They, like Woods, were comfortable not only with their greatness but also in their own skin. At their best, all had in common Tiger's calm focus, his unwavering desire to work and improve and his casual disregard for the sugar traps of money and fame. None shied away from demolishing the records of legends. All understood their responsibility as role models and all were driven to be the best that they could be, regardless of the achievements of others.

Somehow and some way, Tiger retained his grip on humility. 'If you believe you are bigger than the game, you have the wrong perspective,' he said after surviving flu and a wasp sting to win at Firestone.

When *Time* magazine did a cover story on Tiger the Sunday before his epic battle against Bob May in the US PGA Championship, they described him as not only the most accomplished and recognised athlete on earth but also 'the most uncritically embraced person on earth'. Gary Player told the magazine: 'He is a tremendously well-balanced young man. He is a gracious loser. He dresses well. He speaks well. He will be a great influence on generations of people throughout the world.'

It was a burden of responsibility that very few people would feel able to take on. Yet Tiger Woods, once nicknamed Urkel by his Stanford teammates because he was so geeky, wore the mantle of hero, son, role model and world's greatest golfer as if he were born to it. Which, in a sense, he was.

'I don't know if there's ever been another year, worldwide,

like this,' said Byron Nelson, who won 18 titles in 1945, 11 of them consecutively. Lee Trevino bluntly informed Tiger's rivals that they didn't have a prayer. 'You cannot beat a man who is stronger than you, who has more talent that you and who works harder than you do. Tiger Woods is competing against records and golf courses. That's what people don't understand. It's not a foot race. He's racing against the clock.'

'I'm a better player than I was last year,' Tiger said at Firestone. 'And hopefully, I'll be better next year.'

Right then, right there, greatness was defined.